PHOTOGRAPHS OBJECTS HISTORIES

This innovative volume explores the idea that while photographs are images, they are also objects, and this materiality is integral to their meaning and use. It explores the different institutional, political, religious and domestic spheres in which photographs exist through a diverse range of international case studies – from the Netherlands, North America and Australia to Japan, Romania and Tibet. All show that physical properties, the nature of use and the cultural formations in which the photographs function make their 'objectness' central to how we can understand them in new ways.

The contributors come from disciplines including history of photography, visual anthropology and art history, and they have all developed original methodological strategies to engage with the materiality of photographic images. Inspiring and instructive, the book can be used both as a much-needed survey of this exciting new area of investigation and as a handbook for the student or academic on how to understand photographs as objects in diverse contexts.

Elizabeth Edwards is Head of Photograph Collections, Pitt Rivers Museum, Lecturer in Visual Anthropology, Institute of Social and Cultural Anthropology, University of Oxford and holds a Visiting Research Fellowship at the University of the Arts London. Her most recent book is *Raw Histories* (2001).

Janice Hart is Head of Research at the London College of Communication, University of the Arts London, and course director for the MA in Photography: History and Culture. She curates exhibitions and writes on the history of photography and contemporary art practice.

MATERIAL CULTURES
Interdisciplinary studies in the material construction of social worlds

Series editors: Michael Rowlands and Christopher Tilley
Department of Anthropology, University College London

(All the above with Daniel Miller, Department of Anthropology,
University College London, as joint series editor)

PHOTOGRAPHS OBJECTS HISTORIES

On the materiality of images

*Edited by Elizabeth Edwards
and Janice Hart*

Routledge
Taylor & Francis Group

LONDON AND NEW YORK

First published 2004
by Routledge
29 West 35th Street, New York, NY 10001

Simultaneously published in the UK
by Routledge
11 New Fetter Lane, London EC4P 4EE

Routledge is an imprint of the Taylor & Francis Group

© 2004 selection and editorial matter Elizabeth Edwards and Janice Hart;
individual chapters © the original copyright holders

Typeset in 11/12pt Garamond 3 by Graphicraft Limited, Hong Kong
Printed and bound in Great Britain by TJ International Ltd, Padstow, Cornwall

British Library Cataloguing in Publication Data
A catalogue record for this book is available from the British Library

Library of Congress Cataloging in Publication Data
A catalog record for this book has been requested

ISBN 0–415–25441–8 (hbk)
ISBN 0–415–25442–6 (pbk)

CONTENTS

v

CONTENTS

ILLUSTRATIONS

CONTRIBUTORS

Geoffrey Batchen teaches the history of photography at City University of New York Graduate Center, New York, USA. His second book, an anthology of essays on photography and electronic culture entitled *Each Wild Idea: Writing, Photography, History*, was published by The MIT Press in 2001.

Richard Chalfen is Professor of Anthropology at Temple University, teaching in both Philadelphia and Tokyo and currently developing a monograph on Japanese Home Media. He is also a Research Associate at Children's Hospital in Boston, conducting long-term studies of patient-generated video in applied contexts of medical communication.

Elizabeth Edwards is Head of Photograph Collections, Pitt Rivers Museum, Lecturer in Visual Anthropology, Institute of Social and Cultural Anthropology, University of Oxford and Visiting Research Fellow at the University of the Arts London. She has written extensively on photography and anthropology. Her most recent book is *Raw Histories* (2001).

Gabriel Hanganu is a doctorial student at the Institute of Social and Cultural Anthropology, University of Oxford. He has undertaken extensive fieldwork in Moldavia and is currently completing his thesis on the 'social lives' of Orthodox Christian icons in Romania.

Clare Harris is Curator of Asian Collections at Pitt Rivers Museum and Lecturer in Anthropology at the Institute of Social and Cultural Anthropology, University of Oxford, with particular interests in the visual culture of Central and South Asia. Her recent prize-winning book is *In the Image of Tibet: Tibetan Painting after 1959* (1999).

Janice Hart is Head of Research at the London College of Communication, University of the Arts London and course director for the MA in Photography: History and Culture. She curates exhibitions and writes about the history of photography and contemporary art practice, often using the interview as a form of critique.

Susan Legêne is a historian, specialising in Dutch colonial expansion, strategies of representing non-Western culture in the Netherlands and Dutch nation building. Currently, as Head of the Curatorial Department of KIT Tropenmuseum (Royal Tropical Institute) in Amsterdam, she is responsible for re-establishing the museum's semi-permanent galleries.

Mai Murui majored in sociology at Temple University in Philadelphia. She was born in Japan and is now working as a Program Assistant for the Continuing Education Program at Temple University Japan, while taking graduate courses in language and education.

Alison Nordström is Curator of Photography at George Eastman House/International Museum of Photography, Rochester, New York. She completed her doctoral thesis on American travel albums in 2000. She was previously Director of the Southeast Museum of Photography and has written extensively on photography.

Nuno Porto is Lecturer on Social and Cultural Anthropology and Ethnographic Museology, Department of Anthropology, and Coordinator of the Museum of Anthropology, University of Coimbra, Portugal. He recently completed his PhD on the scientific culture of Portuguese colonialism 1940–70, through a case study of the Diamonds Company of Angola's Dundo Museum.

Joanna Sassoon is Research Fellow at Curtin University, writing a history of ideas about heritage in Western Australia. Prior to completing her PhD on the cultural biography of E. L. Mitchell's commercial photography of Western Australia's landscape, industry and Aboriginal peoples, she managed the photograph collections for the State Library in Western Australia.

Joan M. Schwartz holds a PhD in Historical Geography from Queen's University, Kingston, Canada, where she is Queen's National Scholar/Associate Professor in the Department of Art and teaches courses in the History of Photography and Society. Formerly Senior Photography Specialist at the National Archives of Canada, Ottawa, she co-edited (with James R. Ryan) *Picturing Place: Photography and the Geographical Imagination* (2003) and (with Terry Cook) 'Archives, records, and power', *Archival Science* (2002).

Glenn Willumson former Curator of Photography at the Getty Research Institute and Senior Curator at the Palmer Museum of Art, is currently Associate Professor of Art History and Director of Museum Studies at the University of Florida. He is the author of *W. Eugene Smith and the Photographic Essay*.

ACKNOWLEDGEMENTS

This volume has been a long time in the making. Throughout this time we have been indebted to the support of our home institutions and many friends and colleagues: in Oxford, Kaushik Bhaumik, Jeremy Coote, Claire Freeman, Chris Gosden, Chris Morton, Laura Peers, Mike O'Hanlon and Norman Weller; and in London, Angus Carlyle, Katharine Heap, Julian Rodriguez and Eve Waring. We have received cheerful technical support from Haas Ezzet and Malcolm Osman for which we are profoundly grateful. Our families have also borne this uncomplainingly. Christmas 2002 didn't really happen for them as piles of final manuscripts and editorial notes rather than Christmas fare filled the table.

Chapter 11 by Chalfen and Murui originally appeared in *Visual Sociology*, 16(1), 2001, and we are grateful to the publisher Taylor and Francis (http://www.tandf.co.uk) for permission to reproduce it here. We are also most grateful to the following institutions for permission to reproduce photographs in their collections: Boston Public Library; George Eastman House, Rochester NY; John Curtin Prime Ministerial Library, Curtin University; Metropolitan Museum of Art, New York; Museum of Anthropology, University of Coimbra; National Archives of Canada; Pitt Rivers Museum, University of Oxford; San Francisco Museum of Contemporary Art; Tropenmuseum, Amsterdam.

It is surprising how few people have thought about photographs as a form of material culture and were prepared to pick up the gauntlet and think differently about photographs. So finally we should like to thank our contributors who have risen to the challenge and stuck by us loyally throughout – it is they who make the volume.

1

INTRODUCTION

Photographs as objects

Elizabeth Edwards and Janice Hart

> The photograph was very old, the corners were blunted from having been pasted in an album, the sepia print had faded, and the picture just managed to show two children standing together at the end of a little wooden bridge in a glassed-in conservatory, what was called a Winter Garden in those days.
>
> (Barthes 1984: 67)

In one of the most famous and influential descriptions in the whole literature of photography, what Roland Barthes in *Camera Lucida* describes first is not the image of the two children but a material object. It is a photograph that carries on it the marks of its own history, of its chemical deterioration ('the sepia print had faded'), and the fact that it once belonged to a broader visual narrative, pasted in an album, the pages of which were, we can conjecture, repeatedly handled as they were turned, re-enacting its narrative in many different contexts.

The central rationale of *Photographs Objects Histories* is that a photograph is a three-dimensional thing, not only a two-dimensional image. As such, photographs exist materially in the world, as chemical deposits on paper, as images mounted on a multitude of different sized, shaped, coloured and decorated cards, as subject to additions to their surface or as drawing their meanings from presentational forms such as frames and albums. Photographs are both images *and* physical objects that exist in time and space and thus in social and cultural experience. They have 'volume, opacity, tactility and a physical presence in the world' (Batchen 1997: 2) and are thus enmeshed with subjective, embodied and sensuous interactions. These characteristics cannot be reduced to an abstract status as a commodity, nor to a set of meanings or ideologies that take the image as their pretext. Instead, they occupy spaces, move into different spaces, following lines of passage and usage that project them through the world (Straw 1998: 2). As all the chapters here demonstrate in their different ways, thinking materially about photography encompasses processes of intention, making, distributing, consuming, using, discarding and recycling (Attfield 2000: 3), all of which impact on the way in which photographs as images are understood.

For many decades writing on photography has resonated with references to the photograph as object. These references have made tantalizing and fleeting appearances, never to be pursued fully or systematically (a point to which we shall return). Frequently photography's materiality is engaged with only in relation to the coinnosseurial 'fine print' on the one hand and conservation concerns on the other. Despite the clear realisation of this physical presence, the way in which material and presentational forms of photographs project the image into the viewer's space is overlooked in many analyses.[1] The transparency of the medium is such that 'in order to see what the photograph is "*of*" we must first suppress our consciousness of what the photograph "*is*" in material terms' (Batchen 1997: 2). The prevailing tendency is that photographs are apprehended in one visual act, absorbing image and object together, yet privileging the former. Photographs thus become detached from their physical properties and consequently from the functional context of a materiality that is glossed merely as a neutral support for images. As Maynard (1997: 24) has argued, 'Perhaps what has . . . most obdurately stood in the way of our understanding of photography is the assumption that photography is essentially a depictive device and that its other uses are marginal.'

Image content is, of course, fundamental to all the photographs that are discussed in this book. There are several reasons why this is so. Image content is our familiar way of thinking about photographs at the simplest level. Image content is usually why photographs were purchased, collected, exchanged or given as gifts in the first place, for the indexical appeal (that brief moment of exposure of the real world in front of the camera) is one of the photograph's defining qualities. However, the chapters in this volume also argue that there is a need to break, conceptually, the dominance of image content and look at the physical attributes of the photograph that influence content in the arrangement and projection of visual information. Consequently, while the chapters cannot hope to address all the multitude of material forms and performances with which photographic images are entangled, they none the less seek to redress this balance and, as a heuristic device, privilege the materiality of photographs whether in albums, in the museum gallery or in people's daily lives. This is intended not to attempt the impossible – to divorce the materiality of the photographic image from the image itself – but rather to consider in what ways the material influences contain or perform the image itself. Just as Barthes argues that the image and referent are laminated together, two leaves that cannot be separated (landscape and the window pane for instance) (Barthes 1984: 6), photographs have inextricably linked meanings as images and meanings as objects; an indissoluble, yet ambiguous, melding of image and form, both of which are direct products of intention.

While all the chapters discuss images, the arguments are critically focused on the role of the material in understanding those images. In shifting the methodological focus away from content alone, it can be seen that it is not merely the image *qua* image that is the site of meaning, but that its material and presentational forms and the uses to which they are put are central to the function of a photograph as a socially salient object. It can also be observed that these material forms exist in dialogue with the image itself to create the associative values placed on them.

Materiality translates the abstract and representational 'photography' into 'photographs' as objects that exist in time and space. The possibility of thinking about photographs in this way in part rests on the elemental fact that they are things: 'they are made, used, kept, and stored for specific reasons which do not necessarily co-incide . . . they can be transported, relocated, dispersed or damaged, torn and cropped and because viewing implies one or several physical interactions' (Porto 2001: 38). These material characteristics have a profound impact on the way images are 'read', as image content alone. Such an approach militates against the idea that photographs are solid physical objects.

Another model focuses on explanatory or causal history, at least as it is practised within the history of photography, and has tended to focus on origination, instigation and ostensible purpose. In this view one might include the broader analytical views of photography as abstract discourse, related to the analysis of the instrumentality of photographs in state or imperial control (for example, Tagg 1988; Lalvani 1996; Ryan 1997). Indeed, the postmodern angst that saturated many academic disciplines encouraged the examination of the epistemological bases from which images were made, and this was preferenced over other ways of thinking about photographs.[3] Explanatory or causal photography history has of late become extended, drawing from social history or anthropology. In this form such an approach has expanded the factual base of what we know about photography and offered insights into a range of concerns that deepen understanding, such as the use of visual tropes, or the context provided by a specific cultural milieu or commercial market. Such insights help to explain why photographs look the way they do. However, once again, except for those photographic historians who have specifically interested themselves in issues of presentation such as mounting, framing and exhibition display, or such concerns as the circulation of photographs in the networks of collecting and exhibiting (for instance, Poole 1997; Jaworek 1998; Edwards 2001), the explanatory or causal approach has again generally ignored photography's materiality.

Beaumont Newhall's magisterial *The History of Photography* (1949) provided an extensively illustrated, almost seamless narrative of the photographic pioneers, technologies and aesthetic considerations in which the photograph as an object, in the sense in which we are considering it here, is missing. Newhall's emphasis on establishing a factual base and aesthetic canon for the history of photography was an objective also pursued by Helmut and Alison Gernsheim (1969, 1988). Newhall's *History* was written while he was employed by the Museum of Modern Art, New York, and it is significant how many of the overview histories were concerned with the context of an art institution or the world of collecting and connoisseurship (see Willumson, Chapter 5 in this volume). Lemagny's *History of Photography* (1987) is cast in a similar vein but offered considerably more of a social perspective than Newhall's. Even so, Lemagny did not extend this approach to what might now be termed 'the social biography of photographs'. Some of Newhall's later writing does, however, demonstrate his awareness that during the first year of the public announcement of photography, some of the leading proponents could not but be conscious of photography's own materiality (Newhall 1980).

The history of art contains a number of useful models or methodological seeds that prefigure the arguments in *Photographs Objects Histories*. Historical materialism, deriving ultimately from Marx and developed by Lukács and others (see, for example, Marx 1970; Lukács 1971; Althusser 1976), manifested itself in writing about art that emphasised contexts and conditions of production[4] over more traditional art historical concerns such as iconography. The materialist approach was exemplified by Janet Wolff in *The Social Production of Art* (1981), which argues that visual representation of any kind is never separate from its cultural formation, and indeed helps to shape it. In a different vein, Michael Baxandall's groundbreaking *Painting and Experience in Fifteenth Century Italy* (1988) moved beyond issues of process and patronage to enquire into the circulation of ideas and cultural practices in which painting was an integral rather than a separate part. Although differently positioned, in many ways this echoes Pierre Bourdieu's exploration of the social meaning and practice of photography (1990). The philosophy of art also offers some useful pointers. Henri Focillon, in *The Life of Forms in Art* (1984), provides a rich source of ideas about the mutability of objects within cultural formations, drawing on Arsène Darmsteter's (1886) *The Life of Words*. The philosophy of art has also created a number of blind alleys for a material approach to photography. These include Roger Scruton's idea that a photograph is a surrogate for its image content. Interesting as the potential for this idea is, Scruton's theory only explored at an abstract level and did not engage with how people use photographs as surrogates. Philosophy, particularly the writing of Michel Foucault in *The Order of Things* and *The Archaeology of Knowledge* (1989a, b), offers a number of conceptual tools for realising an approach to history and to the study of objects and can be said to have bearing on the models of 'social biography' and 'visual economy'. The first of these concerns origination and the complex question of when something can be said to come into being and have a history made up of a multilayered matrix of interconnected traces.

Conversely, technical history might seem the obvious place to look for an engagement with photography's materiality and in certain respects this is so. Technical history engages with the very physical fabric of photography, such as surface and substrata. It deals with acts of becoming and with agents of change as physics and chemistry interact. However, except for those studies that are concerned with conservation issues such as image fading or decomposition, the marked tendency within technical history has been for the historical engagement to cease once the technical process under consideration is complete. Technology is seen as an end in itself rather than the producer of social salient objects. In addition, although some historians have indeed considered factors such as how various technical originators or the specialist responded to the physicality of photographs and what this says about how photography developed conceptually (for instance, Batchen 1997; Jaworek 1998), most have not explored the potential of using primary source material in this way.

From the 1970s texts began to appear with increasing regularity that located photography within a matrix of production and reception that foregrounded theories of gender and representation. This matrix drew from feminist discourse and especially feminist Marxism and eventually gave rise to theories that differentiated themselves from more mainstream feminist studies, such as queer theory. Likewise, the work of feminist critics of photographs such Jo Spence (Holland and Spence 1991) and Annette Kuhn (1995) focused on family albums as constructed narratives. While the material is implied throughout this work, it is never fully articulated as an analytical category, but none the less is an important precursor of the material turn. An important metaphor that arose out of this intellectual endeavour is 'public/private', because it was seen to have a direct bearing on the experiences of the gendered body and its representation. The importance of this for an argument grounded in the materiality of photography is that a text such as Jane Brettle and Sally Rice's *Public Bodies: Private States* (1994) positions photography as never separable from its relations with the world. This recognition of the reflexiveness of photography is a significant development. However, the line of argument that flowed from this recognition tended in the direction of questioning the moment of photographic truth, the impossibility of defining what is real and an acknowledgement that our outwardly shared experiences are not as much lived as imaged. Although this writing on representation did bring insights into the possibility that photographs move through space and time, it largely buried these and did not initiate a thorough ongoing investigation into the lives that photographs lead after their initial point of inception. However, writing on representation, because it privileged the body and the embodied eye, did pave the way for an approach to photography that acknowledges that it offers a diverse range of body-related engagements.

This concern with embodied relationships with images forms an especially relevant category of writing about photography for a study of materiality. An example of this occurs when Hervé Guibert recalls kissing a photograph of the actor Terence Stamp, in *Ghost Image* (1996). Guibert also remembered acquired film stills, which, when he came to write about them, had been consigned to the bottom of a box, but he described them as bearing the traces of being repeatedly tacked to the canvas that covered his wall, then glued, then unglued from his door. That a photograph was seen to have presence (unlike film, which has to go through the transformation of being screened to acquire presence) took writing about photography in a direction that again resonates here.

A further prescient moment that acknowledges the haptic is located at the border between film studies and photographic theory. Régis Durand's 1995 essay 'How to see (photographically)' specifically identifies a photograph as an object. For Durand a photograph is an object that 'lacks all certainty' because it seems to call for so many different acts of looking, durations of engagement and types of attention depending on whether it is a snapshot in a wallet, a print in a portfolio, reproduced on the printed page or (to bring Durand's thinking forward in time) via a computer screen. But this is not all that theorizing about the ontology of photography and how photography differs ontologically from any other visual medium has to offer those in search of the vanguard of thinkers who recognised that photographs are objects as well as images. The philosopher Alois Riegl's idea of the 'optical-haptic' was taken up by Durand and others to explore the notion that when we look at photographs we often move from pure opticality to the optical-tactile as our attention moves from a thing being represented to an awareness of the texture of that thing (for example, the grain of skin or the weave of foliage), until a point is reached where we identify this with the very texture of the photograph itself.

Walter Benjamin's influential idea that the 'aura' possessed by an original, unique artwork was destroyed by 'mechanical reproduction' cast photography into the role of perpetrator in this process, a position that has resonated through writing on photography from Malraux's (1949) 'Museum without walls' to work such as Baudrillard's (1994) on simulacra. Politically, Benjamin took the view that mechanical reproduction had the beneficial effect of democratising art. However, he did not describe in any detail how this might work and he also avoided the question of whether photography might itself possess auratic properties, a question taken up by Gabriel Hanganu in this volume (Chapter 10). Indeed, it could be argued that the premise of this volume precisely reinvests photographs of all sorts with their own 'aura' of thingness existing in the world.

If Benjamin saw materiality at work in instances such as an altarpiece still *in situ* in the chancel of a church and not in a photograph, for Susan Sontag materiality is a recurring theme in her writing on photography. In *On Photography* (1979) her place-ment of photography within a context of lived experiences – for example, tourists from highly developed work-orientated countries who are described as taking photographs as work displacement activity – enabled Sontag to develop an analysis that was not based on image content alone. In her recent essays on photography published in *Where the Stress Falls* (2002: 218), Sontag considers the varied 'extramural life' that a photo-graph might lead outside the confines of the museum, and cites an example of images that began as prints taking on new identities when reproduced as postcards.

It will be clear then from these examples from a diverse literature that the materiality of photographs has always had a subliminal presence in writing about photographs. Such a knowledge simply strengthens a heuristic resolve to cohere these ideas and bring to the surface the physicality of photographs.

The ubiquitous materiality of photographs

It is impossible for one volume comprising eleven essays to address all the material forms of and interventions with the photographic image, all the presentational forms and social biographies that have mediated photographs and placed them in specific social and cultural discourses. Nor has it been possible to do more than indicate the vast array of culturally specific perceptions of the objecthood of photographs. Our aim is to represent as wide a spread as possible across historical periods and cultural boundaries, with the knowledge that some important material forms and cultural practices are inevitably left out. However, in partial compensation, this section of the introduction provides a reflection on the larger domain of photographic materiality, but one which, in different ways, relates back to the subjects discussed in this book. It is also a reflection of the state of knowledge, for, as we have suggested, there has been remarkably little work that concentrates analytically on the physicality of photo-graphs. Discussions of *cartes de visite* – for instance, by scholars such as McCauley (1985), Poole (1997) or Hamilton and Hargreaves (2001) – have engaged with the material aspects of their subjects, as have writers on albums, especially the elaborate and gendered productions of nineteenth-century women – for instance, Smith (1998) and Crombie (1998), who have addressed the material as part of wider concerns. Conversely, some writing on presentational forms has considered them not as intrins-ically interesting as material culture but as a means to compiling and extending an inventory of the images they contain or support, (for instance, Rinhart and Rinhart 1969; Welling 1976; Wood 1989; Henisch and Henisch 1994). Work by Wolfgang Jaworek (1998) on the reception of presentational forms in the nineteenth century promises to extend this given of investigation into an analytical realm.

Some forms of materiality emerge from specific performative desires for the image. Photographs, as we have suggested, are made for a reason for a specific audience, to embody specific messages and moral values (Schwartz 1995: 42; Attfield 2000: 12). While this applies equally to image content, it is, we argue, essential to see material forms in the same way. For instance, to print in platinum, which is one of the most stable and permanent of photographic processes, as opposed to the volatility and inherently unstable chemistry of silver-based prints, speaks to a desire for permanence. The insistence of the National Photographic Record Association under Sir Benjamin Stone in 1897 that all prints were to be in platinum echoes Cosmo Burton, writing in the *British Journal of Photography* in 1889 that photographs for posterity should be 'unpolluted by silver' (Burton 1889: 668).

Presentational forms equally reflect specific intent in the use and value of the photographs they embed, to the extent that the objects that embed photographs are in many cases meaningless without their photographs; for instance, empty frames or albums. These objects are only invigorated when they are again in conjunction with the images with which they have a symbiotic relationship, for display functions not only make the thing itself visible but make it more visible in certain ways (Maynard 1997: 31–2). This form of materiality, in which image content and presentational form work together, is often dictated by the social uses of the photographs. They 'serve to illuminate the distinctive texture of social relations in which it [the photograph] is performing its work' (Banks 2001: 51) – for instance, wedding photographs in white albums with silver bells printed on the cover, or photographs printed on enamel to withstand the weather in Italian country graveyards. In many ways one can see this as materiality embedding photographs into culturally specific expected or appropriate forms.

Albums in particular have performative qualities. Not only do they narrativise photographs, such as in family or travel albums (see Holland and Spence 1991; Hirsch 1997; Langford 2001; Willumson, Chapter 5, and Nordström, Chapter 6, this volume), but their materiality dictates the embodied conditions of viewing, literally performing the images in certain ways. How are albums used? Are they intended to be read formally? In a large group? Privately? Albums have weight, tactility, they often smell, often of damp, rotting card – the scent of 'the past' (Langford 2001: 5). Large presentation albums require displaying on a table, their contents laid out and presented to the viewer. Such albums, viewed by two or more seated persons with the object spread across their knees, would link the group to one another physically, determining the social relations of viewing. Conversely, small albums, held in the hand, suggest a private relationship with the object: to view jointly with another person would again require very specific and close physical proximity (Edwards 1999: 228–30).

Many presentational forms have a skewomorphic quality referring to other objects with precise social meanings and functions. Albums are made to look like precious books, religious books, such as Victorian albums with heavy embossed covers with gold tooling and gold edged pages that are closed with metal clasps, clearly a reference to medieval devotional books, the *carte de visite* album becoming a form of secular Bible (McCauley 1985: 48). The format was appropriate to an object that was often kept as a book, perhaps, in wealthier households, actually in a library. Modern albums are made to look like leather-bound books, and even the flip case of a plastic wallet has material reference of this kind. Photographs are also produced as commemorative china, mugs and plates, in the tradition of material object that goes back into the Renaissance period and is carried on by high street chemists to this day.[5]

Sometimes material forms reflect the content of the images through reference to other kinds of objects. In this they extend the sense of vision and the indexicality of the photograph itself in a mutually reinforcing sign system. For instance, many colonial albums and their decoration literally set the scene for the photographs and delineate the space in which the reading of the photographs might operate. An album from the Dutch East Indies, dating from about 1890–1900, has wooden cover boards and a half-leather binding that is shaped and painted in imitation of local rice barn decoration.[6] Likewise, an album purchased in the early twentieth century from Farsari of

Yokohama, Japan, has lacquered boards, inlaid with mother of pearl, the whole album being kept in a padded printed cotton box, and closed with traditional Japanese silk and bone toggles (Odo 1997). Other such albums use local craft styles and materials such as ikat, elaborately carved wood or metalwork, underlining the 'exotic' discourses that embed the images and reinforcing their reading (Edwards 2001: 72). At a less elaborate level the thousands of small Kodak albums sold in the early twentieth century, embossed with flowers and the legend 'Sunny Memories', work in the same reinforcing way.

Often material forms reflect public and private functions of images. What is displayed, formally framed in the semi-public spaces of the home, and what is hidden away in boxes, lockets, wallets or family Bibles? This applies equally to the display of photographs. There are profound cultural differences and cultural significances in what is displayed, in what contexts, who has access to it, how long it stays there, when it is superseded and so forth, as Jo Spence, for instance, has suggested in her writing on family albums (Holland and Spence 1991). Morley (1992) has commented on the use of the television as a space on which to display family photographs, the majority of which are formal or studio photographs marking weddings, graduations and the like, often in relation with other auratic objects such as souvenirs and gifts. For instance, silver and leather or 'antique style' frames holding photographs of *rites de passages*, graduations or weddings become public statements of identity and group cohesion, as discussed, for instance, by Gisèle Freund (1980) and Pierre Bourdieu (1990: 31–9). The choice of frame itself may or may not be significant, and sometimes it is selected simply because it fits the photograph, yet the display and the space it occupies remain a significant material presentation of the photographs as social objects, (Banks 2001: 54–5). Conversely, the informal unframed groupings such as displays on kitchen pin-boards or of 'fridge magnets' might be seen as displays of current and shifting identities within the group (Slater 1995: 139). In their material provisionality they are concerned with self-presentation in the present, rather than the future that is suggested in the framing structures of an album or frame, for instance. Photographs are embedded in the flow of the everyday of a consumerist present rather than the non-ordinary. They are objects in a historically marked time.

Materiality is also capable of cutting across these categories. Marks on the photographic object point to the history of its presentational forms and engagements with them, such as is articulated by Barthes's description quoted at the beginning of this chapter. For photographs also bear the scars of their use, as the Hervé Guibert example discussed above showed. Handling damage, the torn and creased corners, fold marks, perhaps text on the back, scuffing and dirt point to the use of images or, indeed, neglect of images. For instance, a small group of photographs of bare-breasted Zulu women purchased by a soldier with the Wessex Yeomanry during the South African War (1899–1902) bear the marks of constant handling: dirty thumb marks, missing and torn corners, a central crease caused by constant folding and unfolding.[7] One senses strongly the embodiment of the colonial gaze, of an image actually being handled, put away, brought out. While such a reading must remain conjectural, it does at least point to an object that was not merely purchased and filed away but used, and engaged with constantly. It bears the marks of its own history as an object. Likewise, albums with missing pages and missing images might be seen in this way. What were the circumstances of this material intervention in the narrative?

Perhaps one of the most widespread social uses of photographs is as objects of exchange. While the image itself is of course central to the act of giving, receiving and utilising, the materiality of the photograph is equally part of the social meaning of exchanges. This is made explicit in this volume in the cases discussed by Porto, Schwartz, Chalfen and Murui and implicit in much of Batchen's discussion of photographic jewellery. The implications of the gifting relationship are in these examples, and many others one can think of, integral to the meaning of the photograph as object in the gestures that recapitulate or re-enact different forms of social relations. Which photographs become exchange objects and within which contexts?

In other relationships photographs are used as votive offerings, as objects of intercession. In many instances layers of photographs accrue around religious figures and shrines: examples can be found almost everywhere in Catholic Europe and in Latin America. Family photographs, wedding photographs, even foetal scans, become votive offerings, objects mediating between peoples and their god. In religious usage the image is perhaps sacralised through its material proximity with a religious figure. At the same time they become a sort of archaeology of photographic practices and photographic usage, the objects scarred by their use, bent, dust covered and cracked. Image-object has moved into sacred space, assuming new meanings. However, these processes are again profoundly culture specific. Both Harris and Hanganu in this volume show how images used in religious contexts become invested with sanctity, and the way in which the indexicality of the image vested is a culturally constructed notion of matter.

Materiality also extends the indexicality of the image through both bodily interactions with the photo-object, especially the tactile, and through interventions with the indexical image. Photographs can be touched or worn or, as Harris identifies in this volume, can involve conjunctures with parts of the body such as the feet, which are inextricably linked to the differentiated cultural specifics of body language. Batchen's chapter in this volume further highlights the importance of touch when he refers to such things as transference of heat to a metal-cased photographic locket as it is held in the hand and to the placing of photographs when worn round the neck, on the hand, on the breast. Photographs that become fetishised are also often subject to touch, and specifically the touch of desire. Frames of carved wood, velvet, silk or fur can work in this way. Likewise, overpainting extends, and moves, beyond the indexical trace of the image itself to add other layers of meaning. Further, material acts on photographs illuminate responses to the indexicality of images. Surface interventions and additive techniques have also permeated photographic practice. At its simplest level this was merely a matter of adding colour to monochrome images, a common practice from the earliest period, as evidenced by hand-tinted daguerreotypes (such as that discussed by Schwartz), ambrotypes, tintypes and later albumen prints, including the fine tinted productions of studios in Japan. However, as Batchen demonstrates, other materials such as hair, or perhaps cloth, might be added to the image, extending its indexicality and thus the understanding and effectiveness of the photographic image.

In some cultures it is sometimes the additive and interventionist techniques applied to photographs that render the image complete and real. For instance, the 'reality' of portrait photographs in India is constructed through material and additive interventions with the surface of the image. Overpainting and collage are integral to the meaning of the photograph. They extend its indexicality, which is seen as a baseline for a photograph, not as the complete rendering of an identity; instead the identity recorded in the photograph is extended and enhanced, revealing a form of inner self through material surface additions to the photograph itself (Pinney 1997: 137). Similarly, as Buckley has shown, photographers in The Gambia cut up photographs, rearranging the surface of the image, or superimposing other images, including publicly available images of pop stars, beauty queens or religious leaders. This aesthetic, called 'double impact' locally, is premised on an exploration of the surfaces and the edges of a person as an expression of identity. Consequently, material edges within these constructed photographic objects become integral to the social expectation and the 'reality effects' of the photographs (Buckley 2000: 81).

While the surface interventions that appear in this book are less dramatic, they none the less can be viewed in the same connection – as extending and focusing the meaning of the image. It is through material intervention and presentational form that people mark their own desires on the machine-produced or mass-produced object of modernity, reasserting the user as author. This is very clear in Nordström's chapter as the traveller Tupper re-authors commercially produced photographs, domesticating them, sequencing them so as to perform materially his own experience, as he chose to present it. In many ways it is the materiality of people's photographs that make them 'their own'.

Conclusion

Postcards, albums, campaign buttons, decorated photographs carried behind the open coffin at Russian funerals, the photographic placards of mass demonstration or political processions, T-shirts or photographs of ancestors worn in the dance in a Native American community – the possible material forms in which photographs are consumed are almost limitless. We have only been able to touch on this ubiquitous and all-saturating world of the photograph-object. There are many ways in which the idea of photographs as material culture might be developed and elucidated – the phenomenological, the sensory, psychology of perception, through enhanced readings of the subjecthood of the viewer, studies of consumption, history of collecting, history of exhibition presentation, the study of both exhibition and domestic frames, the ethnography of photographic practices in many parts of the world. Even in the digital age, when the materiality of many images evaporates into a series of electronic pulses, the desire for the material object remains, as digitally produced photographs are selected for printing, some on photographic paper, others merely printed out at low resolution on ordinary paper, perhaps several to a sheet, and kept in display files with plastic wallets. Even in the digital world these material decisions are integral to the social saliency of the photograph.

Rather than defining a status quo, the intention of this volume is point up some of these possibilities, and, importantly, to inspire further enquiry. We are attempting neither to create a new orthodoxy nor to displace existing theories of photography. Instead we offer shift in emphasis, develop another strand of analysis and provide another theoretical and methodological tool that can resonate through other ways of thinking about photographs. In so many ways it is the material that defines our social relations with photographs. What we hope has emerged is a sense of the centrality of materiality as a formative element in the understanding of photographs as social images. Acknowledging the material makes the act of viewing more complex and more difficult, as the act of viewing cannot any longer be processed in the same way. Instead it has to take account of the materiality of the photograph and the presentational forms in which it is entangled, in a way that will fundamentally cohere the photograph as an image. An approach that acknowledges the centrality of materiality allows one to look at and use images as socially salient objects, as active and reciprocal rather than simply implications of authority, control and passive consumption on the one hand, or of aesthetic discourses and the supremacy of individual vision on the other. They may be these things too, and the examples discussed in this volume can be said to function like this in important ways, but they cannot necessarily be reduced to them unproblematically. The material and social existence of photographs as objects forestalls such a reduction.

Notes

1 There have been two exhibitions dedicated to photographs–objects: *Pop Photographica* at the Art Gallery of Ontario (2003), curated by Dale Kaplan, and, more analytical in approach, *Photography's Objects* at the University of New Mexico (1997), curated by Geoffrey Batchen.
2 In order for the three-dimensional qualities of stereoscopic photographs to be demonstrated to best effect, compositions had to have a clear foreground object and a receding middle and background.
3 The literature abounds with such critiques, from geography (Ryan 1997), criminology (Sekula 1989), anthropology (Green 1984; Edwards 1992; Pinney 1997) and medicine (Gilman 1988) to cite just a few examples.
4 For instance, T. H. Clark (1973) presented the art of Gustav Courbet from this perspective.
5 For instance, Boots the Chemist, found on most British high streets, offers a range of photographic objects: transform your favourite family photographs into mugs, plates, jigsaws, T-shirts, place mats or mouse mats.
6 Tropenmuseum, Amsterdam, Photograph Collection Album 282.
7 Pitt Rivers Museum Photograph Collections PRM.B1A.36.

2

UN BEAU SOUVENIR DU CANADA

Object, image, symbolic space

Joan M. Schwartz

On 14 July 1855 (coincidentally and symbolically, Bastille Day) the French naval vessel *La Capricieuse*, under the command of Captain Paul-Henri de Belvèze, put into port at Quebec City. It was the first naval ship to fly the flag of France on the St Lawrence River since the English defeated the French on the Plains of Abraham almost a century before. Captain de Belvèze (1801–75) was on a mission to restore economic and cultural relations between France and Canada at a time when British free trade policy opened new markets to its colonies and when Britain and France were allied against Russia in the Crimea. During his six-week tour of Canada, de Belvèze visited Quebec, Montreal, Ottawa and Toronto, and held discussions with prominent individuals on a variety of economic, cultural and military matters. When he set sail from Quebec City six weeks later to return to France, he carried with him a daguerreotype, by noted Montreal photographer Thomas Coffin Doane, of a man posed with four boys in historical costumes as a gift for the Empress Eugénie, wife of Napoleon III, Emperor of France.

This daguerreotype (Figure 2.1) warrants close scrutiny as object, image and symbolic space because its shifting cultural meanings are deeply embedded in the complex and dynamic relationships between visuality and physicality, object and narrative, history and memory, author and audience, indexicality and instrumentality. Traditionally valued in curatorial terms as the work of a prominent daguerreotypist on the one hand or the product of an early image-making technology on the other, this *tableau vivant* is also a physical object. Its social functions – as *souvenirs* (memories), as souvenir (reminder of personal experience or commemorative keepsake) and as gift (symbolic offering) – are inextricably linked to its narrative functions: as visual record of a performance of identity, as concrete expression of pride and patriotism and as material residue of an act of communication. Analysis proceeds in a layered and cumulative approach through three sections. The first of these considers the photograph broadly in terms of 'the daguerreotype as physical object'. In the second section, the photograph is examined specifically in terms of 'content and context'. The final section considers more closely issues of 'materiality and meaning'. Approached this way, this enigmatic daguerreotype emerges as a symbolic space of remembrance and resistance, which cannot be fully understood apart from its 'objectness'.

Figure 2.1 Hand-coloured, half-plate daguerreotype of a man and four boys in historical costume, one of two taken following the St Jean-Baptiste Day celebrations in Montreal, 1855. Photographer: Thomas Coffin Doane. (Courtesy National Archives of Canada, Andre L'Homme Collection, 1985–011.)

JOAN M. SCHWARTZ

The daguerreotype as physical object

In this age of electronic images and digital reproduction, when the photograph is often circulated and viewed as a dematerialised, decontextualised image, it is all the more difficult to imagine the excitement and wonder that the daguerreotype inspired when the process was first announced in Paris in 1839. Its unprecedented ability to make detailed images directly 'from Nature' – the phrase commonly used to suggest 'unmediated by the human hand' – challenged the applications to which picture-making had previously been put. Called the 'mirror with a memory' because of its highly reflective silvered surface, the daguerreotype was greeted as 'a discovery as useful as it was unexpected', capable of rendering to both art and science services 'beyond calculation'. Praised as 'the most marvellous invention of the century' and hailed as 'truth itself in the supremeness of its perfection', the daguerreotype attracted the attention of leading artists, writers and critics of the time, including John Ruskin, Edgar Allan Poe and Elizabeth Barrett Browning (see Schwartz 2000: 27–8). Housed in a hinged case of fine leather or nestled between thermoplastic covers with elaborate designs in bas-relief, the infinitely detailed likeness presented a startlingly realistic visual image. More importantly for my argument developed here, it was a unique, precious and profoundly material object.

Produced by deposits of mercury on a highly polished silver-coated copper plate, the daguerreotype required a protective housing consisting of a coverglass, a matte or *passe-partout*, and a frame or case to preserve its delicate surface. Social status and material worth were attached to the daguerreotype's physical presentation and communicated through size, framing, case manufacture and embellishment, all of which have been studied as objects in their own right (see Rinhart and Rinhart 1969; Krainik and Krainik 1988; Berg 1995). Its dimensions corresponded to the dimensions of the camera and were echoed in the dimensions of the case. Its cost, in part determined by the reputation and physical location of the photographer, was also relative to its plate size, the addition of hand-colouring and the intricacies of its housing. Thus, formed on a silvered surface, protected by glass, surrounded by brass or paper, juxtaposed with silk or velvet and enclosed in wood, leather, thermoplastic or gutta percha, the daguerreotype exhibited a combination of materials and confronted the viewer with a variety of surfaces, colours and textures.

Discernible only in raking light, the daguerreotype demanded an embodied relationship with the viewer, a relationship within which the requisite manipulation in the hand as well as the tactility of the case were an integral, if now often overlooked, aspect of a process of meaning-making long presumed to be solely optical in nature. Because reflections from the mirrored surface made direct examination difficult, viewing involved a haptic experience: the case must be picked up, opened carefully, cradled in the hand and tilted slowly, right to left, back and forth until, at just the right angle, the image becomes clearly visible on the surface of the plate. As the image resided not on paper but on metal, and because it was housed in a protective case, size, weight and substance were also a palpable part of the viewing experience. Thus, the 'objectness' of the daguerreotype was central to, and accentuated in, the process of viewing.

Despite these obvious physical characteristics, the daguerreotype has been valued, collected and analysed primarily, if not solely, as a visual image – for its subject matter or for its formal qualities. The reason may be attributed to its visual/presentational form. Taking Suzanne Langer's observation that visual forms 'do not present their constituents successively, but simultaneously, so the relations determining a visual structure are grasped in one act of vision', and extending it to Daniel Miller's notion that objects are typically 'presentational forms' that 'present themselves with all their aspects at one time', it is easy to see how, in the daguerreotype, plate and case present themselves 'simultaneously'. Image and object are, as Langer suggests, 'grasped in one act of vision' (Langer 1957: 93; Miller 1994: 407). This 'subsumption of the tactile within the optical' (Crary 1992: 62), this primacy of image over object, so much an established part of nineteenth-century information gathering and knowledge production, persists today and continues to shape the way we approach photographs, especially daguerreotypes.

If, as is argued here, the daguerreotype is a profoundly material object, then is the visual narrative tied to and transmitted through it one that derives from and depends upon that materiality? This chapter considers how a heightened awareness of the materiality of the daguerreotype as a physical object can inform and enhance our understanding of the meaning of this charming but enigmatic daguerreotype. To do so, we must first attempt to recover the narrative embedded in the visual image through an examination of the daguerreotype's content and context.

Content and context

The whereabouts of the daguerreotype carried back to France by Captain de Belvèze has yet to be ascertained; nor is it known whether the Empress ever received her gift. However, a daguerreotype presented to the National Archives of Canada by a direct descendent of Paul-Henri de Belvèze in 1984 closely matches a description of the daguerreotype sent to the Empress, and will be used as the basis for this inquiry.[1] This delicately hand-coloured half-plate image (measuring 108 × 140 mm) is housed in a fine leather case, lined with green velvet and with a plain brass *passe-partout*, blindstamped in the lower left corner, 'T.C. Doane'. Pinned to the lining is a slip of paper bearing the delicately hand-written inscription *'Au Commandant de Belvèze en Canada'*, with an explanation of the figures in the image and the signature of Alfred Chalifoux.[2] Up to this point, it has been assumed that this daguerreotype was the one originally intended for the Empress; however, careful reconsideration of its materiality has prompted this revised interpretation, predicated upon the existence of two similar gifts.

The daguerreotype destined for the Empress was described in detail in an account published in *La Minerve*, a local French-language newspaper, a week after the departure of *La Capricieuse*.

GIFT OFFERED TO THE EMPRESS EUGÉNIE

The visit of M. de Belvèze to Montreal furnished M. Alfred Chalifoux – so well known for his four small historical characters which everyone was able to admire in our recent celebrations – the opportunity to offer to Her Majesty the Empress of France, a beautiful souvenir of Canada, which is, in fact, a small picture of these characters executed by the daguerreotype process by

Mr. Doane. It is contained in a box of velvet and shagreen,[3] also intended, by the manner of its ornamentation and by the particular style in which it is made up, to enhance the gift offered to Her Imperial Majesty. This delightful idea is due entirely to the zeal and intelligence of Mr. Chalifoux, who also assumed all costs. The following details and notes on this charming piece of Canadian art were provided to us by a person well informed on the subject.

This small picture is accompanied by a silver plaque affixed to the box and bearing in full the following inscription:

To Her Majesty the Empress of the French People:

These small characters who take part in Montreal's national celebrations call to mind all the religious and patriotic memories of the French Canadians. St. Jean-Baptiste, patron saint of Canada, Jacques Cartier who, in the sixteenth century, discovered the country and brought to it the Gospel, the 'Chef Sauvage', who greeted the French at Hochelaga {Montreal}. Finally, to link the past to the present, a young Canadian, bearing the colours of France, is all ready to rejoin his elder brothers at Sebastopol.

The one who accompanies them and has the honour to present them to Her Majesty, the Empress, is her very humble and respectful servant

Alfred Chalifoux
French Canadian

This first box was enclosed in a second, highly decorated box made of birch bark and flawlessly worked and embroidered with porcupine quills.[4] Those who saw it told us that they regarded this work a masterpiece of its kind.

Its decorative design of Beaver, Maple Branch, Rose and festoons was represented in the richest colours, the whole having been due to the skill and truly remarkable talent of a 'demoiselle canadienne'[5] whose name, we regret, we are not authorized to make known.

(*La Minerve* (Montreal) 1 September 1855: 2, col. 1; author's translation)

This account, together with the daguerreotype held in Ottawa, permits closer consideration of the visual image, the objects within the image and the political 'pre-texts' of viewing.

The names of Doane and Chalifoux, along with those of de Belvèze and the Empress Eugénie, in this account frame the historical, social, political and functional contexts in which to explore the significance of this daguerreotype, its meaning(s) as a visual image and its social life as a physical object. Thomas Coffin Doane was Montreal's most successful and sought after daguerreotypist, best known for his portraits of leading politicians and prominent individuals, including Lord Elgin, Governor General of British North America.[6] In 1855, the same year that he was commissioned by Chalifoux to take the daguerreotype for the Empress, Doane was awarded an Honourable Mention at the Exposition Universelle in Paris for his 'portraits au daguerréotype' (Taché 1856: 414, 421; Greenhill and Birrell 1979: 27). His name, blindstamped on the *passe-partout*, brought a measure of professional prestige, an assurance of quality workmanship and a stamp of international recognition to Chalifoux's gift.

Alfred Chalifoux, the man both in and 'behind' the daguerreotype, was a tailor, widely known throughout Montreal for the theatrical *tableau vivant* which he created for the annual *'fêtes nationales'* or St Jean-Baptiste Day celebrations. From the wording on the silver plaque, he viewed himself, certainly figuratively if not literally, as the Empress's 'very humble and respectful servant', as well as an avowed 'French Canadian'.

The daguerreotype as visual image

Doane took this daguerreotype shortly after the *'fêtes nationales'* celebrations, held in Montreal on 24 June 1855, just a few weeks before the arrival of *La Capricieuse*. The boys, in historical costumes made by Chalifoux, had taken part in these celebrations to great popular acclaim, and Doane's *'petit tableau'* cannot be understood apart from the festivities in which the costumed boys figured prominently. These received widespread attention through an account of the proceedings published in *La Minerve*:

> Beginning at 9 o'clock in the morning, the members of the Société St Jean-Baptiste and other benevolent associations marched in large numbers, although more or less separately, towards the parish church to attend Mass, which was celebrated by Monseigneur LaRocque. The officers of these various associations, gathered according to a plan agreed upon in advance, in the rooms of the Seminary, and from there advanced, led by a band, into the church. There, the head of the Société St Jean-Baptiste, flanked by the heads of the other associations, proceeded between the ranks and took his place on a seat opposite the choir; other chairs were laid out on the other side of him for the other heads. Then, in came four small characters in costume. One (Charles Chaput) represented France, having among other remarkable badges, a small flag displaying the colours of the three allied powers, France, England, and Turkey. The second (Mr. Loiselle) represented the patron saint of the festival, St Jean-Baptiste. Another (Theodore Deschambault) posed as Jacques Cartier, and the fourth (Jean Damien Rolland) as an Indian chief. Each one of these small characters was dressed, decorated and armed in an historically accurate manner, and was admired for his beautiful costume and graceful appearance.
> (*La Minerve* (Montreal) 26 June 1855: 2, cols 1–2; author's translation)

The daguerreotype was, thus, not simply a *tableau vivant* created in Doane's studio. Rather, the image was intended to allow Her Imperial Majesty to visualise the role of the costumed characters in the St Jean-Baptiste Day festivities. If the boys' role in the *fêtes nationales* may be considered a performance of the foundational myths of French Canada, then this daguerreotype can be treated as the visual and material embodiment of that performance.

Not only was this daguerreotype a material object in its own right, but within the image were key, culturally significant material objects – headdress, costumes, medals, banner, shield, bow and arrows, flags – each with its own tale to tell: about Alfred Chalifoux, about the four costumed boys and their participation in the commemorative events of 24 June and about French Canadian politics in the mid-nineteenth century. The hand-colouring concentrated on these symbolic objects contributed another layer of materiality; the manual application of colour tints to the surface of the daguerreotype plate not only extended the indexicality of the image, but also emphasised the hand-made nature and originality of the object.

The objects within the image were not only a factual record of Chalifoux's theatrical efforts, they were also the symbolic expression of *'tous les souvenirs religieux et patriotiques des Canadiens-Français'*. Close inspection reveals that the banner held by the small child (left) is appliquéed with the words 'St Jean' and the flag in the hands of the young French Canadian (right) who bears an uncanny resemblance to Napoléon III is most likely not the 'flag of the three allied powers', but the Imperial Standard of the Emperor of France. The medal prominently displayed on Chalifoux's chest proclaimed his membership in the Société St Jean-Baptiste and declared his identity as part of French Canadian society. It also symbolised the historical and cultural roots of the Société St Jean-Baptiste and its *fêtes nationales* in early seventeenth-century New France, when special activities, usually with religious overtones, were organised for 24 June (a legal holiday in the province of Quebec since 1922) as a day for settlers to celebrate the summer solstice and the birth of St Jean-Baptiste, their patron saint. After the conquest of New France by the British, the holiday waned until the founding of the Société St Jean-Baptiste in 1834 by a French Canadian journalist who wanted to stimulate nationalist spirit among francophones and encourage them to defend their language and culture.

At the same time and through its social life as an object, this daguerreotype can be considered in archival terms as the material residue of an act of visual communication between author and audience (Schwartz 1995). It was created with authorial intent and ideological purpose to extend the spectacle of the costumed characters and carry their socio-political narrative across time and space. It survives as tangible evidence of a message from a Montreal tailor with a patriotic desire to confirm to the highest level of political authority in France that French Canadians remembered and celebrated their origins, remained loyal and were willing to bear arms for France. On this last point, it is interesting to note how the inscription on the silver plaque elaborated on the significance of the young soldier at the far right. Key here is the notion of linking past and present and the use of the word *rejoindre* (to rejoin) rather than *joindre* (to join). The former resonates with Stewart's (1984) ideas about the double function of the souvenir, a point to which I shall return in the next section; the latter suggests not simply a willingness to fight with the Allies in the Crimea, but the hope of a long-awaited 'return' to service in the brotherhood of the French military.

The extent to which this daguerreotype represented commonly held notions cannot be determined from the photograph alone. Nor can it be credited with constituting notions of French Canadian identity or strengthening patriotic ties; whereas *'les quatre petits personnages en costume'* were seen by hundreds of spectators, marchers and mass-goers during the *fêtes nationales* in Montreal, the daguerreotype itself was not. As a unique image, as a precious object and as a gift for a specific audience, it did not circulate among the public and had a limited sphere of influence. Nevertheless, Chalifoux, evidently, was not the only one who saw the mission of *La Capricieuse* in historical and patriotic terms, as the effort of the Mother Country to remember the faithful despite loss of contact for almost a century.

At the time of the visit of *La Capricieuse*, Guillaume Barthé, a former member of parliament and an editor of several journals, had just arrived from Paris, where he had recently published a book entitled *Le Canada reconquis par la France* (*Canada Reconquered by France*). Barthé's publication caused de Belvèze concern for its potential to compromise – or divert attention away from – his own mission, which in addition to economic and military matters focused on the struggle of the French Canadian population to preserve its language, its moral standards, its institutions and its religion (De Belvèze Papers 1856: 66–7; in National Archives of Canada, Ottawa). De Belvèze made it clear that he wanted nothing to do with the book, explaining to Barthé that

> its title was contrary to the political intentions of the Emperor and of France, contrary to the interests of his country under a liberal and protective regime that created true independence for him; that if it had occurred to anyone to suspect in the slightest that there existed a link between my mission and his book, I would have been unable to take another step in Canada.
> (*La Presse* (Montreal) 15 March 1905: 1; author's translation)

In the light of these prevailing tensions, this charming, seemingly innocent daguerreotype of costumed children is recast as a serious, politically charged message, an active response to the cultural mission of de Belvèze. Clearly, to understand this daguerreotype, its visual content must be placed in context; yet, never far from the surface of any analysis of the image must be an awareness of its social life as an physical object, for it was through its material form that its message was transmitted.

Materiality and meaning

While the aesthetic qualities, pictorial conventions and historical circumstances of creation, circulation and viewing are important for understanding Empress Eugénie's daguerreotype as a visual image, its meaning did not reside solely in its informational content. Nor was this daguerreotype circulated and viewed purely as a visual image. Instead, its visuality – like that of other cased images, including miniatures on ivory and ambrotypes (or collodion positives) – was inextricably bound up in its physicality; its image and message of remembrance and resistance were tied to, and transmitted through, its materiality as well as its function and trajectory as *souvenirs*, souvenir and gift.[7] Therefore, in addition to its essential nature as a physical object and its message as a visual image, we must consider the meaning-making attributes attached to its materiality, and the ways in which its message of romantic origins, religious and patriotic memories and French Canadian identity, embedded in the visual image and anchored by the textual inscription on the silver plaque, were framed, circulated and comprehended through its physical form.

The daguerreotype as souvenirs, *souvenir and gift*

In the inscription, both on a handwritten slip of paper accompanying the daguerreotype in the National Archives and on the small silver plaque originally affixed to the case sent to the Empress, Chalifoux stated that the daguerreotype called to mind '*tous les* souvenirs *religieux et patriotiques des Canadiens-Français*'; the report on the gift in

La Minerve referred to it as '*un beau* souvenir *du Canada*'. These references open several avenues for interpretation: as image and object, the daguerreotype and its embroidered barkware box functioned, and can be examined, as *souvenirs* (collective memories) and souvenir (reminder of personal experience or commemorative keepsake).

In her oft-quoted study *On Longing*, Susan Stewart suggests that the souvenir exemplifies the 'capacity of objects to serve as traces of authentic experience', adding: 'We do not need or desire souvenirs of events that are repeatable. Rather we need and desire souvenirs of events that are reportable, events whose materiality has escaped us, events that thereby exist only through the invention of narrative' (Stewart 1984: 135). In viewing the souvenir this way, experience and event, object and narrative are inextricably intertwined. In the case of the daguerreotype commissioned by Chalifoux for presentation to the Empress, the reportable event for which it constituted a trace was the costumed performance, enacted on St Jean-Baptiste Day, of the roots of French Canadian identity. The daguerreotype thus functioned as both *souvenirs* and souvenir: the visual image embodied and was intended to evoke the collective religious and patriotic memories of French Canadians, and would have served as a personal reminder of the St Jean-Baptiste Day procession for those who had attended the '*fêtes nationales*'. Importantly, the physical object was also expected to serve as '*un beau souvenir du Canada*', a commemorative keepsake by which to mark and remember the historic visit of *La Capricieuse* and the mission of de Belvèze.

Chalifoux's daguerreotype exemplifies Stewart's (1984: 151) idea that souvenirs are 'magical objects' whose function is 'to envelop the present within the past'. It also fulfilled what she has identified as 'the double function of the souvenir': 'to authenticate a past or otherwise remote experience and, at the same time, to discredit the present'.

> The present is either too impersonal, too looming, or too alienating compared to the intimate and direct experience of contact which the souvenir has as its referent. This referent is authenticity. What lies between here and there is oblivion, a void marking a radical separation between past and present. The nostalgia of the souvenir plays in the distance between the present and an imagined, prelapsarian experience, experience as it might be 'directly lived'. The location of authenticity becomes whatever is distant to the present time and space.
>
> (Stewart 1984: 139)

The past that the daguerreotype authenticated for Chalifoux was the distant, pre-Conquest past of French Canadian identity. The referent was not simply the St Jean-Baptiste parade of 1855, but instead a glorious time – represented by three of the costumed boys – that began when Jacques Cartier, carrying the flag of France and the word of God, was greeted by an Indian chief ('le chef sauvage') at Montreal (Hochelaga) in 1535, and that ended with the fall of Quebec in 1759. The daguerreotype thus authenticated a French past and discredited the British present.

However, the souvenir, as Stewart has also observed, is by definition always incomplete; the object is metonymic to the scene of its original appropriation and it must be supplemented by a narrative 'that both attaches it to its origins and creates a myth with regard to those origins' (Stewart 1984: 136). Writing more specifically about the photograph as souvenir, Stewart (1984: 138) describes it as 'the preservation of an instant in time through a reduction of physical dimensions and a corresponding increase in significance supplied by means of a narrative'. For Chalifoux, for those who witnessed the spectacle of the costumed boys and for readers of *La Minerve*, the materiality of costumed figures in the St Jean-Baptiste Day procession was preserved in the materiality of the daguerreotype and its *tableau vivant*, which carried a narrative of origins, of pivotal moments and principal figures in the collective identity of French Canadians.

But the narrative that accompanies a souvenir 'cannot be generalized to encompass the experience of anyone; it pertains only to the possessor of the object' (Stewart 1984: 136). In this case, the narrative of French Canadian identity and collective memories, so clear and strong in the mind of Chalifoux, did not adhere to the object. The metonymic relationship between object and event did not survive the ocean voyage, and was lost when the daguerreotype was carried across the Atlantic. Even when framed by the accompanying inscription, its narrative of origin would not necessarily have been understood by de Belvèze or the Empress. In the course of its trajectory, the daguerreotype would have become a curiosity with little if any value attached to its materiality as a souvenir.

Part of the meaning of this '*beau souvenir du Canada*' derived from its function as a gift or symbolic offering. As such, this daguerreotype was meant to pass along certain spatial and temporal routes, crossing political realms, geographical boundaries and social spheres in a form that could not be reduced to pure image and that was appropriate for presentation to royalty. Here, while it was the visual image that embodied Chalifoux's notion of patriotic and religious *souvenirs*, it was the aura of the object rather than the information of the image that commanded gift value. Through its combined content as an image, material worth as an object and function as a gift, this daguerreotype was an expression of perceived/desired power relations between (displaced) imperial centre and (former) colonial periphery. Indeed, it was the very 'objecthood' of the photograph that enabled it to operate in this way. Social function was linked to material form in a subtle rather than a rigidly deterministic way.

The meaning(s) attached to the double gift – daguerreotype and barkware box – changed in the trajectory from donor to recipient. In the Imperial household, interest in Chalifoux's gift would have been divided between two collecting interests: one in photographs, the other in indigenous handicrafts. Severed from its origins, displaced socially and geographically, such an object was inserted into new contexts of possession and viewing and was framed by new criteria of value. Old narratives were replaced with new ones.

For Eugénie, the daguerreotype was not a souvenir in the strictest sense. Neither image nor object conjured up familiar collective memories, served as a personal reminder of the St Jean-Baptiste Day celebrations or functioned as a commemorative keepsake of travels. Nor, being intimately acquainted with the daguerreotype (as a French invention), from both sides of the camera lens, would she have assigned great material worth or symbolic value to it as a product of modern technology, as a form of art or as the work of great genius. Whereas the daguerreotype's 'capacity for narrative' as both an expression of collective memories and a personal reminder of exterior sights and individual experience was diminished and transformed once it left the hands of Chalifoux, the fancy barkware box in which it was presented would have been a highly prized collectible. With value derived from its qualities as an object and its mode of production, it took on added significance as a powerful metaphor for Canada, signifying an 'essential' connection to place through references to native tourist arts, as will be discussed below.

Thus the meaning invested in a photograph as souvenir or gift is not fixed and can differ greatly between creator or gift-giver and viewer or recipient. This intersubjective meaning is not simply a function of change over time and space but is contingent upon the pre-texts – the intellectual baggage consisting of values and beliefs, needs and desires – brought to the visual and material encounter. Clearly, then, if the narrative of a photograph, so potent at source, is dissipated by historical, geographical and cultural distance, our understanding of it must start from a strong sense of the mutability of meaning of both image and object, and proceed through careful micro- as well as macro-historical reconstruction to recover, as best we can, its contexts of creation, circulation and viewing.

Diplomatic relations and exchange

As a gift, this 1855 daguerreotype, commissioned to mark a French diplomatic mission to British North America, must also be situated within the larger context of Anglo-French relations and the broader uses of photography that circulated through them. In April of that year, Napoleon III and Empress Eugénie paid a state visit to London, where they were taken to the Crystal Palace, site of the 1851 Exhibition of the Works of All Nations, which by then had been moved from Hyde Park to its new site at Sydenham in north London. Four months later, Queen Victoria and Prince Albert made a reciprocal visit to Paris, where they, in turn, were taken to the Palais de l'Industrie, site of the Exposition Universelle. These visits, which constituted the larger context in which the visit of *La Capricieuse* must be situated, had great symbolic significance. Allied in the Crimea, England and France enjoyed a new friendship, which had replaced longstanding enmity between nations and their rulers. The visits symbolised and cemented the alliance between the two former enemies (Dimond and Taylor 1987: 96). Part of the diplomatic glue of these new Anglo-French relations consisted of the taking, viewing and giving of photographs.

Both Victoria and Albert and Napoleon and Eugénie were avid collectors and enthusiastic supporters of the new medium, but the role of photography in these 1855 visits goes beyond collecting and patronage. In April, the Royal and Imperial couples were photographed seated on the dais in the transept of the Crystal Palace on the day of their visit, by the London firm of Negretti and Zambra, Photographers to the Crystal Palace Company (Dimond and Taylor 1987: 96). Four months later, when Victoria and Albert visited France, the Queen presented the Emperor with two stereoscopic views taken when he and the Empress visited Sydenham as a souvenir of his visit and a token of friendship. She also bought, and took with her to Paris, photographs of the Crimea, taken by Roger Fenton, to present to Napoleon III to 'effect a diplomatic rapprochement' (McCauley 1994: 312). As she reported in her journal, 'After dinner . . . we [Victoria and Albert] sat with the Emperor, Prince Napoléon, and the children, talking and looking at some of my photographs of the officers, &c.,

in the Crimea, which I had brought on purpose' (quoted in Daniel 1994: 263, note 108).

Among these photographs was one of *The Council of War on the day of the taking of the Mamelon Quarries, 7 June 1855*, showing Lord Raglan, General Pelissier and Omar Pasha sitting together. The content of this photograph offered visual evidence of Anglo-French military cooperation; the viewing of it brought together the rulers of England and France physically, to share a symbolic space of military alliance, political accord and mutual understanding. As Anne McCauley (1994: 312) has observed, 'That the rulers of two of the most industrialized countries of the world should have come together over albums of photographs in 1855 indicates both the novelty of the paper print and its acceptance as evidence.'

Before her departure from Paris, the Queen was presented with a magnificent album of photographs as a souvenir of her visit (Daniel 1994: 43–54, 238). Commissioned by Baron James de Rothschild, president and principal investor in the rail line between Paris and Boulogne, it showed views of towns, stations and sites along the route between Paris and the English Channel. Bound in red leather with raised panels and gold leaf embossing on the cover, it contained: a decorated title page in watercolour and silver leaf; two maps, each ornately embellished with coats of arms and an elaborate cartouche inset with a photograph; and fifty rich, salted paper prints, almost all by leading French photographer Édouard Baldus. In his careful analysis of its contents, Malcolm Daniel (1994: 54) argues that the album addressed 'the issues and aspirations of the epoch', and showed the Chemin de Fer du Nord as 'the physical embodiment of the theme that underlay the entire state visit . . . the linking of the two nations'.

In this atmosphere of Anglo-French *entente*, and in the context of the photograph as an object and space of diplomatic relations, the Chalifoux daguerreotype emerges as a visual statement of patriotic remembrance and political resistance. Drawing on sociologist David Cheal's notion of a gift as a 'tie-sign', it is easy to presume that Alfred Chalifoux saw the visit of *La Capricieuse* as an occasion 'for confirming attachments', the significance of which 'would seem to be strongly related to the theme of demonstrating unbroken attachment in the face of separation' (Cheal 1988: 96). However, the attachment confirmed by the gift was not between Victorian Britain and Second Empire France, but between the loyal descendants of sixteenth-century New France and the reigning order of the former Mother country.

Shagreen and barkware

Significantly, the Doane daguerreotype destined for the Empress was housed in a case not of leather but of 'shagreen' or sharkskin, an exotic material of subtle beauty, used along with ivory, rare woods and other prime materials for both utilitarian and decorative items. Made popular in eighteenth-century France by a master leather-worker for Louis XV, it was used in the embellishment of eyeglass holders, toiletry sets, 'objets d'art', furniture, jewellery boxes, cigar cases, sword hilts and a variety of other prestige articles, made even more precious by the use of shagreen. Both beautiful and functional, its tough and textured surface was especially popular for use as a covering for scientific instruments and high-status items that symbolised wisdom and wealth in the Age of Enlightenment. As highlighted in the description in *La Minerve*, the choice of shagreen was a particularly meaningful aspect of the material form of a gift that was further enhanced by its ornamentation and style, and bound up in yet another layer of materiality by its placement in a fancy barkware box.

From the report in *La Minerve*, we know that the cased image was originally housed in a second box, made of birchbark and richly embroidered with a colourful design of beaver, maple branch, rose and festoons. This presentation would have carried particular significance during the 1850s, for such fancy barkware was a gift of choice for diplomatic visitors to Canada. During the second half of the nineteenth century, when important visitors went to the Indian village of Lorette (now Wendake) in the vicinity of Quebec City, they were regularly presented with birchbark scrolls on which were written welcome addresses with moosehair floral motifs embroidered in the margins. More broadly, it was customary in the mid-nineteenth century to present such dignitaries as Prince Maximilian von Weid and Lord Elgin, Governor-General of British North America, with moosehair or quill embroidered objects; equally, their purchase by aristocratic visitors, military or colonial officials and travellers of the mid-nineteenth century was common.

Such fancy barkware items were presumed to represent the essence of Canada because they were made of native materials, according to craft processes, both of which were identified with indigenous peoples. The motifs with which they were decorated – images of either native people or flowers – were read as signifying the natural, the pure, the feminised and the beautiful – all attributes ascribed to indigenous people according to the romantic construct of the noble savage (R. B. Phillips, personal e-mail communication 5 June 2002; see also Phillips 1998: 155–96). However, as Phillips has pointed out, moosehair embroidered barkware novelties were first made and presented by the Ursuline nuns during the early eighteenth century as gifts for their supporters, donors and other important people they wished to honour or please. Later, the medium became fashionable among genteel ladies from the late eighteenth century to the 1860s (Phillips 1998: 125–7).

If, in the daguerreotype as *souvenirs*, past was linked to present, then in the dual material nature of the gift, the present was nested in the past, the modern was juxtaposed with the primitive. Both daguerreotype and box were unique, original, hand-crafted: the image was the product of a modern technology of French origin; the fancy barkware box was presumed to be an ancient art of native origin. Known only through its description in *La Minerve*, the birchbark presentation case, claimed to be the handiwork of an unidentified French Canadian woman ('*une demoiselle canadienne*'), had its roots, appropriately, not in aboriginal art, but in early French Canada. Yet, regardless of maker or design, the embroidered birchbark box would have been considered a quintessentially Canadian production, more closely associated with native peoples than with the Catholic nuns who first trafficked in them or the genteel Euro-Canadian ladies who subsequently made them. Chalifoux's gift was, thus, an object within an object; the parts, separately and together, carried symbolic meaning(s) attached to their respective modes of manufacture, physical form and iconographical content within the prevailing cultural circumstances of gift-giving and exchange.

Conclusion

This chapter has focused on a single daguerreotype and the ways in which it was invested with, and generated meaning through, its visuality, its materiality and its function and trajectory as *souvenirs*, souvenir and gift. A tribute to Chalifoux's skill as a tailor and evidence of Doane's talents as a daguerreotypist, this daguerreotype is of historical interest as a record of the costumes worn in the St Jean-Baptiste Day parade in 1855 and as a reflection of prevailing cultural notions and national aspirations. It represents the use of photography to preserve and extend the spectacle of one event (the St Jean-Baptiste Day parade) and to commemorate another (the visit of *La Capricieuse*). Its narrative of origins and collective memories, framed by Alfred Chalifoux's personal vision, by the boys' participation in the *fêtes nationales* and by de Belvèze's mission to Canada, manifested the cultural aspirations and political hopes that, for some, cast the mission of *La Capricieuse* as the effort of the Mother Country to remember and redeem the faithful. But, as I have tried to show, the visual facts captured by Doane on a silvered plate were not inert; nor did they circulate as pure image. In this daguerreotype, object and image combined to form a symbolic space of cultural remembrance and political resistance, the significance of which was intimately and inextricably tied to and transmitted through its material worth as a thing, its social life as an object and its haptic encounters as a concrete form.

Until the advent of photo-mechanical reproduction, the materiality and the visuality of the photograph were inseparable aspects of its meaning-making capacity. However, with the development of the halftone process and the subsequent proliferation and sophistication of technologies for copying and printing photographs, for publishing them alongside letterpress text in newspapers, books and magazines, and for recording, circulating and viewing them electronically as wholly dematerialised virtual images, with the visual homogenisation of photographs as standard size prints on catalogue cards in archive, library and museum collections, and with increasing academic analysis of vision and modernity, 'scopic' regimes and the visual turn, the meaning-making aspects of a photograph's objectness have been marginalised.

Yet, for some, the daguerreotype has never lost the allure of its material form. On the sesquicentennial of its first appearance in France, rekindled enthusiasm for the beauty, delicacy, sensuousness and immediacy of this 'middle-class art form with a wide mass appeal' inspired one passionate admirer to celebrate the daguerreotype's unique place in the history of art and image-making:

> The daguerreotype is not a photograph, nor was it a stage in the development of photography . . . . The daguerreotype, like any other art form, demands its own critical vocabulary, its own way of being seen, and its own way of being appreciated.
>
> (Wood 1989: 8–9)

Part of that critical vocabulary, part of its way of being seen and appreciated, involves its physicality. Whether or not the daguerreotype can be accorded a place on the continuum of the development of photography depends to a great extent on the criteria by which we judge it: as the product of a technology, as the by-product of a social practice, as a mode of communication, as a form of artistic expression, as a way of seeing across space and time. However, it is clear upon reflection that the daguerreotype, so often described in strictly visual terms, is not simply an infinitely detailed image; it is a profoundly material object.

Notes

This research was undertaken with the assistance of doctoral and postdoctoral fellowships from the Social Sciences and Humanities Research Council of Canada and education leave from the National Archives of Canada. This chapter is a substantially revised and expanded version of a case study in Joan M. Schwartz, 'Agent of sight, site of agency: the photograph in the geographical imagination', unpublished PhD thesis, Queen's University, Kingston, Canada, 1998. An earlier version appeared in *The Archivist*, no. 118, 1999: 6–13 (National Archives of Canada, Ottawa) and was reprinted in *The Daguerreian Annual*, 1999: 75–9. I thank my colleagues at the National Archives of Canada: Brian Carey (1986), who first carried out research on this daguerreotype, and George Bolotenko (1992), who subsequently discussed it in his exhibition and publication, *A Future Defined: Canada from 1849–1873*. I am particularly indebted to Dr Lynda Jessup (Department of Art, Queen's University) for suggesting that I pursue the broader significance of the birchbark box, and to Dr Ruth Phillips (former Director of the Museum of Anthropology, The University of British Columbia) for generously sharing her enthusiasm for, and knowledge of, fancy barkware.

1 This daguerreotype was presented to the National Archives of Canada by General André L'Homme on the occasion of the official visit to Canada by Laurent Fabius, Prime Minister of France. The National Archives of Canada also holds a report by de Belvèze on his travels and discussions with prominent individuals: see Paul-Henri de Belvèze Papers, MG 24, F 42 (National Archives of Canada).

2 The original inscription reads:

> Au Commandant de Belvèze
> en Canada
>
> ---
>
> Ces petits personnages qui figurent dans les
> Fêtes nationales de Montréal rappelent tous les
> souvenirs religieux et patriotiques des Canadiens
> Français
>
> ---
>
> St. Jean-Baptiste, Patron du Canada
> Jacques Cartier, qui au XVIe siècle découvrit
> le pays et y apporta l'Evangile
> Le chef sauvage, qui accueillit les Franc^s à Hochelaga
> Un jeune Canadien, portant les couleurs
> de la France
> *Alf^d Chalifoux*

3 The term 'shagreen' originally meant hide from a variety animals; while often mistaken for leather, shagreen came to refer to the untanned, leatherlike skin of sharks and stingrays.

4 According to Ruth Phillips, it is more likely that the box was decorated not with porcupine quills, but with moosehair embroidery (personal e-mail communication, 5 June 2002). The two materials were (and still are) commonly confused, but Phillips's research indicates that porcupine quillwork was not done in Quebec. Instead, it was used to decorate birchbark containers by the Anishnabe people of southern Ontario and the central Great Lakes, as well as by the Mi'kmaq of Maritime Canada (Phillips 1998, 1999, 2001).

5 The word 'demoiselle' can be translated as either spinster or young (unmarried) woman.

6 Born in Barrington, Nova Scotia, Doane first advertised as a 'Professor of Photography' in Yarmouth, Nova Scotia, in May 1842. He set up in partnership with William Valentine in St John's, Newfoundland, in 1843, and eventually established a gallery in Montreal in 1846. He retired from photography about 1865, and moved to Boston and then to New York, where he spent the remainder of his life as a portrait painter. Doane daguerreotypes can usually be identified by his crest embossed in gold leaf on the front cover and/or cut into the velvet lining of his plain but fine morocco leather cases.

7 This discussion is informed by the work of Suzanne Langer (1957), Susan Stewart (1984), Daniel Miller (1994), Elizabeth Edwards (1999) and Marius Kwint (1999), among others.

3

ERE THE SUBSTANCE FADE

Photography and hair jewellery

Geoffrey Batchen

The object

A locket lies here in my hand, coldly at first, and then gradually warming as it absorbs and begins to return my own body heat. Its bronze surfaces are articulated with incised patterns, a combination of star and fleur-de-lis on one side and an abstracted open flower on the other. Designed to be touched, this object touches back, casually grazing the pores of my skin with its textured surfaces. In this mutual stroking of the flesh, object and image come together as one; I behold the thingness of the visual, the tooth of its grain, even as I encounter the visuality of the tactile, the piercing force of its perception. Already, then, a number of my senses have been engaged. For this is an object that has both an inside and an outside, and to be fully experienced it must be handled as well as looked at. A small button on the top of the locket, perhaps a remnant of the watch that it once contained, invites me to press down. When I do, the two halves of the locket spring apart. Opening to an angle of ninety degrees, this mechanism adds an extra geometry to the locket's original circular form and reveals an interior to my gaze for the first time. Suddenly I am made aware that this thing in my hand is in fact a photographic object. On one side of the interior lies a portrait of an elderly man, in the form of a circular tintype behind glass. On the other, also behind glass, is a small clipping of human hair (Figure 3.1).

So what are we to make of such an object? How, in particular, are we to incorporate it into a history of photography? Perhaps the question itself is at fault. Why not instead turn it around and ask another: how have established histories of photography fallen short of this kind of object?[1] For there is surprisingly little published on photographic jewellery as a genre, and this despite the large numbers of these objects that were produced during the nineteenth century.[2] They receive no attention in most survey histories of photography.[3] This last absence is the more easily explained. Since the turn of the twentieth century, photography's published history has largely adopted the logic of art history and this has neatly excluded most photographs from their own epic. Organised around a canon of presumed masters and masterworks, with original-ity, uniqueness and aesthetic innovation as its principle tropes, photography's art history has tended to ignore ordinary, commercial photographic practices, of which photo-jewellery is certainly one. It has also privileged images over their casing or frames, presenting reproductions of daguerreotypes, to take but one example, floating miraculously free from the surrounds that always informed their actual experience in the hand or on the wall.[4] Most importantly, vernacular practices like photo-jewellery are presumed to have few intellectual or aesthetic qualities beyond sentimental kitsch, and therefore apparently do not deserve the spotlight of historical attention or critical analysis.

Given all of this, it is tempting, especially in the context of this volume, to abandon the discipline of photo-history altogether and adopt in its place the methods and concerns of material culture, a mode of analysis that explicitly addresses itself to the social meanings of artefacts. I want to resist this temptation, however, and instead keep working towards changing photography's history from within (Batchen 2001: 78–9). Otherwise the genre of photographic jewellery will continue to be left out of photographic histories, finding itself confined to the relative ghettos of social history or cultural anthropology, or lost in a vast continuum of related, but non-photographic, representational practices. I want, in contrast, to concentrate on the particularities of my locket's 'photographicness'. For this reason, and for others that should become clear at the conclusion of this chapter, I would prefer to start by regarding this locket in the same way that I might, say, a photograph by Alfred Stieglitz, and then see what happens from there.

We should begin, perhaps, by establishing some sort of genealogy for this locket. Bought on the Internet auction service Ebay.com, it comes into my hand without any information about the identity of either its makers or its subject. All we know is that it is very probably of American manufacture and was made in the later nineteenth century, at some time between about 1860 and the 1890s. A hundred or so years later, it speaks first and foremost of its age, of the undeniable aura of the antique. But then so do all nineteenth-century photographs, to greater or lesser degrees. This one is tintype portrait is unremarkable in pose and features, showing the bust of an elderly man looking directly, almost quizzically, into the camera, his greying hair slightly askew. The collected wisps of fine hair that face him on the other side of the locket have a reddish tint, suggesting that they may have been taken from a younger head – perhaps from this same man several years before his photograph was made, or perhaps from a loved one wanting to stay close to at least this man's image. Already we enter into the seductive realm of speculation. Could it be that this object was put together by a loved one after this man's death, combining a watch locket, a sample of hair taken in the man's younger years, and a photograph made late in life? This would make it a memorial or mourning object rather than a token of ongoing love or friendship. It would also make this locket the intersection of at least five distinct moments (its original manufacture, the taking of a hair sample, the making of a photograph, their later combination in this object and its perception now, here in my hand). Demonstrably collapsing any distinction between being and becoming, my locket demands that we acknowledge that all historical identity is a manifestation of this kind of temporal oscillation.[5]

Photographic lockets

Whatever its intended meaning, this locket now functions as a representative of a genre rather than as a portrait of a known individual or an exceptional masterpiece by a famous photographer. Even the genre itself is unexceptional, for there are frequent

Figure 3.1 Engraved silver locket containing a tintype portrait of a man and human hair
c. 1855. Diameter 4 cm. Unknown American maker. (Private collection.)

references to such photo-lockets in nineteenth-century advertisements and newspaper stories. *The Scientific American* of 1865, for example, reports that a Mr E. N. Foote of New York City had been awarded a patent by the United States Patent Office for a miniature gold locket in the shape of a photographic album, 'with leaves for pictures of friends, so made that each of the golden leaves receives two ferrotypes or other pictures, the number of leaves being varied with the size of the locket'. The reporter mentions seeing an example that held eight portraits, each pair opening out in its leaf like the pages of an album, and with the exterior surfaces 'chased and engraved with elegant designs'. Thanks to this inventor's ingenuity, the writer concludes, an owner 'can have with him always, in this elegant locket, the faces of his dear kindred and friends'.[6]

Lockets are also mentioned in any number of earlier advertisements taken out by photographers to attract new customers. Indeed, from the evidence of such advertisements, it would seem that photographic jewellery was a staple product of the professional portrait photographer of the mid-nineteenth century (Figure 3.2). George Barnard, working in Oswego, New York, informed his fellow citizens in August 1847 that 'he is prepared to take PHOTOGRAPHIC MINIATURES, unsurpassed by any artist in the country . . . and neatly set in Morocco cases, lockets, breast pins, and in a few minutes'. In January 1852, J. H. Fitzgibbon of St Louis, Missouri, encouraged his potential customers to 'secure the shadow ere the substance fade, let nature copy that which nature made'.[7] Having made good use of one of photography's most familiar exhortations, he advises that he can provide 'pictures taken by the most Improved Method, and Colored true to Nature, from the finger ring to the double whole size plate, and put up either in cases or frames, to suit tastes'. Augustus Washington, an African-American daguerreotypist working in Hartford, Connecticut, advised his loyal customers in April 1853 that 'he has also on hand 100 fine GOLD LOCKETS, from six different manufacturers, of every size and variety, suitable for one, two, three or four pictures, which he will sell cheaper than they can be bought at any other establishment'. A Miss M. MacFarlane, of Belfast, Maine, took out a similar advertisement in the *Maine Free Press* in April 1857 to report that her daguerreotype 'miniatures' could be 'neatly inserted in Pins, Lockets, Bracelets, etc.' In September 1854, *Humphrey's Journal* reported that Willard Ellis Geer, 'who is Daguerreotyping on wheels', had written a catchy poem to attract new customers. According to Geer:

> I can put them in Rings, in Keys, or in Lockets;
> Or in nice little Cases to slip into your pockets;
>
> In a word, I've Cases of all kinds, single and double,
> Lockets too, of all sizes, which saves you all trouble
> Of looking any farther than my Daguerrean Gallery.[8]

The consistent use of the word 'miniature' to describe these early photographic portraits is a reminder that the practice of carrying a small portrait of a loved one predates photography itself by quite a few years. By the late eighteenth century, small portrait paintings of members of the aristocratic class were frequently being incorporated into jewellery and especially into mourning jewellery (a type of ornament that itself goes back to at least the seventeenth century) (see Frank 2000). It was logical that, following the invention of photography in 1839, calotypes, daguerreotypes, ambrotypes, tintypes and albumen prints would also find their way into the pins, rings, pendants, brooches and bracelets that were then so fashionable (Figure 3.2). In a sense, photography allowed the middle classes to adopt a cheaper version of the visual affectations of their betters. There are certainly many examples of daguerreotypes showing their portrait subjects wearing brooches and bracelets that themselves contain photographic portraits. Judging by these and the numerous surviving pieces of photo-jewellery, they came in many shapes and sizes, and varied considerably in cost and fineness of finish.

They also seem to have fulfilled a range of different functions and, indeed, the same piece of jewellery might signify different emotions in different contexts. Often, for example, these objects are clearly organised as declarations of love, or at least of marriage. A single necklace pendant might have portraits of husband and wife on either of its sides, lying back to back, never to be parted. For the object to be experienced in full, it has to be turned from side to side, a form of perpetual caress preordained by its designer. Other examples include photographic lockets containing two facing but separate portraits, such that the man and woman inside initially lie hidden, kissing each other in the dark until liberated into the light of a loved one's gaze. But whatever their exact form or meaning may have been, these are all photographs that turn the body of their owner into an accessory. One displays one's affections in public, wearing them not on the sleeve but as pendants against the chest or hanging off the ears. This is a photography that is literally put in motion: twisting, turning, bouncing, sharing the folds, volumes and movements of the wearer and his or her

Figure 3.2 Tintype portrait of a young woman in an elliptical metal pendant on a chain, with two samples of human hair, *c.* 1860s. Pendant 3.4 × 2.5 cm. Unknown American maker. (Private collection.)

apparel. No longer seen in isolation, the photograph becomes an extension of the wearer, or, more precisely, we become a self-conscious prosthesis to the body of photography.

Although it is tempting automatically to associate these types of object with mourning (as I have already done with my locket), apparently only about 20 per cent of such objects were used for that purpose. But there is no doubt that these are the ones that still tug at the heart. Mourning was a carefully calibrated social ritual during the Victorian period, with fashion, jewellery and photography all playing important roles in the public representation of grief.[9] In fact, the popularity of photographic jewellery as a mourning device is often traced to its adoption by Queen Victoria after her consort Albert's death in 1861 (although she was wearing a daguerreian bracelet featuring his portrait from at least 1848). According to Heinz and Bridget Henisch (1994: 140), 'a memorial ring was designed for the Queen, containing a micro-photograph of the Prince Consort, made in 1861 and attributed to Mayall'. A cabinet card dated 1897 shows her with right arm raised to reveal a portrait of Albert still firmly encircling her wrist, 36 years after his death.[10]

Although there is evidence that adding hair to jewellery was not an exclusively feminine activity, it was certainly one dominated by women. By the mid-nineteenth century, American women in particular were being charged with new social roles as keepers of memory, as mourners and as home-based teachers of religious belief. Even non-Catholic American homes were decorated with religious artefacts of one kind or another, and this pervasive Christian context invests hair lockets like this one with a distinctly sacred aura.[11] The advent of the American Civil War in the mid-1860s added a certain urgency to the practice. Many young men from both sides of the conflict had their photographs taken before heading off for war, perhaps suspecting it might be their last chance. These photos were consulted hopefully in their absence and then, should they die, were incorporated into appropriate ornaments designed specifically for mourning purposes. One striking example comprised a matching set of black and white onyx brooch and earrings, in which an ambrotype of a young man in uniform could be swivelled back and forth, in and out of public view, depending on the context (Kaplan 1998).

The addition of human hair to such objects was already a common practice by the early decades of the nineteenth century.[12] As Thomas Laqueur notes, hair began to enjoy a new prominence as the raw material of memory. 'It became the corporeal auto-icon par excellence, the favoured synecdoche – the real standing for the symbolic – perhaps not eternally incorruptible but long lasting enough, a bit of a person that lives eerily on as a souvenir' (Laqueur 1992: 16–17). Hair, intimate yet easily detached, is of course a convenient and pliable stand-in for the whole body of the missing, memori-alized subject. Women in particular were encouraged to use hair in their domestic handicrafts, beginning with horse hair and then, as their skills improved, working with the finer human hair, either bought for the purpose or gathered from friends or even from their own heads. This amateur practice ensured that the hair being used was from an 'authentic' head, there being some fear that professional braiders were not so particular about this. But it also turned the natural hair into a cultural sign, while allowing the braider to involve herself physically with the body of the other as well as with the act of remembrance that braiding entailed.

Custom-made braiding tables were available to facilitate the production of complex patterns, which included pictures of flowers, landscapes and the feathers associated with the late Prince of Wales.[13] The 1856 book *Elegant Arts for Ladies*, for example, devotes a whole chapter to the complex art of 'Weaving or plaiting hair ornaments', including subsections on 'Plaits for rings, lockets, and brooches' and on 'Mourning devices'. The accompanying text underlines the gender-specificity of this practice, while stressing once again hair's memorial function.

> Hair, that most imperishable of all the component parts of our mortal bodies, has always been regarded as a cherished memorial of the absent or lost. Impressed with this idea, it appears to us but natural, that of all the various employments devised for the fingers of our fair country-women, the manufacture of ornaments in hair must be one of the most interesting. Why should we confide to others the precious lock or tress we prize, risking its being lost, and the hair of some other person being substituted for it, when, with a little attention, we may ourselves weave it into the ornament we desire? And the dainty and very tasteful handling hair-work requires, renders

it as truly feminine an occupation as the finest crochet or the richest embroidery.[14]

My locket is actually one of the simpler presentations of this material, its lack of visual sophistication suggesting it was put together by a relatively unskilled hand. Some brooches, by contrast, feature a portrait on one side and on the other two artfully organised filigrees of hair behind glass, each teased into exquisite plant-like designs and tied with tiny pearls or precious stones. Samples of hair from two different heads are often woven together in this manner or are simply conjoined in permanent communion with one another, obviously a metaphor of friendship and love or a discreet act of courtship. Thus hair could signify either love or death (or both), and refer simultaneously to past and present. Some oval-shaped brooches were made with a photographic portrait on one side and a small glass viewing-window on the other, so that a sample of the subject's hair could be permanently placed in its own mini-sarcophagus. One elliptical silver brooch, for example, features a tintype portrait of the bust of a young woman on its public side and then behind glass on the other side are two samples of hair woven together, with yet another 'natural' sample laid on top of that. These representative pieces of another's body are thus worn tight against one's own, creating a permanent but entirely private bond cemented by the act of touch. Of course, being behind glass, the hair in this locket offers only an imagined touch of the absent body it signifies. But a pair of bracelets woven from human hair, each with an inset daguerreotype portrait (one of a man and the other of a woman), allow that touch to become real and continuous, resting on the skin of our wrist as a physical, permanent and public reminder of the missing subjects, our relationship to them and their relationship to each other (Figure 3.3).

Hair was also sometimes plaited into a thick knot of interlinked braids, or, alternatively, woven into a tight grid pattern, so fine that it looks like a piece of cloth. In other instances, human hair was given a functional as well as a symbolic role. In one particularly striking example, the hair was braided into a seven-inch-long ribbon from which hangs a small medallion-shaped tintype. Particularly poignant are those posthumous portraits accompanied by a fragile circle of baby hair and a handwritten text ('Angel on Earth – an Angel in Heaven. Fell asleep with a sweet smile'). In others, a lock of hair is tied up with a simple scrap of silk and placed inside the case next to the photograph, waiting to be encountered (to be touched as well as seen) whenever it is opened.

There is sometimes an intriguing play between the visibility and invisibility of the hair in such objects. One cased tintype shows a soldier sitting in his Union uniform with his hands clenched in his lap. This young man has at some point been given a spectacular headdress of real blond hair, carefully placed around his image under the front glass. This hair cascades down each side of the man's body from a point just above his head, the assembled strands looking gigantic in relation to the reduced scale of the photograph they now frame. Any respect for the integrity of the photograph, and in particular for its reality-effect, has been firmly discounted in favour of a respect for its subject, by the need to memorialise his presence in the owner's life. Conversely, in other examples, memorial locks of hair are placed behind or underneath the image and therefore out of sight (unless the whole object is taken apart). Its existence known only to the owner, this hair remains buried beneath the photograph, part of the total object's signifying morphology but haunting it exclusively in the mind's eye of a single privileged viewer.

Figure 3.3 Daguerreotype portrait of a woman's head set into a bracelet of woven human hair, *c.* 1850. 7.5 × 3 cm. Unknown American maker. (Courtesy of George Eastman House, Rochester, NY, [69.214.10].)

Extending indexicality

So what is it doing there? What does added hair, whether visible or not, actually do to the photograph that it accompanies? First and foremost the hair serves a metonymic memorial function, standing in, as we have already noted, for the body of the absent subject. So why isn't the photograph alone enough to fulfil this function? The person pictured has, after all, represented himself or herself through that wondrous intercourse of object, light and chemical reaction that is the photographic process. The body of the subject (be it human, building, landscape or still life) is present as visual trace even when absent as material thing. So why adulterate this already magical process with something as carnal and common as a lock of hair? Perhaps the answer takes us back to where we began, to the reasons why photo-jewellery is worthy of study. Could it be, for example, that the addition of hair to all these otherwise ordinary photographs is a vernacular commentary on tracing itself, on photography's strengths and limitations as a representational apparatus?

This deserves some further consideration. More than any other medium, photography promises an unhindered immediacy of representation. It could even be argued that photography is the manifestation of a desire for a pure opticality, for a visibility without mediation. In a photograph, the thing pictured is automatically transformed into a portable visual sign (mobilising it, but also completing that thing's commodification). But much the same could be said about the photograph itself. For the photograph is certainly nothing if not humble, so ready is it to erase its own material presence in favour of the subject it represents. In most contexts, we are asked to look through the photograph as if it simply isn't there, penetrating its limpid, transparent surface with our eyes and seeing only what lies within. Posing as pure sign, or even as no sign at all, the 'good' photograph offers minimal resistance to this look. Invisible to the eye, it appears to provide a representation generated by the referent itself.

Around the turn of the twentieth century, the American philosopher Charles Sanders Peirce formalised this observation in his taxonomy of fundamental relationships between a sign and its referent. According to Peirce, an iconic sign looks like the object it denotes, whereas an index 'is not the mere resemblance of its Object . . . but it is the actual modification of it by the Object'. Photographs, Peirce argues, 'are very instructive, because we know that they are in certain respects exactly like the objects they represent . . . But this resemblance is due to the photographs having been produced under such circumstances that they were physically forced to correspond point by point to nature. In that aspect, then, they belong to the second class of signs, those by physical connection' (Peirce 1985: 8, 11). As a footprint is to a foot, so is a photograph to its referent. As Allan Sekula (1983: 218) puts it, photographs are 'physical traces of their objects'. Likewise, Susan Sontag (1977: 154) says that the photograph is 'something directly stencilled off the real', while Rosalind Krauss (1984: 112) describes it as 'a kind of deposit of the real itself'. Indexicality, then, is a major source of photography's privileged status within modern culture. For, unlike other systems of representation, the camera does more than just see the world; it is also touched by it.

Roland Barthes makes much of the physicality of photography's connection to its subject in his 1980 book *Camera Lucida*. 'The photograph is literally an emanation of the referent. From a real body, which was there, proceed radiations which ultimately touch me, who am here . . . a sort of umbilical cord links the body of the photographed thing to my gaze' (Barthes 1980: 80–1). For Barthes, photography's indexical system of representation provides 'a new, somehow experiential order of proof', a 'certificate of presence', of '*what has been*'. According to Barthes, the reality offered by the photograph is not that of truth-to-appearance but that of truth-to-presence, a matter of being (of something's irrefutable place in space/time) rather than resemblance. And, for Barthes, this is an important distinction. 'For resemblance refers to the subject's identity, an absurd, purely legal, even penal affair; likeness gives our identity "as itself", whereas I want a subject – in Mallarmé's terms – "as *into* itself eternity transforms it". Likeness leaves me unsatisfied and somehow skeptical' (Barthes 1980: 102–3). The indexicality of the photograph allows it to transcend mere resemblance and conjure a 'subject', a presence that lingers (the sidelong reference to ghosts and haunting seems no accident). No wonder certain photographs have such a strange effect on him: 'neither image nor reality, a new being, really: a reality one can no longer touch'. These sorts of photographs tantalise Barthes with a nearness made insurmountably distant, 'a mad image, chafed by reality' (Barthes 1980: 115).

Could the addition of a tactile portion of the subject's body to his photograph be an effort to bridge the distance, temporal and otherwise, between viewer and person viewed and between likeness and subject? Contaminating visibility with touch, my locket might then be regarded as an effort to bring the 'mad' photograph back to earth, or at least back to the body of the subject. Truth-to-presence is joined by the actual presence of a portion of the body being signified. In its combination of hair and photograph, my locket has therefore become an indexical sign twice over, two physical traces of the same referent brought face to face, first with each other and then with ourselves.[15]

We could point to many other examples of a doubled indexicality involving photography. Wedding certificates in the nineteenth century often incorporated albumen prints of bride and groom, and sometimes the celebrant as well, together with the signatures of all concerned. This intersection of image and hand is also found in a daguerreotype case containing a handwritten inscription and a lock of hair woven into a circle (both once hidden away behind the image). 'OCala – Florida – July 20th 1859 – "Little things bring back to mind Thoughts of happy bygone times" – Kate – (Dinna Forget).' A portion of Kate's body nestles beneath that same body's photographic imprint, once again bringing touch into the picture and adding a trace of the real (as well as the animation of her presumably Scottish voice) to the simulation of the image (Batchen 1997: 2–11). Barthes suggests throughout *Camera Lucida* that photography allows an imagined exchange of touches between subject, photograph and viewer. In one object's combination of daguerreotype and fabric, this normally invisible exchange is made manifest and thereby repeated for real. It is a daguerreotype portrait of a young girl in a case, taken in about 1850. At some point, a square of cloth from her dress has been added to the inside of the case. We are thus invited literally to touch a piece of the cloth that, we can see from the photograph, once also touched the skin of this long-departed girl (Isenburg 1989: 77). We touch what she touched, turning this square of fabric into a membrane conjoining past and present, the living and the dead. By this creative contrivance, absence and historical distance are temporarily bridged by a moment of shared bodily sensation, turning the remembrance of this girl into an experience at once optical and haptic.

So what are the effects of a doubled indexicality, as opposed to a single one? The photo in my locket is presumably thought to be lacking something that the addition of hair fulfils, but, equally, it would appear that the hair alone is also deemed to be not quite enough – apparently, neither is as effective an act of representation without the other also being present. Like a photograph, the hair sample stands in for the whole body of the absent subject, turning this locket into a modern fetish object; as a mode of representation it 'allow[s] me to believe that what is missing is present all the same, *even though I know* it is not the case' (Durand 1995: 146).[16] A talismanic piece of the body is used to add a sort of sympathetic magic to the photograph, an insurance against separation, whether temporary or permanent. By this means, as we have seen, a secular object is given a potentially sacred aspect. But the hybridity of this object also makes for a stronger portrait experience. By adding a lock of hair to the subject's photograph, the indexical presence of that subject is reiterated and reinforced. The studium of mere resemblance (and the portrait in my locket is of the formulaic kind that offers little more than this) is transformed into the punctum of the subject-as-ghost (a figure simultaneously absent and present, alive and dead). This sorcerer's animation of the missing subject has a temporal component as well. A photograph usually functions as a memory of the past (the moment in which the photograph was taken), while this hair sample stolidly occupies the eternal horizon of the present. The photograph speaks of the catastrophe of time's passing, but the locket as a whole speaks of the possibility of eternal life (a message embodied in its circular form). In short, no matter what its actual size, the combination of photograph and hair turns this locket into a monument to immortality.[17]

All this also enhances the locket's capacity to conjure memory. We usually imagine photographs and memories to be synomymous. The American writer Oliver Wendell

Holmes called photography 'the mirror with a memory' as early as 1859 (Newhall 1982: 54), and the Eastman Kodak company has extensively promoted this notion ever since: '[Kodak] enables the fortunate possessor to go back by the light of his own fireside to scenes which would otherwise fade from memory and be lost' (Frank 2000). And so we have taken our photographs, voraciously and anxiously (Americans take about 550 snapshots per second), as if to fail to do so would be to let our precious memories fade away into the mists of time. The irony in all this is that some of photography's most insightful critics have argued that in fact photography and memory do not mix, that one even precludes the other. Barthes, for example, claimed that 'not only is the Photograph never, in essence, a memory . . . but it actually blocks memory, quickly becomes a counter-memory' (Barthes 1980: 91). Following Proust's lead in *Remembrance of Things Past*, Barthes bases his claim on the presumed capacity of the photograph to replace the immediate, physically embracing experience of involuntary memory (the sort of emotional responses most often induced, before conscious thought, by smells and sounds) with frozen illustrations set in the past; photography replaces the unpredictable thrill of memory with the dull certainties of history.[18]

However, in the examples I have been discussing here, the photograph's capacity to erase memory has been countered by its transformation into an overtly touched and/or touchable object-form. In the process, the subject of each photograph has been similarly transformed, from something merely seen into someone really felt, from just an image set in the past into an exchange you are emotionally (as well as physically) touched by, right now, in the present. The addition of a piece of hair repeats and accentuates this appeal to the mnemonic capacities of touch. Turned into fetish objects devoted to the cult of remembrance, hybrid photographs such as these pieces of jewellery ask us to give up a little something of ourselves if they are to function satisfactorily. They demand the projection on to their constituent stuff of our own bodies, but also of our personal recollections, hopes and fears (about the passing of time, about death, about being remembered only as history and – most terrible of all – about being forgotten altogether).

All this enhances the photograph's capacity to conjure memory, and this at a time when, according to Richard Terdiman, memory itself is in a state of crisis. Of course, memory is always in crisis, always in fearful struggle with its other, with the encroachment of amnesia (Sturken 1997: 7, 17). But Terdiman regards the nineteenth century as a period in which this perpetual memory crisis takes on a more social and systematic character, driven by the often bewildering changes wrought by political revolution and industrial modernity. He argues that Europeans of this period 'experienced the insecurity of their culture's involvement with its past', a type of memory crisis in which 'the very coherence of time and of subjectivity seemed disarticulated' (Terdiman 1993: 3–4). He points to, among other nineteenth-century texts, the commentary in Karl Marx's *Capital* on commodity fetishism, suggesting that, 'because commodities suppress the memory of their own process . . . essentially, "reification" is a memory disturbance: *the enigma of the commodity is a memory disorder*' (Terdiman 1993: 12). Indeed, memory is one of those abstractions increasingly reified in the nineteenth century, turned into lucrative commercial objects of exchange such as keepsakes and souvenirs. One might regard the invention and proliferation of photography as a response to this memory crisis but also as its embodiment and reproduction. The photograph remembers a loved one's appearance, but it is a memory 'hollowed out', disconnected from the social realities of its own production, and also from us, who are doing the remembering.

Might we regard these various examples of photo-jewellery – in which the photograph is touched, worked on, added to, transformed into a personalised, hand-made and often hand-held object and into a multisensory experience – as an attempted resistance or counter to this same memory crisis? They all enact a practice that breaches the virtual walls of the photographic image, forcing us simultaneously to project our mind's eye back and forth, into and out of, the photograph they incorporate. They punctuate the 'chafed reality' of time, for Barthes (1980: 89) the *noeme* or essence of the photographic experience, with the more immediate and tangible realities of physicality. They collapse looking into touching, and history into memory, and, by making their photographs relatively minor, if never incidental, elements of a larger ensemble, they refuse to privilege a pure photography over other types of representational experience.

But the addition of hair to these lockets is not only a modification of the photograph's indexicality and capacity to induce memory. It also constitutes a commentary on photographic representation in general. We have already seen that photography has long been privileged as a direct trace of the real. It is this special form of visuality that allows the photograph itself to pose as invisible, as a 'message without a code' in Barthes's (1977: 17) famous words. But in my locket the real is treated as but one more of these traces, as something not outside the play of signification but very much part of it. The hair sample, for example, is a piece of reality that doesn't just stand in for the symbolic – here, it *is* the symbolic. Equally, this particular photograph is no longer allowed the pretence of invisibility. Turned into a three-dimensional object by its locket frame, that framing, as we have already seen, makes us self-consciously aware of the photograph's thingness by involving our hands as well as our eyes in its perception. Framed in bronze, and then framed again by the embrace of a loved one's hand (and now by my own), the photograph cannot help becoming a sign of itself as well as of its referent. For here it is but one mode of representation among others. We are also made to reflect on the relationship of the image to this referent, a relationship repeated twice over in the confines of this locket. To repeat something is explicitly to declare it as coded, as sign (two knocks on the door signify very differently from just one). This locket thereby takes indexicality to its logical conclusion: 'the thing itself is a sign . . . from the moment there is meaning there are nothing but signs' (Derrida 1976: 48–50). And this declaration could be extended to encompass all the identities incorporated in the locket (hair, photograph, subject, viewer); real and representation are each made continually to signal and (de)generate the other, a physical manifestation of, in Jacques Derrida's words, 'the impossibility for an identity to be closed in on itself, on the inside of its proper interiority, or on its coincidence with itself' (Derrida 1981: 94).

Lockets and photographic history

The same could be said for the identity of the history that would exclude this locket from its purview. It should by now be clear that vernacular photographic practices issue a serious challenge to that history, calling not simply for inclusion in the medium's grand narratives but for the total transformation of the narrative itself. It should be equally clear that if my locket is indeed to be included in photography's story, an art history centred on origins, great individuals and purity of medium will no longer be adequate. We need to invent a mode of photographic history that matches this object's complexity, and that can articulate its intelligibility both for the past and for our own time. We need also to develop a way of talking about the photograph that can attend to its various physical attributes, to its materiality as a medium of representation. As we have seen, the production of this locket represents certain nineteenth-century social and cultural rituals; a little historical context enhances any reading of it. However, in this particular case we know nothing specific about it, nothing about its subject or owner or their intentions, nothing except what is implied or enacted by the locket's form and design. Refusing to give up its meanings easily, the locket demands I supplement its existence with my own: the locket's meaning amounts to 'an addition: it is what I add to the photograph and *what is nonetheless already there*' (Barthes 1980: 55). My locket thus lends itself to a measure of speculation, to an empathetic, phenomenological style of historical writing that can bridge the temporal and emotional gap between us and it – a century's gap that is, after all, not yet an abyss.

This is a kind of writing already well established in photographic discourse (see Barthes's *Camera Lucida*), but under the guise of a name like Visual Culture it has managed to generate some vigorous opposition in recent times. What is it that makes Rosalind Krauss, Hal Foster, Abigail Solomon-Godeau and other pillars of the postmodern establishment so nervous?[19] Irit Rogoff has described Visual Culture as a shorthand term for 'the critical theorization of visual culture'. and argues that its effort to speak *to* as well as *about* particular objects alters 'the very structures by which we organize and inhabit culture . . . It is clearly one of the most interesting aspects of visual culture that the boundary lines between making, theorizing and historicizing have been greatly eroded and no longer exist in exclusive distinction from one another' (Rogoff 1998: 17–18). Foster, for one, sees this as a dangerously 'ethnographic turn', accusing a generic Visual Culture of failing to distinguish subject from object, good art from bad and even art from non-art (Foster 1996: 104). He fears, in other words, the capacity of my locket, and the discourse it generates, to collapse all such binary oppositions into its dynamic supplementary logic.

His argument is not simply against the potential disruptions of deconstruction (although that is part of it) but also attempts a defence of the political function of the avant-garde within mass culture. The artistic avant-garde, so this argument goes, represents a space of resistance to the blandishments of globalised capital. Good historical criticism should privilege this space, thereby offering an alternative model of practice (both artistic and social/political) to that continually propagated by and embodied in the products of a normative capitalist culture. My locket, according to this reading, represents nothing more than Victorian bourgeois sentiment in material form and therefore does not deserve the attention due to, say, a print by Julia Margaret Cameron or Stieglitz. Such an argument of course privileges the sensibilities of the upper middle classes over those of their poorer cousins (both then and now), but it also continues to assume that political agency rests with the object rather than with its reading. It ignores the symbiotic authorial economy described by Rogoff (and before her by Roland Barthes), an economy that in fact pertains to all historical writing and not just the sort that claims the name of Visual Culture (Barthes 1977: 142–8).

But it also turns a blind eye to the contradictions and spaces of critique inherent in all of capitalism's products, including this one. At a time when all things, including memory, are being turned into prescribed commodities, my locket represents a moment of personal resistance to this process. In its unruly turning from life to death and back again, collapsing visuality into touch, and forcing modernity to cohabit with magic, this photographic hair locket conjures an intensely private, unpredictable and even unknowable experience, an experience outside the capacity of capital to control (or, at least, no more in or out of its control than is avant-garde art). For this reason, on top of all the others, I believe my locket deserves our respect and critical attention.

Notes

Thanks go to Bill Jay, Danielle Miller, Monica Garza, Julie Coleman, Catherine Whalen, Anne Ferran, Mary Trasko, Janice Hart and Elizabeth Edwards for all their help with the research and writing of this essay.

1 I have borrowed this reversal from Meaghan Morris's work on women and modernity. She has been cited as saying, 'I prefer to study . . . the everyday, the so-called banal, the supposedly un-or-non-experimental, asking not "why does it fall short of modernism?" but: "how do classical theories of modernism fall short of women's modernity?"' (cited in Burns 1999: 310) For a broad discussion of the place of the vernacular in the history of photography, see Batchen (2001: 199–204).

2 Among the few publications specifically written on this genre of photography are Kappler (1982), West and Abbott (1990: 136–200) and Spies (1997: 36–40). For more general histories of jewellery in the modern era, see Cooper and Battershill (1973) and Luthi (2001).

3 Photo-jewellery, for example, is not reproduced in prominent survey histories of photography by Newhall (1982) and Rosenblum (1984). Frizot (1998: 33, 747) reproduces a daguerreotype button and some twentieth-century photo-badges, but discusses neither.

4 In terms of reproductions in photographic histories, the image is consistently privileged over a daguerreotype's casing, not only in the various editions of Beaumont Newhall's *The History of Photography* (1949–82), but also in the much more recent Lowry and Lowry (1998). In contrast, the work of German historian Wolfgang Jaworek (1998) concentrates on the history of the presentation of photographs in frames. Burns (1995) has also emphasised the frame as a means of dating his collection of painted tintype portraits.

5 For a consideration of the historically contingent nature of identity, see Hall (1990).

6 Thanks are due to Bill Jay of Tempe, Arizona, for supplying a copy of this publication.

7 The same phrase, 'secure the shadow ere the substance fade', appears, for example, in the advertisement taken out by Noah North in September 1845 in the *Livingston County Whig* of Geneseo, NY. This advertisement is quoted in Fink (1990: 56). The phrase also appears in an 1843 advertisement published by 'Alvah Ames, Daguerrian Artist', held in the collection of Matthew Isenburg in Connecticut.

8 These examples come from Gary Ewer's invaluable daily Internet DagNews service (http://www.daguerre.org/resource/dagnews/dagnews.html: 1998–2000). See also Palmquist (1980) for an advertisement from a 1902 *Sears Roebuck Catalogue* promising 'an ever present reminder of your relatives or friends, in the form of a photograph on the dial or back cap of your watch . . . done by the Photographic Enamel Process'. He reports that a photographer working in northern California was offering a similar service as early as 1869: 'what could be more appropriate than having the miniature likeness of very dear friends on the dial of one's watch, which would meet the gaze whenever the watch was taken out to tell the time?'

9 For overviews of this tradition, see Morley (1971), Snyder (1971), Meinwald (1990) and Ruby (1995).

10 As the Henisches report, in 1862 Garrard & Company, Goldsmiths to the Crown, supplied Victoria with 'nine gold lockets for photograph Miniatures, with Crown loops and black

pearl drops'. Queen Victoria, like Prince Albert, had a keen interest in photography. See Dimond and Taylor (1987).

11 Pointon reports that 'the use of hair in jewellery seems to begin during the Middle Ages and seems to be a peculiarly Christian practice'. She suggests that the practice may stem from a particular reading of the book of Revelations, such that a lock of hair becomes a sign of a possible reunion with the deceased in the afterlife (Pointon 1999a: 198–201, 293). McDannell (1995) mentions gloves, rings and hair art (all pertaining to touch and the hand) as being among those tokens typically exchanged in order to remember the deceased. She also reproduces a mass-produced 1877 certificate designed to memorialise the dead, with this example personalised by the addition (in a vignette space originally intended for a photograph) of a ring of hair tied with a ribbon. Thanks go to Catherine Whalen for directing me to these references.

12 By 1862, advertisements for 'artists in hair' were appearing in such journals as the *Illustrated London News*. In 1855 a full-length, life-size portrait of Queen Victoria, composed only of hair, was exhibited at the Paris Exhibition (O'Day 1982: 36). In England hair jewellery continued to be popular until the 1880s, when, following Queen Victoria's agreement in 1887 to wear some silver jewellery on state occasions, the mourning period for Prince Albert was considered to be at an end and 'hair jewellery was now regarded as being in the worst possible taste'. See Luthi (2001: 29).

13 See O'Day (1982: 36–7) and Trasko (1994). American women were informed by the influential *Godey's Lady Book* of the availability of hair bracelets with clasps made to hold ambrotypes (Kaplan 1998: 9). Particularly instructive is Mark Campbell's *Self-Instructor in the Art of Hair Work: Hair Braiding and Jewelry of Sentiment with a Catalog of Hair Jewelry* (1875 edition). Campbell provides a vast range of possible designs to be made from human hair, including a number that surround a glass-faced locket suitable for photographs. In his Preface, he stresses hair's potent memorial function. 'Persons wishing to preserve, and weave into lasting mementoes, the hair of a deceased father, mother, sister, brother, or child, can also enjoy the inexpressable advantage and satisfaction of *knowing* that the material of their handiwork is the actual hair of the "loved and gone".'

14 *Elegant Arts for Ladies* (1856: 3–4). Interestingly, this book also comes with three pages of advertisements for such things as 'Barnard's Photographic Watercolours' and 'Barnard's Photographic Powder-Colours'.

15 In the context of a memorial locket, hair is an index of the body from which it has been taken because, in Peirce's words, 'it necessarily has some Quality in common with the Object, and it is in respect to these that it refers to the Object'. An index is 'in dynamical (including spatial) connection both with the individual object, on the one hand, and with the senses of memory of the person for whom it serves as a sign, on the other . . . Psychologically, the action of indices depends upon association by contiguity' (Peirce 1985: 8, 13).

16 On this question of fetishism, see Pointon (1999: 39–57).

17 In *Camera Lucida*, Barthes states: 'Earlier societies managed so that memory, the substitute for life, was eternal and that at least the thing which spoke Death should itself be immortal: this was the Monument. But by making the (mortal) Photograph into the general and somehow natural witness of "what has been", modern society has renounced the Monument' (Barthes 1980: 93).

18 See Barthes (1985: 351–360), Keenan (1998: 60–4) and Edwards (1999). I make a parallel argument to the one in this chapter in Batchen (2003).

19 For instance, Krauss and Foster (1996), Foster (1996), Solomon-Godeau (1998: 33, 39–40). For an overview of this debate, see Moxey (2001: 103–42).

4

MIXED BOX

The cultural biography of a box of 'ethnographic' photographs

Elizabeth Edwards and Janice Hart

The box in the museum

This chapter considers perhaps the most ubiquitous and therefore invisible of material objects: a box with things in it in the reserve collections of a museum. It explores how, by enclosing specific photographs in conjunction with one another, materiality becomes integral to the meanings of images. We hope to demonstrate how, through seeing photographs as material objects to which things happen, we might come closer to understanding ways in which photographs operate as visual objects within the discursive practices of, in this case, anthropology and anthropological museums.[1]

The art historian Norman Bryson sums up a methodological problem that is central to the concerns of this chapter when he writes about the way in which the act of looking is caught up between the conjuncture of a disappearing past and an emerging present:

> Surrounding those forms of looking that have given rise to the discursive configurations that actually figure in the archive, are other submerged series of procedures that addressed other needs. Such series will include codes of viewing that represent residual practices edged out by the rise of those latter codes that are hardly yet formed, emergent ways of seeing whose coherence has not yet been established and whose energies have not yet taken root, still tentative and altering configurations that still have to find each other and lock together.
>
> (Bryson 1992: 36)

The specific focus of this chapter is Box 54 in the 'Mixed Geographical' series of the photograph collection of the Pitt Rivers Museum, University of Oxford (Figure 4.1). It is a synthetic object of linked but separate parts (the photographs on their card mounts) that have interacted, and continue to interact, with each other and with the institution in which they are housed, to produce a succession of meanings that are broader and more complex than a simple sum of the various parts. What has gone on and what is going on in the succession of mediations around the object that determine and are determined by meanings? What are, to follow Bryson, the submerge

Figure 4.1 Box 54, the cards interleaved with archival paper. Photographer: Malcolm Osman. (Courtesy of Pitt Rivers Museum, University of Oxford.)

procedures? How are the box and its constituent presentational forms – the cards – related to the discursive whole in making historical, anthropological and micro-political meanings?

This exercise will also reveal the archival or museum object not as stereotypically dormant and clouded by the dust of ages, but as an active socially salient entity that exists within contexts that shift and sometimes dramatically change over time. From this perspective, museum objects are seen to be subject to the often tense atmosphere of a curatorial dynamic that attempts to hold an uneasy sway of order over the chaos of things and their associated bodies of knowledge. While taxonomic meanings of the archive have been explored in general (for example, Sekula 1989; Isles and Roberts 1997), and the concept of collecting, the museum and the archive, especially the colonial archive, and their relation to configurations of power and the politics of representation have also been explored (for example, Vergo 1984; Coombes 1994; Elsner and Cardinal 1994; Bennet 1995; Barringer and Flynn 1998), the *material objects* themselves which make up 'the archive' have been largely invisible, naturalised within insti̶t̶utional structure, their own social biographies as objects obscured and ̶̶̶̶̶̶̶̶̶̶̶̶̶̶̶̶critical attention.

̶̶̶̶̶̶̶̶̶̶̶̶̶̶̶̶̶̶̶̶̶̶̶̶̶̶̶̶institutionalised object, organised intentionally out of serendipitously ̶̶̶̶̶̶̶̶̶̶l, look as it does? What processes of thought and action have separ-̶̶̶̶̶̶̶̶̶̶vely, shaped its current state of being? What was the relationship ̶̶̶̶̶̶̶̶̶̶tical activities of bureaucracy, collections management, anthropolo-̶̶̶̶̶̶̶̶̶̶d desiring poetics? To answer these questions requires a methodo-̶̶̶̶̶̶̶̶̶̶hat does not necessarily follow a chronological line of enquiry but aims to establish what Foucault has termed 'rules of formation in order to define the conditions of their realization' (Foucault 1991: 79). Thus we are concerned not so much with the photographs themselves simply as *images*, as with the changing archival and museological environments that enabled the photographs to operate within a shifting discourse and assume the presentational form they did. Kopytoff's biographical model is important here: 'the cultural responses to . . . biographical details reveal a tangled mass of aesthetic, historical and even poetical judgements and of the convictions and values that shape our attitudes, to objects' (Kopytoff 1986: 67). Thus, while the image content of the photographs contained within Box 54 dictated their identity as 'ethnographic' long before they reached the institution, the museum itself was the source of resonant associative values, constituted through the nexus of anthropological, photographic and museological concerns that imparted order through schemes of organisation.

Past orderings, of course, rarely fit with current ideas about what to do with objects. Indeed, they can be objects of fascination in themselves precisely because they are so different from how we construct order now. However they might appear in the present – logically, ideologically, culturally or aesthetically – past orderings cannot be ignored or suppressed. They constitute accretions of meaning, layers formed by their very institutional existence, which become part of the constitution of the object as if they were initially intrinsic to it. While these accretions are not necessarily clearly visible because they are under the surface of what we see now, close study can reveal the traces of past orderings as a succession of never entirely discrete layers, in which the past orderings might still disrupt the present.

A central concern in this study of Box 54 has been the methodological needs of an object that might be termed 'synthetic'. Some objects enter archives and museums and remain in them as discrete singular entities. For the purposes of our argument here, they can be termed 'natural' – an old master drawing, for instance, a run of correspondence in private papers or an album of photographs. Synthetic objects are those objects upon which sense and order have been imposed in their institutional lifetimes, creating something that was not there before, making a new entity both intellectually and physically in a way that goes beyond simple taxonomic description, moving into a set of changing values and, further, into a framework of policies, strategies and practices. Within this set of definitions, museums and archives themselves are arch-synthetic objects. They do more than put objects in their proper place or make a place for them. They are active environments for participating in the histories of objects, active environments that ultimately shape histories, through the preserving contexts that they themselves constitute.

Box 54 is such a synthetic object. It is a mixed box in all of its topological, typological, taxonomic and indeed semantic senses. A succession of institutional and curatorial mediations with it have created a sequence of overlapping frameworks of internal logic to form and reform the material object. At some point in the various histories of the individual photographs, and sets of photographs, that now make up the box, a decision was taken to bring them together for the first time. At a slightly later date, this containerised assemblage was formally categorised as a 'mixed box' and given a number so that it formed part of a series: Box 54 in the 'Miscellaneous Geographical' series. It still answers to this name when called. However, in a recent decision to integrate the number system of the object and photograph collections and all that this implies, the box underwent another shift in identity to 1998.254, the 54 being the residue of its previous identity.[2] Finally, early in 2002 the Museum's database describing Box 54 became available on-line, a textual reconstitution in cyberspace.[3] The identity of Box 54 has never been stable and there is no reason to think that this condition of flux will alter with time.

One of the initial research tasks was to establish the origins of Box 54. One approach to this was to date Box 54 to the moment of its inception as a box of photographs in the early 1930s, a point to which we shall return. However, at the same time, to date its inception to a unique moment of archiving along these lines was inadequate. As Foucault has suggested, the historical beginning of things is not the 'inviolable identity of their origin', but the 'dissension of other things', the 'simultaneity of myriad events' that grow out of 'the exteriority of accidents' (Foucault 1991: 79), resulting in strata that are 'superimposed, overprinted and enveloped in each other' (Derrida 1996: 22).

The contents of the box

If we take Box 54 from its shelf today, what do we think we are looking at? Did it emerge in answer to a specific set of questions and imperatives within an institutional structure, and does it embody a matrix of the histories of anthropology and photography? If so, how might these contributing developments be understood? While individual elements of this matrix have been well explored – for instance, the analysis of specific semiotic forms within images – what interests us is what we might find if we keep our theory close to the ground and subject Box 54 to ethnographic scrutiny.

Pitt Rivers is relatively unusual in terms of European ethnographic museums in that it collected photographs from its foundation in 1884 as an active policy as opposed to an ephemeral accrual.[4] This is not to say that the photographs within the institution have an even history of linear progression. What is significant are the historical traces laid down in the box of photographs, which enable us to subject it to interrogation as a piece of material culture on the one hand and as a series of historical re-engagements in curatorial terms on the other. These point to the nexus of the status of photographic object as a provider of visual information, and as a testimony to anthropological thinking and curatorial practice. How are *these* considerations manifested through the material and presentational forms of this object?

Box 54 contains 203 photographic images of Native American peoples, from nine cultural regions of the United States and Canada, dating from between *c.* 1870 and *c.* 1926. Their processes include albumen prints, gelatin silver prints and glossy develop-out papers. They are grouped and mounted on 32 cards (Figures 4.2 to 4.4). Almost one-third are from the Plains region and another 20 per cent each from the Southwest and Northwest Coast. Another sizable group, 26, are from the Northeast/Woodlands. The photographs come from five donor sources. The largest number of images (ninety-one) came from Beatrice Blackwood[5] and comprise photographic portraits of scientific reference, made during fieldwork in 1925–6. These are the Northwest Coast and the Southwest series. About 40 per cent (seventy-five) were originally a gift from the Bureau of American Ethnology to Oxford Professors E. B. Tylor and H. Moseley in 1886.[6] The third largest body is a series of albumen prints from Carl Dammann, a Hamburg photographer working for the Berliner Gesellschaft für Anthropologie,

Ethnologie und Urgeschichte in the 1870s, the residue of this project being purchased for the Museum in 1901 after the descendants of the photographer had approached Professor Tylor seeking to dispose of the collection (Theye 1994–5; Edwards 1997). The two remaining donors were Henry Balfour (six), first curator of the Pitt Rivers Museum, and Mrs J. Crosby-Brown, a musicologist, Americanist and major donor to the Metropolitan Museum of Art, New York (three).

Box 54 was selected at random for the purposes of this study and its very typicalness is an important defining feature. This ordinariness, at least at the simplest level of analysis, can be extended to the photographs in it. In terms of canons of photography Box 54 contains no widely acclaimed icons of influence, although in terms of public interest, the subject matter, Native Americans, has assumed a certain iconic status. Native American material is one of the most frequently requested subjects by general researchers using the Pitt Rivers Museum in both the photographic and object collections. Indeed, the growing tensions presented by the increasingly ambiguous relationship of canonical to non-canonical histories of photography has been central to the development of curatorial agendas in many ways.

The condition of the majority of the photographs in Box 54 is on the good side of fair. They lack those qualities sought in the 'fine print' in art market terms, although some may legitimately be described as 'vintage prints' in that they are prints broadly co-temporal with the making of the image. The images are not matted and window mounted on carefully selected archival boards as one would expect images of this kind to be were they accessioned and archived within curatorial agendas today. They are simply stuck on card mounts, each measuring 12×18 inches, usually more than one to a card, with various annotations and numbering systems recorded in different hands, and comprise a palimpsest of curatorial thinking and acts of description.

The photographs have surface damage consistent with them having been soaked off their original mounts but written information from the mounts or on the back of the prints appears to have been meticulously transcribed on to the new boards in 1931.[7] The photographs are arranged broadly, but not entirely consistently, by cultural region. The larger half-plate albumen prints are arranged in symmetrical grids, four to a board. The Blackwood photographs are grouped on separate cards, often sixteen or eighteen to a card. These photographs are mostly arranged in pairs, which suggests the intention of making comparisons that may relate as much to Beatrice Blackwood's original intentions in making the images for her project as to later curatorial organising principles.[8] This is accented by the way in which two negatives are printed on one piece of photographic paper, side by side. There are gaps on some of the cards and this may be because it was understood that other photographs would be added later, or it may be the residue of a taxonomic decision now obscured.

The making of the object

What was the mix of anthropological, photographic and curatorial thinking that made such a configuration possible? As already suggested, the box contains material collected relating to very different agendas. To some extent Box 54 charts the shifts in the use of visual material within anthropology itself, from being a shared visual resource – for instance, here, the sharing of material between the Bureau of American Ethnology and the Pitt Rivers Museum – to a more fieldwork-specific concentration such as Blackwood. These are not merely developments in access and opportunity presented by the exchange of photographs, but they represent whole paradigm shifts,[9] the noise of which is suppressed within the homogenising rubric of Box 54. The historical and cultural specifics of all the images are presented in a spatial and temporal continuum of equivalent meaning, in a rationale of image arrangement that, for example, breaks continuity between stereoscopic pairs, or distorts and suppresses potential nuances of iconography in the studio portraits (see Figure 4.2).

However, we must go back a layer and look at the currency of photographs of Native American peoples within the institution before the emergence of Box 54, for it is only with reference to this, to the constituent parts of Box 54 as separate images, separate collections and separate agendas, that we can comprehend the shifting value of the photographs as images and objects moving through different anthropological and curatorial spaces.

The first layer might be termed the acquisition of living/dying cultures. In 1886 seventy-one of the photographs were donated as part of two duplicate sets of photographs sent as gifts to Tylor and Moseley for the Pitt Rivers Museum, although the distinction between the personal and the institutional was not finely drawn at this period. The donor was John Wesley Powell, Director of the Bureau of American Ethnology which had been formed by Act of Congress seven years earlier, to record and describe the native peoples of North America and their cultures.[10] The photographs were part of a gift of material culture, especially pottery from the Southwest, which, in anthropological terms, marked the ongoing relations of intellectual reciprocity and shared interest between Washington and Oxford. Here we have photographs as exchange objects within the social process of proto-modern anthropology. The photographs were duly treated as objects and entered in detail in the Museum's accession registers.

The 1886 acquisition material comprises mainly portraits, including photographs by Charles Milton Bell, Alexander Gardner and John K. Hillers.[11] While the portraits are individually strong in aesthetic terms, the relentless repetition of their stylistic conformity constitutes, at another level, an oppressive and repressive discourse (Sekula 1989: 345; see Figure 4.3). Within the museum space this might be read in Foucauldian terms as the transformation of the individual person into the objectified anthropological commodity arranged for the appropriating gaze. This is accentuated by the arrangement of the photographs in grids, inviting a discourse of equivalence (Poole 1997: 133–4) that, through the regularity of size and arrangement, stresses the meaning within a comparative discourse. However, Box 54 cannot necessarily be reduced to such a reading. The contents were never wholly dehumanised. Paradoxically, the documentation practices of successive regimes of museum culture retained contextualising information. Individualising elements, such as name and age, act to authenticate and impart individual difference to the object of study. While the 'noise' of such individualising detail might be quietened by other appropriating institutional practices and concerns, these processes of documentation leave a space through which voices might emerge for future engagements with Box 54.

The photographs thus started their existence as separate, specific, individual items that became conflated within the homogenising rubrics of an anthropological museum. The 1886 acquisition formed the core of the Native American images in the Pitt Rivers Museum. Some are in Box 54, while other parts of the acquisition appear

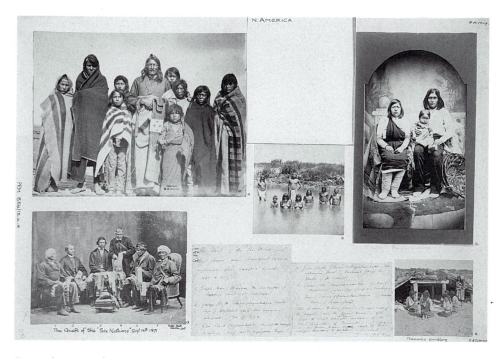

Figure 4.2 Box 54, Card 13. Miscellaneous photographs mounted to form a sequence, including two separated stereoscopic photographs. (Courtesy of Pitt Rivers Museum, University of Oxford.)

in other boxes in the same series. They were added to in 1901, through the purchase of the residue of the Dammann project with the Berliner Gesellschaft, which comprises earlier images from *c.* 1865–75, a decade before the founding of the Pitt Rivers Museum. Dammann was a Hamburg photographer who copied and disseminated photographs of 'anthropological' interest on behalf of the Berliner Gesellschaft. Published between 1873 and 1874, Dammann's *Anthropologisch-Ethnologisches Album in Photographien* comprises ten sections of five folios each, containing in all over 600 photographs (Theye 1989: 70–2). This latter project was in conceptual terms not unlike the making of Box 54 in its provisional and serendipitous nature, which none the less had an internal logic and coherence that formed a nexus of description and ideological authority (Edwards 1997). A wide range of images from different sources and in different photographic dialects from the domestic to the political were absorbed into unifying discourses, endowed with an equivalence of meaning. What links these collections conceptually is the movement of images as 'immutable mobiles' of indexical certainty and scientific data into the learned institutions of anthropology (Latour 1986). Their equivalence of meaning within a comparative structure resonates with André Malraux's *Museum without Walls*, where individuals reduced to photographs become pieces of comparison capable of being refigured in endless combination, flotsam brought together, moving in the same direction to make certain forms of meaning (Malraux 1949).

There is little evidence of how the photographs were kept or how they functioned within the institution at this stage. Early reports of the Pitt Rivers Museum displays

Figure 4.3 Box 54, Card 5. Six portraits of Native American elders by Charles M. Bell, arranged in a grid. (Courtesy of Pitt Rivers Museum, University of Oxford.)

suggest that photographs were used in an explanatory and authenticating way within displays of other kinds of material culture objects (Temple 1886: 173). Those not actually on display in the galleries were probably simply kept as loose prints in boxes. It was in this form that material labelled 'duplicate' was found during the restorage project of the early 1980s. This material comprised prints that appeared elsewhere in the mixed box series and that had clearly been deemed surplus to requirements in 1930–1, as the informational elements of these photographs were clearly considered to be 'covered' in the one print contained within the main series.

It seems that the functional or evidential use of the photographs did not have any formal articulation at this point. For it was in 1930–1 that the idea of function was given formal expression in constituting a synthetic material object, Box 54. It constitutes a frozen moment in anthropological time. It represented an amalgam of classification and visualisation in the order and cohesion of a field of knowledge, and reduced a series of differentiated individual photographic objects to a synthetic unitary object. It is the defining moment of Box 54 and sets the photographs contained within on the trajectory that we are tracing. This development was described in *The Pitt Rivers Museum Annual Report* for 1931–2 as follows:

> Card index catalogues have been brought up to date. The extensive collection of ethnological photographs, which have generally accumulated, was taken in hand, and a start was made to have them uniformly mounted and classified for arrangement in a series of cases. When completed this collection will be very valuable for reference.
>
> (Pitt Rivers Museum 1932: 1–2)

These cards were then placed in green solander boxes specially purchased for this use. This statement in the *Annual Report* marks the genesis of the trajectory of Box 54 as an object of material culture that reflects an attempt to establish a single closure of meaning through its spatial organisation and presentation.

It was at this point that the Beatrice Blackwood material was added to the existing North American photographs that were being constituted as Box 54. These prints were made from negatives from her 1925–7 fieldwork in the Plains of the United States and Canada and the peoples of Canada's Northwest Coast. Their intentionally strong anthropometric reference of full-face and profile is accentuated materially, the two images being printed on the same piece of photographic paper for ease of comparison within the broad discourses of physical anthropology (Figure 4.4). They dominate the other photographs in the box not only formally but materially in the printing paper: the visually arresting black and white glossy finish of their develop-out silver prints stands in stark contrast to the matt brown–yellow tones of ageing albumen prints. Because of their visual impact and the specificity of their content, their inclusion sets the conceptual agenda for the reading of the other photographs in the box. This is more than a stylistic correlation. As we have already suggested, it evokes a series of meanings about collective and individual identities that emerge from the dynamic material relationships within Box 54 in creating equivalences through the regularity of statement in the photographic iconography and formats. Thus, despite the differences in the photographic concepts, ranging from studio photographs to fieldwork photographs, the individual statements cannot be disassociated from one another: they conform precisely to Foucault's notion of 'homogenous fields of enunciative regularities' that characterise a discursive formation (Foucault 1989: 144–5).

Further, for the 1930–1 project, new prints were made from the Dammann wet collodion plates of copy negatives for which no prints existed in the Pitt Rivers Museum. These were printed using the same high gloss black and white paper as the Blackwood prints, probably printed by the same person at approximately the same time. The 'enunciative regularities' of both style and process here endorse the temporal slippage and equivalence of meaning inherent in the synthesis that created the epistemological framework for Box 54 at this formative moment.

It can be argued that value is accrued by objects according to their insertion into a classification legitimised by 'institutional strategy', rather than by the act of creation

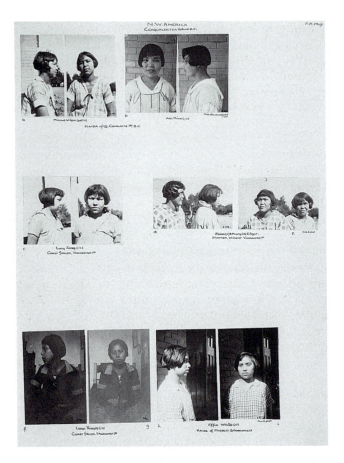

Figure 4.4 Box 54, Card 9. Pairs of photographs printed on single pieces of paper. (Courtesy of Pitt Rivers Museum, University of Oxford.)

in itself (Shelton 1990: 83). The shape of Box 54 as given in 1930–1 is dictated precisely thus. It would appear that when the photograph collection was divided into series during the 1930–1 project, the division followed the typological and comparative classification of General Pitt Rivers, which arranged comparative technologies together; for instance, pottery, food quest, houses, watercraft or ornament.[12] These were privileged as the defining taxonomy in the organisation of the photographs resulting in massive series of images arranged by technology.[13] The contents of Box 54 belong to a residue of images that could not be classified according to this arrangement of objects under comparative technologies within the institution, and the photographs were therefore arranged by geographical areas, and by implication racial types, contrary to the normal institutional practice. Sometimes the decisions are not easily comprehended retrospectively. Why, for instance, was clothing not privileged in the photographic content analysis? Nevertheless, this residual nature of the images perhaps cautions against over-emphasis on the racial classificatory elements that suggest themselves to any modern analysis of Box 54. While racial agendas are undoubtedly present, it would be a mistake to see the classification of race as causal in any primary way to the structuring of Box 54. Instead, the structuring should be seen as a matrix of both racial and cultural elements and those tensions between narration and categorisation. The legitimacy of the racial and the cultural, in terms of past institutional readings, only stresses the indeterminacy and ambiguity of the photograph, even at a time of taxonomic confidence. Thus Box 54 constitutes an example of the way in which classifications are articulated by prescribed registers, through selection, exclusion and arrangement.

Refiguring the object

The material form of Box 54 constitutes a fusion of form and function. But, paradoxically, it would appear that at the moment of formal expression within the museum function, the photograph collection was removed from the main body of the Museum (the object collections), first to the 'Book-Room' where they were difficult to use (Pitt Rivers Museum 1948: 1) and then in 1950 to the first floor of a new library facility, 'arranging them for easier consultation' (Pitt Rivers Museum 1950: 6). This physical removal stressed the instrumental and informative aspect of the photograph rather than the intrinsic value as historic objects. Further, it reflects in broad terms the marginalisation of visual material in anthropology. Although this was never as marked in museum ethnography as it was in social anthropology, there was none the less a devaluing of visual material as it was relegated to a visual notebook, the reactive product of fieldwork rather than a central process of interrogation. This bears out the comment in the *Annual Report* quoted above that the series will be valuable 'for reference' (Pitt Rivers Museum 1932: 1).[14]

But what of Box 54's social biography after its emergence? It remained as originally constituted, in a large green solander box, and significantly, was not engaged with curatorially for another thirty or forty years. It is difficult to gauge the use of the material at this period, although clearly Box 54 was in use, as the hinging fabric became frayed and weak, needing to be reinforced with linen adhesive tape. The *Annual Reports* of the Museum give no indication of numbers of research visitors to the photograph collections; nor is there any indication as to whether those who used the photograph collection were subsumed into object research visitors to the institution or were simply unrecorded. Nevertheless, Box 54, by merely continuing to exist in dormant form, carried its taxonomic and curatorial agendas into the newly constituted curatorial worlds.

The period 1960–75 might be characterised as the 'ascendancy of the document'. This constitutes a period of both intellectual and practical realisation and reactivation for museums, including the Pitt Rivers Museum. A broad awareness of the potential of visual material began to emerge in the 1960s, with mounting excitement around the historical potential of photographs (Samuel 1994: 315–47). While this was not especially marked within anthropology there was none the less an increasing interest in anthropology's own history.[15] The major curatorial initiative in the photograph collection during this period was to produce a handlist for the larger part of the photographic collections, including Box 54. No primary research was carried out and documentation was merely transcribed from the mounts or backs of photographs, so in many ways it was a reformatting of the 1931 work. The contents of each box were listed, the cards numbered and ordered (we have no way of knowing if this was the

1931 order), an inventory was produced, documenting the card number, the number of images on the card, the tribal group and/or cultural area, and the sources of the images, all were entered along one line. However, no attempt was made to record the photographers' names or the dates when the images were made, unless this information was already on the original mount or photograph in the form of a signature or studio mark and could be easily transcribed.

While this information constituted the bare minimum, it nevertheless, in creating new and easily accessible lists, recognised the value of one level of meaning, the evidential level. While it might well have been the case that conscious articulation of further meaning was not considered, the attention given to the photographic collection at this time does suggest that it was to some extent conceived within the cultural and historical ambience that identified the broad historical possibilities of the visual image at this time. This recognition went beyond informational value, which is fixed by content. It moved towards a concern with evidential value, which itself is neither absolute nor static but various in a multiplicity of circumstances, carefully including what production and collection information was available. While questions of the evidential may not have been overtly articulated, it represents a development that extended abstract intellectual control over the photograph collection through engagement with it.

The period after 1980 saw another shift, which one might term the primacy of photographic curatorship. This constitutes the surface layer, which partially obscures the historical layers on which it depends and that have been our focus so far. This surface layer is characterised by the recognition of the photograph as a cultural object. This was also in part a response to growing awareness of the needs of photographic conservation: the people in white coats were no longer in the darkroom but in the conservation laboratory. But this itself was premised on a re-evaluation of historical photographic sources over a number of related disciplines – for instance, anthropology, geography, cross-cultural and colonial history and art history. This functional shift of Box 54 is articulated by a radical development in its material form. As part of a restorage project for the whole photographic collection in 1981, the cards of photographs were removed from their acidic, non-archival solander boxes and placed in an archival storage box specifically made for the long-term storage of photographs. So, although the object Box 54 remained conceptually, the actual physical object changed. It is constructed of board with a high level of purity, free of lignums and other acidic, oxidising chemicals. The card mounts are now interleaved with sheets of silver-safe paper. Further, the collection was moved out of temporary out-housing (where it had been for several years) back into the central body of the Museum and housed in environmentally controlled stores.[16] The photographs themselves have been catalogued on an electronic database and conservation copy negatives have been made for the whole contents. The care lavished on the photographs in Box 54, in curatorial terms, represents a dramatic paradigmatic shift in thinking about anthropological photographs. In some ways reverting to their treatment as objects in the early days of the Museum, the photographs are now treated as precious objects worthy of preservation rather than merely, in simple evidential terms, reproducible and transparent documents of something else.[17]

The change from image-based perception to object-based perception has had major implications. In museum terms, photographs other than those classified as 'fine art' had traditionally been marginalised through their very lack of uniqueness and obvious aesthetic value. However, a conflation of alternative histories of photography, including cross-cultural histories, material culture studies and the exploration of broader cultural processes of uses, meant that it was recognised that it was essential to preserve and intellectually engage with the process of such transformations. The shift is precisely that characterised by Foucault (1989: 7), in that photographs no longer operate at a purely informational level through which past culture can be reconstructed.

The paradoxes inherent in this position are illustrated through the fate of mass-produced half-tone reproductions of the Rinehart photographs. These were removed from the main photographic series of Box 54 in *c.* 1979–80 (another material change). This was rationalised as a conservation decision (they were not 'photographic' in 'technical terms' and therefore required a different and lower level of preservation input). However, it also points to an increasing purification, in curatorial terms, of the photographic object. The move away from picture/image resource to 'photographs' in their own right excluded such an object, yet their value has been restored in a further shift from 'photographic object' to 'cultural' object. The latter precisely restores the perception of these mass-produced reproductions as cultural performances of photographic image-objects. Thus one can argue that subtle shifts in photographic curatorship can be traced through the history of this one excluded, then reabsorbed, item.

Conclusion

The plurality of histories and meanings accruing to the photographs in Box 54 have now become its salient characteristic. The understanding that photographs are objects that move through different spaces and that context is more than background information (Edwards 2001: 108–9) represents a substantial paradigmatic shift in both museum thinking and practice. Further, it is one of gradual accrual, in which there is an 'accumulation of traces, each layer being deposited on the former only when confidence about its meaning is stabilised' (Latour 1986: 17–18). While the photographs have been largely seen as documents, which has been part of their complex, ambiguous and paradoxical 'archaeology', one could argue that the distinction between artefact and document is artificial (Lubar and Kingery 1993: ix–xi). A photograph or box of photographs treated as an object in its own right can provide new arguments and a level of support to the intellectual and cultural environment of making and meaning that a mere 'photograph as document' approach cannot accomplish.

As Kopytoff argues, 'an eventful biography of a thing [Box 54 and its contents perhaps] becomes a story of the various singularisations of it, of classifications and reclassifications in an uncertain world of categories whose importan᷉   ᷉th every minor change in context. As with persons, the drama lies in ᷉ valuation and identity' (Kopytoff 1986: 90). Charting of the / which gathered the minor and successive shifts that refigured B᷉ and intellectually position the box within the dynamic temporal the Museum and testify to its relationships with varying discou the Museum's confines.

While the notion of grouping within a photographic colle in some ways serendipitous, each space through which the pr various ways in which they come together within collection᷉ a set of classificatory meanings and reclassify them within a new space in accordance with evolving strategies and values. However, while new meanings emerge, they none the less exist within a meta-narrative that assumes the institutional relevance is intrinsic to the photographs in the first place (Shelton 1990: 93–4). This is so because these objects were selected from a wider class of related objects; for instance, photographs of white North Americans, or railroads on the Plains, whether chosen by the Bureau of American Ethnology or by Dammann as suitable material, or a suitable subject for photography in the case of Blackwood's. All selections constitute an informed discrimination, grounded, of course, in an assumed criteria of museum value (Shelton 1990: 93–4).

In this chapter we hope to have demonstrated how the *object* in the archive or museum can be read as a closely woven palimpsest of shifting values within curatorial practice and, by implication, shifting meanings in material culture. We have argued that Box 54 and its contents have inextricably linked meanings as images and meanings as an object, an indissoluble yet ambiguous melding of image and presentational form, both of which are the products of layers of intention. The material form of Box 54 continues to perpetuate its meaning long after intellectual reclassifications have suggested other readings because of the persistence of past material traces. The life of things is in reality many lives, winding through each other, no more so than for photographs. Box 54 is an amalgam of indexical traces of the physical world and cultural objects projecting those traces embedded within shifting patterns of ownership, organisation and use.

Notes

1 It might be argued that our engagement with this box of photographs is another moment in its cultural or social biography.

2 This was part of a rationalisation project bringing all institutional numbering systems in line with one another.

3 http://www.prm.ox.ac.uk/databases/

4 General Pitt River's founding gift to the Museum included photographs and it continued to collect systematically. In the early days of the Museum photographs were accessioned as objects.

5 Beatrice Blackwood was on the staff of the Pitt Rivers Museum from the 1920s until 1975.

6 E. B. Tylor (1832–1917) was appointed to teach anthropology at the University of Oxford as part of General Pitt Rivers's gift in 1884 and was one of the most influential anthropologists of his generation. Moseley was Linacre Professor of Human and Comparative Anatomy, University of Oxford, and had been Chief Naturalist on the HMS *Challenger* Expedition of 1873–7. Both were closely connected with the Museum in the late nineteenth century. Some of the photographs were actually given by Mrs W. Sollas. Moseley died in 1891 and his widow married the geologist Professor W. Sollas as her second husband in 1914.

7 Moseley's set is not in Box 54 but is still on its original mounts elsewhere in the collection. It is a reasonable assumption that both sets were similarly mounted and that Tylor's set was removed from the mounts during the making of Box 54. The sets of photographs from Charles Milton Bell's Washington studio in the collections of the National Anthropological Archives, Smithsonian Institution, are on similar mounts.

The photographs were made during Blackwood's fieldwork as Laura Spelman Rockerfeller Memorial Fellow, investigating hereditary and cultural issues among mixed-race women in American communities in Canada and the United States. Like much of the work that the Foundation supported after its establishment in 1918, Blackwood's work had application as a contribution of human biology to the study of human socio-cultural differences and ultimately to social welfare, which the Foundation believed should have a firm base in social scientific research (Stocking 1985: 116–17).

9 For consideration of the shifting relationship between anthropology and the visual see Pinney (1992), Edwards (1998) and Grimshaw (2001).

10 For a history of the Bureau of American Ethnology, see Hinsley (1981).

11 Hiller's landscape photographs from the US Geological Survey expedition of 1879 also formed part of the gift but were kept in a separate series.

12 The Pitt Rivers Museum arranged, and continues to arrange, objects not by cultural or geographical arrangements but typologically, by type of object. For a description of the classification and schedules see Blackwood (1970).

13 Box Series C1 and C2, totalling thirty-five large boxes.

14 It is significant that the dormancy of Box 54 coincides with the nadir of material culture studies in anthropology, possibly exacerbated by local conditions in Oxford, where the Institute of Social Anthropology, under A. Radcliffe-Brown, was anxious to distance itself entirely from the Pitt Rivers Museum (in fact the older institution), which was seen as a relic of the 'old anthropology'. The treatment of photographs in these conditions began to suggest the broad shift in function, and even form, that Kopytoff (1986: 67) has identified with the 'end of usefulness'.

15 In 1980 The Royal Anthropological Institute produced a ground-breaking exhibition, *Observers of Man*, which drew attention to the photographic legacy of anthropology. This period also saw the publication of some influential works on the history of anthropology (e.g. Slotkin 1965; Burrow 1968; Stocking 1968; Asad 1973; Kuper 1973; and, from 1973, *History of Anthropology Newsletter*). *History of Anthropology*, under the editorship of George Stocking, first appeared in 1983.

16 This represents a considerable financial investment, which in itself has political implications.

17 The overall shape of this shift was articulated institutionally at a national level with the Museums and Galleries Commission *Curatorial Standards for the Care of Photographic Collections in Museums* (1986).

5

MAKING MEANING

Displaced materiality in the library and art museum

Glenn Willumson

Introduction

Although they are initially treasured for their ability to reproduce a person, an event or a location, the passage of time is not kind to photographs. As connection is lost and memory fades, photographs are quickly stored in boxes and albums. They are moved to attics and basements until, eventually, they become merely discarded objects. Over the decades a few hundred thousand survive as they pass through a series of commercial exchanges from private hands to those of booksellers and antique dealers. Of those preserved images, a few tens of thousands are of enough educational or aesthetic merit to rate the attention of a cultural institution such as a library or art museum. Of these, a small fraction is judged to be of high enough quality or great enough rarity to enter into the permanent collections of these cultural institutions. This movement and shifting from private to public, from commercial commodity to a confined social meaning and back to commodity on the art market, marks the photo-object.[1] Too often this socio-cultural inscription suppresses the materiality of photographs as they are squeezed within the rhetorics of canonical histories of photography and their concomitant spaces of collection and exhibition. Historically, even when attention is paid to the materiality of photographs, as is the case with the fine art print by the master photographer, it is submerged beneath the discourse of aesthetics.

Moving through time and across our cultural horizon, manifesting themselves at different moments and in diverse places, photographs are marked by their trajectory. In using this term I am thinking not of the sharp, straight lines of geometry, but of the incomplete, soft-edged outline of a vapour trail. This ephemeral trace is difficult to track in some places, more clear in others and obvious at its intersection with the object. It delineates not only the biography of the photograph but also the histories of the persons and places that house it. Until recently, scholarship had been so dazzled by the luminescence of the image that it ignored the photograph's physicality and the evanescent trail that it had left in its wake. This chapter explores the materiality of the image and its supporting medium (album page, cardboard mount or museum mat) and outlines its trajectory. Furthermore, it discusses those historical moments that can still be seen in its atmospheric trail and how these gossamer traces suggest the evaluation of photographs as different kinds of historical objects whose meaning changes in different social situations. It analyses three different photo-objects – the sequenced album, the stereographic series and the large format image – and different locations, particularly the library and the art museum. As this chapter will attempt to demonstrate, these artefacts can only be understood as products of a contest between their trajectories and their institutional frameworks. As such, 'thinking materially' reveals and elucidates a number of aspects of institutional culture.

A photographic album

For most photographs, redemption or rejection comes not in the institutional locations of official culture but in the domestic setting of the home, that treasure trove of imagery. Most of these individual images, of children or holidays, are filed away and eventually lost. Surviving longest are those images that have been given personal attention by individual family members and added to a photo album.[2] This framing of the photograph is intensely personal and replete with memory. In the nineteenth century, before the advent of mass-produced cameras and film, many of the images placed in albums were purchased, rather than made, by their consumers. The trajectory of photographs away from commerce is significant, in part because it marks the moment when the photograph as commodity became domesticated within the sphere of the personal.

Photo albums demand our attention as unique cultural products for several reasons. In these cultural artefacts, unlike others that will be discussed later, who produced the photograph is of less relevance than the creator of the object in which the photographs reside. The performance of thumbing through the photographs, selecting and sequencing, and gluing them into an album breaks the bond of the materiality of the photograph from its links in commerce and mass production. In choosing, sequencing, organising and captioning the photographs for the album, the person responsible transforms the meaning of selected images into an intensely individualistic expression. At the moment of creation, the photo album is a personal artefact, a record of people and events that are rich with biography and personal memory (see also Nordström, Chapter 6 in this volume).[3]

Photographic albums transcend private, personalised circumstance when they are clearly marked by the traces of their owners and their practices. The way in which particularised cultural authority permeates the pages of the book can be seen in an extraordinary set of albums in the Getty Research Institute. Kept by D. M. Seaton, an American industrialist, they are blue-lined composition books that have been transformed into photo albums.[4] They are relatively small for their purpose (33 × 21 cm), with thick cardboard covers, cloth or leather bindings and descriptive labels pasted on to the front cover. Many of the pages include photographs or reproductions glued down and surrounded by hand-written text. Often, because of the reduced size of the ledger albums and Seaton's desire to keep the orientation of the photographs consistent with the text, he glued only half of the photograph on to the album page (Figure 5.1). To protect the photograph and to make it fit inside the closed cover of the book, Seaton folded the image in half and reinforced the back of it by pasting graph paper behind the exposed half of the image. Carefully placing these commercial photographs on to certain pages and surrounding them with his cursive text, Seaton created a new object from the material production of the commercial photo gallery, an album that is personal and memorable.

In the photograph, handwritten annotations read:

platform still

Half speed

Full speed

Below the photograph, handwritten text reads:

*just to ride on that sidewalk.
It pleases the children — young
people like it — and old people laugh
with joy when they get on it.
Shows, swings, towers and
all other kinds of amusements
are not in it with this moving
sidewalk — It is only a succession of
cars on small wheels and the platforms so arranged
and connected together as to all the time make the smooth walk.*

Figure 5.1 D. M. Seaton European Travel Albums, 1898–1902, volume 5, page 95. (Courtesy of Getty Research Institute, Research Library.)

Seaton assembled seven albums during an extended trip through Europe between 1898 and 1902. Most of the text was written as a lengthy correspondence to relatives, particularly his sister Mollie. Within the narrative framework of the letter, Seaton described the location of each photograph and his relationship to the place depicted in the image. His pictures and text are personal recollections that relate and illustrate the day-to-day events of his European sojourn, provide a sense of the physical spaces through which he travelled, and comment on the national traits of the people and countries he visits. Sprinkled throughout are maps on which he noted the photographic perspective. The photographs themselves are often numbered so that they may be more easily integrated into the text. In the back of his volume on the Paris Exposition of 1900, for example, Seaton included a street map of the city. On it he wrote numbers that correspond to photographs set in the pages of his album-journal. His accompanying text alludes to these numbers in his description of place. Using the map in this way situated the photographs in the context of urban space, at the same time that it established the writer in the context of the photographs. This effort added an additional layer to the complex materiality of the Seaton albums.

Seaton made the albums for his daughter Alice, who accompanied him on his European excursion. As objects, they demand an active viewer/reader who sits at a well lit table and slowly deciphers the cursive script of the writer. To appreciate the album fully, the viewer has to reach into its pages and carefully open the photographs, unfolding the experiences and the memories captured in these image and text combinations. The volume devoted to the Paris Exposition shows how complicated this process of viewing could be. Here the reader not only had to open the photographs but also had to correlate them with the map in the back of the album, flipping back and forth between map, image and text. This high level of haptic participation in the activation of the album marks its unique materiality as a personal memoir and its value as a cultural artefact.

Over time, however, the albums' tie to personal history and significant memory was broken. For while the evidence of buckled pages and damaged spines suggest that the albums were well used, at some point they were relegated to storage. With the death of the inspiration for the albums, Alice Seaton's family lost their connection to the photographs and the personal memories that they contained. Consequently, the albums again moved from one social space to another, becoming commodified examples of pictorial and cultural oddity. They were consigned to the auction house: in 1989 Swann Gallery in New York put them up for bid as photographic curiosities.[5] Their purchase by the Getty Research Institute marked a new path for the artefacts, as public, rather than private, objects.

Significantly, the physical nature of Seaton's travel albums dictated their trajectory: first, in their particular pathway into the public sphere, and, second, in their ultimate location in the Getty Center special collections library. Aesthetically situated between the visual and the book arts, the albums found the Swann Gallery to be their most comfortable entrée into commerce. Swann had made its reputation in the book trade and, as an extension of its library interests, had been one of the first major auction houses to offer photography for sale. The Getty Center in Los Angeles includes both the Getty Research Institute and the Getty Museum, a collecting institution of international repute with a world-renowned collection of photographs. The Seaton albums, however, did not match the museum's defined collection criteria. Specifically, they were wanting in the material form normally associated with the tradition of the 'fine art print' – qualities concerned with the surface of the photograph, an issue to which I shall return later. They also lacked a canonical maker, and the images themselves had been folded and dog-eared from years of use. Although the Seaton albums did not meet the museum's standards, the library valued the albums for the interaction between text and image, for the personalised voice and construction of them as objects and, at a primary evidentiary level, for the information that they contained about Europe and America at the turn of the twentieth century.[6] In short, placing the albums in the library collections acknowledged their significance in specific epistemological contexts in relation to the history of photography and encouraged scholars to pay special attention to the material physicality of their embedded photographs as multifaceted objects.

The shift of the cultural position of the Seaton albums is typical of the photographs' trajectory as they move from the commercial photographic outlets ubiquitous in late nineteenth-century Europe, to the personal memory construction that constituted the artefactual qualities of albums, back to the world of commerce and the auction house and, finally, to the institutional location of the library. Just as the domesticity of the album transformed the reception of the material qualities of the photographs, so the library altered the understanding of the albums. In the special collections of the library at the Getty Research Institute, the Seaton albums became new objects. From repositories of memory and personal connection, they now are valued as a 'type', representative of a genre, the personal travel album, and as a source of pictorial and linguistic information about Europe at the turn of the twentieth century. In the Getty library, this latter dominates. The albums are classified using an organisational model that tethers them to subject matter. For example, archivists noted each of the countries visited and were particularly interested in the volume devoted to the Paris Exposition of 1900 because of the significance of the event. As the example of the Seaton albums suggests, artefacts are mobile objects that are embedded in particular social locations and are subject to rigid organisational rules. Both the location of the object and the discipline under which it is arranged privilege certain aspects of its materiality, in this case informational content, while ignoring other possibilities, such as the interaction between image (photograph and map) and text as they are placed in the pages of the album. The transformation of the photo-object by an organising system has significant implications for its materiality, its meaning, its social effect and the way such objects have been assessed within the history of photography.

Stereographic cards

From the questions raised by the photo album and the ambiguous status of the object, I want to consider another genre of photography that is perceived as belonging to the library: the stereograph (Figure 5.2). The material shape of stereographic photographs is determined by their function as a form of nineteenth-century 'virtual reality' and the technological requirements for this effect. They are made with a twin lens camera that produces two images, one two and a half degrees to the left of the other. The resulting prints are relatively small (approximately 8 × 8 cm) and in order to be viewed properly are glued on to a specially made cardboard support (approximately 9 × 18 cm). Placed in a specially made viewer, a stereoscope, the two images merge into a single image of three-dimensional depth.[7] Stereographs were enormously popular in the nineteenth century and have left a vast visual legacy. For a variety of reasons that will be discussed later, most stereographs found their institutional home in the library. There the paired images are treated like exact duplicates and are collected, filed and conserved for the information contained in the photograph. This method of organisation and classification ignores the special material qualities of the stereograph, dictated by the intention to reproduce a three-dimensional effect, and treats them in a way not dissimilar from books. By narrowly defining their interest in the stereograph, libraries ignore not only the aesthetic quality of the image but also the traces of historical trajectory.

Figure 5.2 Alfred Hart, 56. Rounding Cape Horn. Road to Iowa Hill from the River, in the Distance, 1866. (Private collection.)

The ways in which materiality must be read into the meaning of photographic objects can be demonstrated through the example of a series of stereographs of the Central Pacific Railroad (CPRR), which, following the various vicissitudes of the company, eventually fell out of use. However, the stereographs became entangled in a new phase of their trajectory as collectable objects within an institutional domain. Thus the CPRR stereo-cards acquired by the California State Library were subject to a cultural order that diverged significantly from that of the railroad that commissioned and used them.

Made between 1865 and 1869, there were originally 364 stereographs. They were mounted on the standard cards, the verso carrying printed titles in elaborate borders. 'Photographed and Published for the Central Pacific Railroad Company' or 'The World as Seen in California' are two of the most popular logos. On the front of the card, beneath the right hand image, letterpress numbers and titles, printed on small pieces of paper, have been glued on to the surface. The titles record the subject depicted, the geographical location and the distance from the railroad's origin in Sacramento, California.

Considering first the verso of these stereographs, one uncovers important historical clues with regard to their intended audience. These signs are easily overlooked when the photographic object is valued for the informational quality of the photograph alone. Here image and support are inseparable, constituting a single object produced to fulfil a specific social function. At first the stereographs do not appear to have been commercially available but were used in the CPRR directors' lobbying efforts that thrust them into corporate boardrooms, federal government agencies and newspaper offices. From the evidence of their material production it is clear that they were incontrovertible evidence of railroad success, produced to create a particular affective tone and, as such, served the needs of the corporation as it raised public and private money to build the first transcontinental railway across the United States. The transition of the stereographs from private testimony to public commodity is evident in the logo printed on the verso: 'Photographed and Published for the Central Pacific Railroad Company'. As the success of the railroad became evident in 1868 the stereos were available for public sale and a new verso was put into play. 'The World as Seen in California' indicated a different audience: the imagined tourist market.

Turning to the front of the stereographic cards, one finds an equally important form of materiality. Each cardboard mount in the CPRR series contains a number and title beneath the right image. In the space of the modern library, this label is small and insignificant. It is the more prominent information offered by the image that dominates the stereo-card and is the source of the library's organisational priorities. If the card's intended reality as a three-dimensional image were in play, however, a different order would be enforced. Looking at a stereograph requires the eyes to be enclosed by the viewfinder of the stereoscope. As the two images merge in the visual field, all visual stimulation outside of the image is eliminated. This creates an encompassing reality effect as the image fills the whole visual frame, rather than the normal experience in which the viewer perceives the spatial limits of the photograph. In stereoscopic viewing, the field of vision is enveloped by the three-dimensionality of the photograph and by the strategically placed number and title beneath the image. Because the labels lack visual dominance outside the stereoscope, the sequence of the CPRR stereographs is too often ignored and the images are scattered and grouped with other stereographs on the basis of subject matter. A case in point is the dividing up of a series of stereocards (numbers 321–325 in the sequence) that dealt with the railway's progress through the Humboldt desert in Nevada, the march of 'civilisation' through Shoshone Indian territory. The original impact of the series of oppositional markers of the 'primitive' and 'civilised' in the photographs, represented by a juxtaposition of native encampments and trains, is destroyed by the disregard for the narrativity that is the basis for the numbering system and the titling of these photo-objects.

In the library they were valued for the information the images contained about a specific moment of American chronology, not as narratives of American history. Because they were of manageable size, the stereographs were often filed together in specially designed cases that looked much like the drawers for catalogue cards.[8] Disregarding the physical evidence of the printed cardboard on which the images were glued, the library reassembled the stereographs like book collections, into essentialising themes and subject headings: 'Indians', 'Transportation', 'Landscape', 'Bridges', 'Portraits', 'Towns' etc. This organisational model is rooted in the library's concern for its contemporary audience and its familiarity with a text-based system of organisation. With its visitors in mind, the library ignored the physicality of the stereo-cards and transformed the stereographs into visual text rather than material culture, into subjects rather than objects.

In the gallery

Stereographs suit the library because libraries are first and foremost collecting institutions. They accumulate books, photographs and ephemera with the understanding that their primary purpose is to act as a repository of data. The stereographic format makes them easy to collect and to organise reductively into categories of information. The art museum, however, is a significantly different institution. It is not only a venue for collections but also, and primarily, an institution of exhibition. Whereas the library exists to collect objects of informational importance, the museum is called upon to show objects of significant cultural value. Historically, this mission has been performed on the stage of aesthetics and these values have been played out through the material practices of the museum. The traditional exhibition practice of matting and framing images behind glass effectively calls attention to the visual aesthetics of the large single photograph, but it cannot easily encompass the presentational demands of the stereograph, thus making it difficult for it to enter the gallery space of the museum. There are several reasons for this neglect. Stereographic aesthetics,[9] the representation of three-dimensionality in the stereograph, requires a physical interaction between the materiality of the photograph and the viewer. This is not possible within accepted art museum practice. Put another way, the privileging of the aesthetics of the image that is the basis for fine art museum exhibitions denies the body of the viewer, just as it denies the physicality of the object exhibited. In the case of stereographs, on those rare occasions when they are included in the art museum context, they are made to perform the values of 'fine art photography'.

To demonstrate the problematics of the materiality of the stereograph in the halls of the art museum, I should like to consider a recent exhibition of American landscape photographs. *Carleton Watkins: The Art of Perception* offers an example of one of the more innovative inclusions of the stereograph within the walls of the art museum.[10] Organised by the San Francisco Museum of Modern Art, this retrospective of arguably the greatest photographer of the American West included over 175 photographs, almost a third of which were stereographs. Not only did the exhibition include many examples of Watkins's stereographic work, it also used innovative technology to present the three-dimensional aesthetics of stereography.

Shown in the last room of the exhibition, the stereographic photographs were transformed into digital images that were viewed on computer screens through specially designed glasses.[11] This innovative presentation allowed viewers to see easily the three-dimensional aesthetics of an extended sequence of stereographic images. This effort was significant, but it achieved its end by divorcing the image from its support and its material context, for the material translation from stereo-card to digital was obscured, and the two presented as equivalent forms (see Sassoon, Chapter 12 in this volume). Rather than providing insight into nineteenth-century stereographic photography, this presentational mode served the traditional needs of the museum: the promotion of a decontextualised aesthetics that was divorced from the materiality of the object and the physical interaction of the viewer. The materiality of the stereographs was eliminated and their effect was reproduced.

Even more to the point, the inclusion of so many stereographs was used to reinforce the aesthetics of the museum and submerge the stereograph's materiality.[12] With the exception of a few examples of stereographs placed in stereographic viewers in the centre of the galleries, those stereographs included in the core of the exhibition were matted and framed behind glass, giving no sense of the intended visual impact (Figure 5.3). The presentational mode was the same as that of the large format prints that made up the bulk of the exhibition. This display technique served a decided aesthetic purpose. Within the imposed order of the exhibition the smallness of the stereographic cards enhanced the impressive size and aesthetic monumentality of the large images (38 × 51 cm). The selection of identical or similar locations in both stereographic and mammoth formats made even more evident this pronounced aesthetic difference.

Figure 5.3 Installation view of *Carleton Watkins: The Art of Perception* at the San Francisco Museum of Modern Art, 1999. (Courtesy of San Francisco Museum of Modern Art.)

The juxtaposition of format was another of the ways in which the museum signalled its commitment to the traditional cultural order.

In addition to their role as counterpoints to the high art aesthetics of the large format prints, the inclusion of stereographs served yet a third purpose. Although important aspects of their physicality were denied, the stereographs none the less served to validate Watkins as a canonical photographer by establishing his versatility and the breadth of his artist oeuvre. As has been noted by Rosalind Krauss and others, this traditional art historical model fits uneasily as a criterion for judging photographic production (Krauss 1989). None the less, it continues to be used extensively by art historians and curators. In the case of the Watkins exhibition, this move is played out not only in the juxtaposition of sites in both stereographic and large print formats, but also in the selection of photo-objects and the aesthetic discourses these practices create.[13]

The most noteworthy example is the exclusion of the CPRR stereographs. Although Watkins was not the photographer who had made the images, he had come into the possession of the negatives shortly after the completion of the railway in 1869, and for the next thirty years he printed and published them on card stock imprinted with his name. The inclusion of Watkins's CPRR stereograph production would have allowed the museum to examine critically his practice as a photographer. Instead, this material aspect of Watkins's oeuvre was omitted from the exhibition because including these examples of his work would draw attention to the commercial nature of his photographic practice and would distract visitors from the museum's production of Watkins as a fine artist.

Despite the inclusion of 'low cultural objects' such as stereographs, the Watkins exhibition reasserted the notion of photographs as high-status commodities. It reproduced the material manifestations of 'value' through presentational form, juxtaposition and selection. These exhibition techniques called attention to the high art status of the finished print and masked the commercial status of the photographer in order to elevate him unproblematically into the canon of artistic practitioners. This mark of acceptance privileges one form of materiality, the cult of the fine print by a great artist, but it ignores the historical framing evident in the photograph's support and presentational form and consequently rejects its history and its socio-cultural trajectory.

Making art objects

Twenty-five years earlier, in 1975, the Metropolitan Museum of Art organised one of the first art exhibitions to include a significant number of Watkins's photographs. *Era of Exploration* was a groundbreaking selection of nineteenth-century landscape photography of the American West (Naef and Wood 1975). In addition to a national tour, an extensive and well researched catalogue ensured that the impact of the exhibition would be long lasting. The resulting public and scholarly success raised the status of western landscape photography and established a canon of photographers, with Carleton Watkins, Timothy O'Sullivan, Edweard Muybridge, Andrew Russell and William Henry Jackson singled out for a special portfolio in the back of the catalogue. The accompanying essays highlighted Watkins as the most important photographer of the group. This event called attention to the aesthetic qualities of the photographs made by these practitioners, and began the transformation of their work from socially significant information to that valued for their aesthetic qualities.

The social function of the museum, then, consisted of two elements: discovery and assurance. The museum acted in its role as explorer when it unveiled previously unknown or overlooked examples of the fine art aesthetics in photography. In the institutional history of photography, actions of this kind were of greatest importance during the 1930s and 1940s, a period when photography struggled for recognition. The 1970s witnessed an upsurge of museum interest in collecting photographs and with this shift, new cultural values emerged in relation to photography. Museums began to offer reassurance of photography's status by refining the canon and articulating high and low forms of the medium. This latter distinction was often a direct result of the material properties of the print. Rich tonality, large format, consistent compositions and articulated aesthetic control were among the criteria used to assure a sceptical museum public that photography was indeed a fine art. With exhibitions like *Era of Exploration*, the museum established a new trajectory for the library's photographic collections from the nineteenth century.

This elevation of certain photographs had economic as well as aesthetic implications. Increasing significantly the commodification of photography, this shift to the art museum caused a re-evaluation of the functional holdings of libraries throughout the country. One of those institutions was the University Club in New York City. While completing a commissioned appraisal of the library, Swann Galleries discovered two albums of mammoth-plate photographs (40 × 53 cm) by Carleton Watkins. The first of these, entitled *Pacific Coast*, consisted of 49 albumen prints of California. The second, an even more rare compilation of images titled *Columbia River and Oregon*, was composed of 51 mounted prints. Realising the increased value of the albums, the University Club decided to put them up for auction in order to augment operating funds,[14] thus marking another move in the albums' trajectory from commodity to artefact and back again.

Contemporaneous with their production in the 1860s, Watkins's large format prints were offered for purchase from his studio in San Francisco. In this aspect of their trajectory the Wakins photographs are not dissimilar to those purchased by Seaton for his albums. They were redeemed from the vicissitudes of commerce when the University Club added the two elephant-folio albums to their library. For the institution, the albums were not dissimilar to books in that both conveyed information about the western United States to their readers. Over time, the proliferation of mass-produced imagery of the West, however, devalued the albums' status as a unique source of knowledge. Interestingly, it was undoubtedly their obsolescence as an information resource that assured their high market value. Because the albums had received so little use, the photographs inside showed few signs of normal material degradation, and most images still retained the rich purple colour of fine gold toning. When, a century later, a new library committee discovered the value of the albums not as information but as aesthetic objects, they returned the photographs to the arena of commerce. The two Watkins albums were sold in New York at Swann Gallery on 10 May 1979. At that time, they were the most expensive photographic objects ever sold. The Hastings Galleries in New York purchased the *Pacific Coast* album for $98,000 and The Weston Gallery in Carmel bought *Columbia River and Oregon* for $100,000.[15]

What so shocked contemporaries was not the price paid for the photographs, however (the average of $2,000 per photograph was well within the market's range). In the late 1970s Watkins's mammoth photographs sold for as much as $4,000, and it was widely acknowledged that these were among the finest prints to come on the market. What was so surprising was the willingness of two dealers to acquire so many photographs by the same photographer at this relatively high price.[16] This circumstance was made possible by the museum. By exhibiting Watkins's photographs as fine art to an increasingly interested public, the museum offered assurance of the photographs' value as high status commodities and, thereby, confirmed for dealers that there would be a market for the prints. As it turned out, however, this was only possible if the albums lost their uniqueness as objects. This, too, was indirectly supported by the museum.[17]

Museums collect photographs as objects for exhibition. The Watkins photographs in the *Pacific Coast* and *Columbia River and Oregon* albums seemed ideal. They were large format, richly toned prints by the acknowledged master of Western landscape photography (Figure 5.4). The problem was their serial presentation in the bound album. As was discussed in connection with the Watkins exhibition of 1999, the presentational aesthetics of the art museum favour large format photographs hung in single file on museum walls. This practice finds its history in the display of other precious graphic forms such as Old Master drawings, and like Old Master drawings, to enter the halls of the museum, the collection of photographs needed to be disbound.[18] This served exhibition practice, but the transformation of the album into single prints offered other advantages to the museum.[19]

Figure 5.4 Carleton Watkins, *View on the Columbia, Cascades*, 1867. (Courtesy of Metropolitan Museum of Art, Warner Communications Inc. Purchase Fund and Horace Brisbane Dick Fund.)

The materiality of the album, and the reproduction of its narratives, required a physical connection to the viewer that was possible in the library, but was not available in the museum. Albums, especially an elephant-folio, demand an intimacy with the viewer because their size and weight are such that one must have physical contact with the artefact by supporting the album and carefully turning its heavy cardboard pages as each new photograph is revealed. This can take place in the library because it is a place for bound books of an informational nature. The art museum intentionally removes the body of the viewer and its accompanying tactility. It does this in order to preserve the object, but at the same time this practice removes any trace of the artefact's previous trajectory. The museum cannot afford to pay attention to the traces of the object's history because it would distract from the photograph's reception as a work of art in the current moment. Because it desires objects on to which curators and viewers can write their own stories, museums do not want objects pre-inscribed by history.[20] Consequently, the disbinding of an album, like the one containing the Watkins photographs, serves to make the images accessible for easy exhibition and, at the same time, available for effortless reinscription by curators and audiences.[21] The bound album is also problematic because its large number of photographs, regardless of their quality, remind visitors that photography is a reproductive medium and that its origins are in commerce. Single prints re-enact the sensibility of the elite cultural object. Reinvented and scarce, the Watkins photographs from the University Club albums slipped effortlessly into the collections of the very institutions that had been responsible for the elevation of their status. Just as the museum displays enact the disembodiment of the viewer, so exhibition policies enact the disembodiment of the photograph. We must recognise, however, that the practice of cultural ordering that transformed the Watkins albums into objects of fine art and that supported *Carleton Watkins: The Art of Perception* is not a natural occurrence, but the result of historical practices codified earlier in the twentieth century.

(In)visible materiality

In the United States, the elevation of photography into the sphere of the art museum is intertwined with the defined history of the medium. This process allowed photographs (always suspect because of their connection to mechanical reproduction) to move beyond amateur collectors and hobbyists and to attain the status of high cultural production. In the 1930s, the medium was of particular interest to the modern art museum because of its connection to technology and its availability to the popular imagination. These factors marked it as emblematic of the new machine age that was being celebrated by artists in the United States and Europe and by the Museum of Modern Art in New York. Although the medium was of interest to cultural institutions, questions about criteria for collecting and ordering photographs within existing institutional structures and forms of hierarchical discrimination had not been resolved for the museum.

Until late in the nineteenth century, the majority of photographs produced in society were commodities intended for sale. In their efforts to legitimise photography as a fine art, curators mask this history behind formal criteria based on the tradition of the fine art print. Beaumont Newhall at the Museum of Modern Art articulated the methodology that addressed these issues and that shaped the curatorial practice towards photography in the United States.[22] His exhibition *Photography 1839–1937* and its associated publications codified a history of photography within a practice rooted in contemporary art historical methodology. Based upon formal analysis, attention to the moment of production and a concern for the contemporary audience, this set of practices brought attention to the surface quality of the photograph.[23] Although material quality defined the fine historical print, its 'thingness' was absorbed unarticulated into an aesthetic discourse. These criteria became the centrepiece for the collecting practice and the cultural ordering that were accepted for photography collections in United States art museums. However, this methodology and practice were contingent and historically determined.

Because photography was a medium of mechanical reproduction, and, perhaps, even more damning, one whose history was associated with commerce, in the early twentieth century practioners, such as the Linked Ring in England and the Photo-Secession in America, embraced accepted and universally approved art principles in an effort to elevate photography to the realm of fine art. As Ulrich Keller (1984, 1985) has pointed out, the resulting photographs mimicked accepted motifs, practices and even formal qualities of painting. While leaders such as Alfred Steiglitz soon abandoned the Pictorialist approach, which had endowed photographs with painterly qualities and which was favoured by many at the turn of the twentieth century, he continued to battle for the recognition of photography in the hallowed halls of the museum. In the United States the breakthrough came in early 1936 when Museum of Modern Art director Alfred Barr invited Newhall to organise an exhibition in celebration of the first one hundred years of photography.

The principles and understanding that Newhall brought to photographs came from his study of art history at Harvard University. Particularly influential was the museum course taught by Paul Sachs, associate director of the Fogg Art Museum. Between 1922 and 1947 Sachs taught 'Museum Work and Museum Problems' to Harvard graduate students, many of whom would become prominent museum directors and curators in the American museum community.[24] One of those former students was the director of the Museum of Modern Art, Alfred Barr.[25] The centrepiece of his methodology was a requirement that students describe and assess the attributes of individual objects that Sachs gave them for analysis. Premised on close observation of an artefact, the student was expected to articulate the exact formal qualities that were identifiable in the materiality of the item. This discernment in the face of the object was at the centrepiece of Sachs's belief in connoisseurship. The exercise of selecting the most important aspects of objects, defined in terms of aesthetics, and verbally articulating those qualities to one's peers provided Sachs's students with confidence that they could quickly engage objects with little outside preparation.

This emphasis on the articulation of objects in terms of a rarified aesthetic discourse was supported by contemporary socio-cultural trends outside of academia. For a variety of social and economic reasons, the newly emerging wealthy class in the early twentieth century embraced collecting and museum philanthropy as its preferred social endeavour. These people were collectors of rare and beautiful objects: artefacts removed from their contexts and transported across the ocean to the United States. Following their supporters' lead, art museums shifted their focus from education to collection development (Weil 2002). To do this effectively, however, a new class of museum worker was needed, one whose training promised the kind of sophisticated knowledge and expertise that the industrialists serving on museum boards had come to value in their own collecting and corporate enterprises. Sachs's museum course trained and certified those individuals who could fulfil this role. In addition to attending to the formal qualities of beautiful objects, Sachs insisted that students cultivate relationships with important dealers and collectors. Sachs was astute enough to recognise that this training enabled his students to be outstanding collection developers and to enter easily into the shifting paradigm of the contemporary art museum. Their combination of skills prepared the Harvard students to work with this new class of museum supporter, to select the finest aesthetic objects and to lead art museums with a new emphasis on collection development.[26]

In organising his exhibition at the Museum of Modern Art and in writing and rewriting his catalogue, Beaumont Newhall acted within this framework as he formulated criteria for collecting photography in the art museum. For this first exhibition of the history of photography, Newhall organised 841 photographs into a linear progression based on technological innovation and exemplary practitioners (Newhall 1937).[27] His text reveals Newhall's commitment to the art historical tradition. Regardless of their period, the best photographs, he argued, demonstrate a careful crafting of the image that displays the photographer's intimate knowledge of the medium – evident in the colour, texture and fine detail of the finished print. Later, using contemporary photography as his touchstone, Newhall championed the materially pure, unretouched and sharply focused photograph as the aesthetic ideal (Newhall 1938).[28] This principle favoured photographers such as Alfred Steiglitz, Paul Strand and Edward Weston. In making this move, however, Newhall embraced a framing discourse that divorced the photographic object intellectually from its materiality and its context. It made photography's transition into the museum less problematic, in that it imitated traditional models of museum practice and art historical methodology, and it allowed him to pull into his fine art orbit the work of other photographers such as Berenice Abbott, Margaret Bourke-White and, later, Lewis Hine, all of whose work shifted category to fit more easily into the fine art museum. With a framing discourse that embraced aesthetic judgement of the single print and its surface qualities, Newhall's criteria may have been effective, but they established a practice that minimised the presentational mode and the materiality of the photographic object, by translating, as we saw with Watkins, for example, the material into a series of abstract aesthetic values.

The extent to which this aesthetic framework has ingratiated itself within museum practice is made evident in the more recent discourse surrounding the 'vintage print'. Although there is no universally accepted definition for this term, for the most part, it is agreed that 'vintage' prints are those made within ten years of the exposure of the negative, tying specific objects – negative and print – into a historical relation of physical production that is invested with certain values. Later prints from the same negative are considered 'non-vintage'. Although on the surface this distinction seems to serve the purposes of commerce, elevating the price of certain images from the same negative, it also serves the rationale of the museum.

The idea of the 'vintage print' allows the museum to bridge a number of gaps in its aesthetic criteria. It highlights photography as a print-making process and thereby unites it with other accepted art practices, such as etching, lithography, engraving, serigraphy and mezzotint, to name just a few. It also ties the exhibited print to the production of the negative. This has two effects. On the one hand, it connects the museum object with an individual practitioner. The vintage print is essential, so the argument goes, because it exhibits the closest affinity between the idea of the photographer/artist and the object in the museum. Later prints, while they may be aesthetically appealing, do not have this direct connection of concept and primal moment. This association allows the museum to do something else that is critical to the history of photography: establish a canon of master photographers.[29] With the rise of this rarified museum and market discourse has come a determined critique.

Over the past twenty-five years, art historians have turned away from the exclusive privileging of formal analysis in favour of photographs whose cultural value is rooted in social function. Arguably the most dramatic effect of this new methodology has been to decentre art history's relationship with the museum and its objects. For art museum curators, connoisseurship and a canon of master practitioners continue to be of primary importance. It is equally clear, however, that this approach locates value on the surface of the print, not in the support, presentational forms or its historical consumption. Releasing academics from the canon, on the other hand, has allowed scholarly attention to move from an exclusive concern for the production of the photograph to an active interest in the consumption of the image, which has forced a precise articulation of the material aspects of the photograph. These new critical studies, with their attention to reception at particular historical moments, are difficult for the museum to absorb. This methodology calls for a new set of criteria rooted in the material existence of the photo-object at specific historical moments, and, thereby, runs against the grain of the museum's cultural ordering of its objects for exhibition and its embrace of a contemporary audience.

There have been other broad-based socio-cultural pressures on the museum's tradition of aesthetics over materiality. The elite support on which Sachs and his students could rely in the 1930s and 1940s is no longer sufficient to maintain art museums. Increasingly, museums in the United States have, of necessity, turned to local, state and federal governments for funding. In turn, these agencies have required the art institutions to demonstrate new outreach activities to an increasingly broad cross-section of social constituencies.[30] As they approach these new audiences, however, museums are in a difficult position. Having collected the most rare and beautiful objects available, museums must now make their collections relevant to a constituency for whom these elite objects have little relevance.

These challenges to the traditional strategies of selecting artefacts for preservation and cultural ordering in storage, exhibition and publication are not easily resolved. One solution would be to reorient the museum's thinking about the relationship between its objects and its audience. Instead of privileging an aesthetics of production and exhibition value, museum practice might engage questions of object trajectory and historical reception. The single masterworks that are individually framed and hung in straight lines on white museum walls encourage contemplation, but in the future, exhibitions that engage materiality might foster historical inquiry. The museum should consider the potential benefits of conceptually replacing historically disengaged museum visitors with a consideration of the audiences contemporaneous with the making of the photograph, and thus engage with the 'thingness' of photographs: their albums, frames, cases and reproductions. These shifts would involve a radical reconsideration of the art museum, including its collection development policies. In particular, this new conceptualisation of museum practice would demand a renewed respect for the physical properties of the object, an interest in the trajectory and historical trail of those objects over time and attention to the circumstances of specific collisions between object and audience throughout the photograph's history.

Furthermore, by denying the historical trajectory of the object, the museum fails to engage a critical link between the institution, the artefact and the visitor. Masking the physical properties of the object at different moments of history and ignoring its cultural positioning in different social locations damages the relationship between the museum and the visitor. Treating the photograph as an organic thing that has a history whose trajectory can be traced like a personal biography offers to the popular audience experiences that are familiar. Not only would museum objects be invested with a past, a present and a future, just like the visitors themselves, but such a practice would also unmask the role of the museum as producer of socially relevant artefacts. This cultural activity is appropriate because it is common. All museum visitors will have had the experience of deciding which photographs to save and which to discard. Many people, for example, have had to clean out the house or apartment of a deceased relative – throwing out certain objects while keeping others. As discussed at the beginning of this chapter, these acts of selection represent the formation of a cultural organisation of personal memory. Like these special objects, museum artefacts are socially located through a similar process, but one that is based on contemporary social and cultural factors rather than a singular, personal memory.

Whatever the answer to the issues that surround the art museum at present, solutions will involve more than rehanging the galleries and changing the label text. All photographs, especially those in the museum, have age and consequently history. Especially for photographs from the nineteenth century, their trajectory includes the social and cultural shifts of the image between commodity and artefact as it changes hands and accrues exchange value. This interaction between the past and the present is manifest in the physicality of the artefact. Considering photographs not only as objects of fine art but also as objects with histories and spatial and geographic trajectories recognises the possibility that meaning can be found in the presentational forms of photographic prints, in the uses to which they are put and in their cultural trajectory from public to private, from common to singular, from commodity to culture (Kopytoff 1986). It is in these historical transitions that one locates the human and social contexts that help to activate cultural meaning, and that might suggest the elements of more socially aware collection and exhibition policies.

Conclusion

This overview of the problematic relation between the art museum and the materiality of the photograph has been able only to indicate the shape of the debate. Any one aspect could be usefully developed further. The recognition that cultural evaluation is contingent opens up new directions for thinking about photographs – pathways in which the material evidence of the image, its support and its presentational mode can serve as a beacon to the underappreciated social and cultural role that photography has played historically, and that it continues to play today. While past efforts have saved for future generations countless examples of pristine and beautiful photographs, they have also served to structure cultural values and social relations. Within contemporary museum practice, however, those traditional values and audiences have changed. With that shift will come a necessity to reconsider the objects that a museum collects and the reason why it collects them. This new evaluation will take into account a fresh set of criteria, with the materiality of the photograph and its trajectory over time as the primary consideration for inclusion. It will bring renewed attention to overlooked presentational forms such as the photographic album and the stereograph and their inherent and inseparable 'thingness'. With the passage of time, this approach will become central to new formations of photographic collections and new articulations of photographic history.

Notes

1 For the transformation of culture artefacts in space and time and particularly the way in which they are located and ordered in and by particular societies see Straw (1998) and Appadurai (1986).
2 On the construction of personal family albums see Spence and Holland (1991) and Langford (2001).
3 For the relationship between photographs and memory see for example Edwards (1999) and Langford (2001).

4 *D. M. Seaton European Travel Albums*, seven volumes, Getty Research Institute, Special Collections, 89.R.22. Seaton was a successful San Francisco lawyer in the latter part of the nineteenth century when a client suggested that they go into a manufacturing business together. Over the next few years, Seaton patented over one hundred refinements and inventions for the loom. As his albums make clear, his trip to Europe was as much for promotion of his machines as it was for his pleasure.

5 Swann Galleries (1989) (24 April), lot number 492.

6 For an extended discussion of the albums in the Getty Research collections see Willumson (1998).

7 For a basic history of the stereograph see Darrah (1977). For a more recent consideration of the social implications of stereographic viewing, particularly its relationship to modernity, see Crary (1990).

8 For a discussion of the theoretical framework of the library and archive see Sekula (1986). These ideas are theorised in a discussion of a photographic archive of worker portraits in Sekula (1983).

9 Its technical and material forms dictate the formal aesthetics of the stereograph. To emphasise its three-dimensionality, the composition demands a strong foreground and a receding middle distance with a prominent midground object. The deep space of the stereograph provides a backdrop against which the foreground and midground subject matter is silhouetted.

10 Nickel (1999). The exhibition was well received and travelled to the Metropolitan Museum of Art in New York and the National Gallery of Art in Washington, DC.

11 These comments about the installation are based on the author's experience of the exhibition at the Museum of Modern Art in San Francisco.

12 This message is made explicit in the text in which Nickel (1999) advances the argument that the oscillation between the stereograph and the large format prints was a central element in the development of Watkins's aesthetic.

13 For a discussion of photographs as objects of study within the market system see Solomon-Godeau (1991).

14 The circumstances of the sale of the albums are outlined in Alinder (1979). My thanks go to Weston Naef for bringing these albums to my attention.

15 Swann Galleries, 10 May 1979, Rare Books Auction, Sale 1141, lot numbers 226 and 227.

16 My thanks go to Stephen White for giving me this information and for sharing his insight and experience as a photography dealer in the 1970s.

17 Before the *Columbia River and Oregon* album was disbursed, it was photographed and published by the Friends of Photography (Alinder 1979).

18 For a discussion of the history of the museum as a system of classification and ordering see Hooper-Greenhill (1992).

19 Significantly, this practice is reproduced in storage, where single prints are matted to standard sizes in order to be easily stored in commercially produced solander boxes.

20 Donald Preziosi (1996) argues that the purpose of the museum exhibition is to define our expectations, discipline our desires, and provide both a past and future dominated by the visitor's sense of presentness.

21 Eileen Hooper-Greenhill (2000) discusses the process through which objects are made meaningful as a relationship between the viewer and the object.

22 For a discussion of the constructions of histories of photography before the museum, see Gasser (1992) and McCauley (1997).

23 For details about Newhall's 1937 exhibition and the importance of Sachs's course in its planning see Bertrand (1997).

24 Sachs taught his museum course from 1921 to 1947 and placed 160 students in 85 of the most important museums in the United States. Of these placements 42 were directors, assistant directors and administrators, and 45 were curators (Kantor 1993).

25 On Alfred Barr's career and the influence of Sachs see Kantor (2002).

26 For the latest biographical sketch of Sachs and his course, including a brief outline of the specifics of his pedagogy, see Tassel (2002).

27 Phillips's (1989) argument that Newhall's first exhibition was influenced by Bauhaus principles and by Moholy-Nagy in particular is convincing. None the less, Newhall's catalogue essay was more traditional in its approach (Newhall 1937). His tendency towards aesthetic classification was made manifest when the catalogue essay was rewritten in the following year (Newhall 1938).

28 Since the original publication of *Photography 1839–1937*, Newhall's text has undergone four revisions and been translated into several languages. It remains a standard survey text.

29 There have been several recent critiques of museum practice and the way in which it constructs the canon and controls its visitors; for example, Sherman and Rogoff (1994), Duncan (1995) and Wallach (1998).

30 In his concise history of museums in the United States, Harris (1999) pays particular attention to the 1960s when public funding replaced private support.

6

MAKING A JOURNEY

The Tupper scrapbooks and
the travel they describe

Alison Nordström

Introduction

Between 1891 and 1895, William Vaughn Tupper, a Brooklyn financier, visited Europe and North Africa with his wife and two daughters. He was one of the millions of middle-class Americans who travelled abroad for pleasure at this time, and, like many of his compatriot counterparts, he returned with photographs, in his case nearly two thousand of them. Almost all of them are the mass-produced albumen prints found in most travel-related collections of the period, depicting monuments, street scenes, landscapes and local costume, and bearing the names of such familiar commercial photographers as Alinari (Florence, Italy), Beato (Egypt), Dimitrou (Greece), Sebah (Turkey), Sommer (Italy) and Zangaki (Egypt), whose images had a massive distribution in the late nineteenth century (Figure 6.1). Tupper organised his collection into 46 handmade scrapbooks, embellished with detailed annotations, drawings and inclusions of ephemera that describe and delineate his travels with the particularity of a diary. Unlike many such volumes that have survived, these merit attention precisely because they are not associated with a famous person. The photographs in them are likewise commonplace, and are of little economic or aesthetic value. On one level, these are profoundly mundane objects, thick with the ordinary marks of their making, but it is precisely this that permits them to reveal multiple aspects of the complex culture they inhabited and the meanings they have held since they were made.

Travel albums from the nineteenth century are so common a system for the storage, organisation and display of photographs that they are sometimes invisible, yet as material objects they offer a rich subject for analysis, extending our knowledge of what photographs meant to their earlier users. They are deeply individual, yet they survive as a material example of the broader context in which certain images were once used and understood, and they continue to shape our understanding of these images today. This chapter aims to demonstrate these general assumptions through the close reading of the Tupper scrapbooks, for their structure as material objects was made for a specific reason: to communicate specific narratives to a particular audience (Schwartz 1995: 42). There is a substantial literature on travel photographs (see, for example, Adam and Fabian 1983; Perez 1988; Zannier 1997) and on travel represented as an abstract discourse of cultural practice, concerned with metaphors, for instance, of displacement

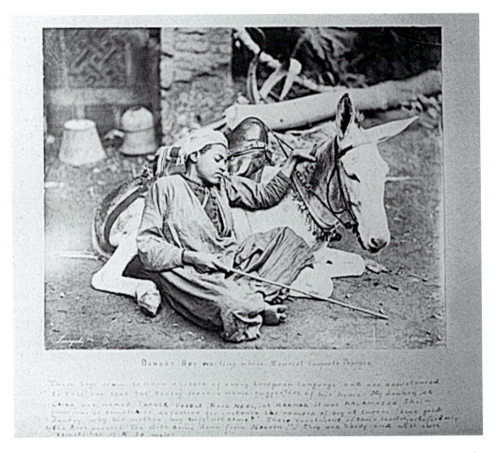

Figure 6.1 'Donkey boy waiting while tourist inspects Temple' (T31.31). Photographer: Zangaki
studio. (Courtesy of Boston Public Library, Print Department.)

and desire (see, for instance, Pratt 1992; McClintock 1995; Grewal 1996; Kaplan
1996; Clifford 1997). While these ideas inform my analysis at a deep level, my
intention here is to undertake a detailed analytical description of a material object –
Mr Tupper's scrapbooks – that puts flesh on the bones of the abstract. As material
objects these scrapbook albums manifest a system of knowledge through the structuring of their pages that represent, contain and domesticate the foreign worlds they
display. Resonating with the authority and structure of the book, they present a
personal journey as something true, certain and complete, and one that is formed by
its linear structure as a sequential narrative with an air of inevitability, yet, as I shall
argue, this material structure re-engages with the spatial and temporal ambiguities of
photographs to cast them in a specific narrative that is both personal and creative.

This chapter, therefore, emphasises the Tupper books as objects. Their material
form is what fixes the meaning of the photographs they hold; the story they manifest
is discrete and exclusive. These scrapbooks are utterly personal and particular, yet a
close examination reveals the larger world of which they are both a part and a reflection. Their content, sequence, layout and material qualities perform a complex act of

organisation and meaning-making that reveals relationships between tourism, photography, visuality, memory and collective knowledge in the earliest period of American mass travel abroad.

Mr Tupper's travels

We may extrapolate the rough shape of the Tuppers' actual journey from the dates on the covers of 15 of the 46 scrapbooks. The earliest volumes show the family to have been in London in 1891 (T24).[1] That year they appear to have taken a short tour to Chester, Stratford-on-Avon, Warwick and York, between 29 July and 5 September, with an additional trip to Scotland, between 8 August and 1 September (T39). In the spring of 1892, they were briefly in Algeria (T1, 14 April to 5 May) and they were in London again that year as well (T24). The volume *Vienna, November 25–December 12, 1892* (T45) suggests a winter trip across central Europe that ended with a season in Egypt, as indicated by the volumes Tupper titled *Cairo Mosques and Schools, December 21–28, 1892* (T9), and *Lower Egypt and the Pyramids, December 21, 1892–March 8, 1893* (T26). Undated books titled *Egypt, Luxor, Karnak* (T27), *On the Nile, Cairo to Luxor* (T31) and *Luxor–Philae* (T32) suggest an extended itinerary during their Egyptian sojourn. The party apparently returned to Europe via Greece, as shown in *Athens, March 12–29, 1893* (T3) and the undated *Greece* (T21). The summer of 1893 included at least a brief trip to the Netherlands, indicated by the two books *Amsterdam and Marken, July 27–August 1, 1893* (T2) and *Holland, July 27–August 10, 1893* (T22) and it is possible that their trip through Belgium, described in two undated volumes (T5 and T6), also occurred that year. They returned to London again for part of the year (T24) and apparently undertook short excursions from there to popular English tourist destinations, recorded in *Isle of Wight, Southampton, September 2–9, 1893* (T23) and *Canterbury. Salisbury. Stonehenge. Oxford. 1893* (T11). There is a return to the Continent indicated by *Austria, November–December, 1894* (T4). The titles and contents of the remaining, undated, volumes suggest that the Tuppers travelled widely in Europe, visiting France, Germany, Spain and Gibraltar, the popular regions of Italy and the Alps.

The pattern of travel that emerges from these volumes is the conventional one established by the guidebooks of the times. Starting out in England and using it as a familiar base from which to take short journeys, the Tuppers spent a fashionable winter season on the Nile, and summers at various seaside resorts. Their itineraries were shared by thousands and the infrastructures that supported this massive volitional migration include numerous institutions to connect the buyers and sellers of photographs. The ubiquitous Baedeker guides list a variety of places where photographs were for sale, under headings as various as 'Photographs', 'Photographers for Artistic Purposes', 'Booksellers', 'Stationers', 'Bookbindings and Albums', 'Art Dealers and Showrooms' and 'Shopping'. Some clues to Tupper's likely sources are suggested in a few of the photographs he collected, such as the image he identifies as an 'Old Elizabethan House' (T13: 26), which shows a variety of souvenirs, including photographs, displayed for sale in its windows. A similar possibility is suggested by the first image of the volume titled *The Rhine Heidelberg Nuremberg* (T36). The large image has Cologne Cathedral as its focus of attention but a small photographer's shop is also visible in one corner of the frame. Its multilingual sign reads 'Th. Creifelds

Photographische Anhalt, Atelier Photographique, photographs mounted and unmounted in every size, largest selection of Cologne and the Rhine'. Displayed in the windows are large photographs of the cathedral.

In a different instance, a commercially produced cabinet-sized image of a quaintly costumed man (T2: 36) figures prominently in the book dedicated to the Tuppers' excursion to Marken, an island of fishermen near Amsterdam popular with tourists for, in Tupper's words, its 'peculiarly interesting . . . costumes, manners and houses [that] retain the old Dutch customs' (caption T2: 34). Tupper identifies the portrait as 'Our Skipper', suggesting that this boatman may also have provided souvenir images of himself, a practice that links him not only to his counterparts in other parts of the world (Brown 1895: frontispiece), but also to the practice of selling portraits that was common to the sideshows and other human novelty displays of the time 1938: (Taft 149–50; Bogdan 1988: 13–16).

The books of photographs themselves are thus what remain of William Vaughn Tupper's travels. Importantly, the material form here constitutes a narrative sequence of photographs that is viewed by turning the pages, thereby creating an embodied relationship with the viewer that retemporalises the experience and establishes an affective tone that centralises him or her. Travel photographs served to define, value, commodify and validate the travel experience; their organisation into books fixed, cohered and materialised it. Once made, these complex photographic objects constructed the journey that should have been, one without boring moments, bad weather, late trains, pickpockets or lost luggage. The foreign worlds depicted were composed only of significant monuments, sublime views and picturesque or exotic inhabitants. The narrative to which the pictures contribute is limited to (and by) the travellers' knowledge and inclinations, so, in reading photographs, we must recognise what they do and do not show. Satchell Hopkins, whose tour of Egypt took place just five years before the Tuppers', describes some of his photographic purchases as deceptive:

> Some of my photographs were of children, and I note they are all too clean and good-looking – indeed in their best and full holiday attires instead of every day half or perfect nakedness. The flies too are missing. Nor do they show distinctly, if at all, the sore eyes that are certain to be there.
>
> (Hopkins 1887: 7)

Some images in the Tupper collection demonstrate their maker's desire to offer images of what tourists had seen or expected to see even when their photographic production was technically impossible. Thus the image of Vesuvius that Tupper mounts like a frontispiece to his volume *Naples* (T29: 1) bears a distinguishing plume of smoke skilfully drawn in on the negative, and colour has occasionally been added to images of views and costumes (T2: 3–9, T2: 30, T37: 8, T41: 23, T44: 3), probably most often by the photographer, but sometimes with a crudeness that suggests an amateur hand. Tupper's choice of pictures also includes images outside his own experience, like the image of Athens covered with snow (T3: 20) in a book describing a trip made in high spring. While Tupper's choice of photographs extends his experience of travel, the interventions with the physical traces of the images aid this extension beyond the reality experienced.

Beyond their individual images, the books themselves structure journeys that are quite different from those that actually occurred. The albums are organised by place, rather than chronology, so that, for example, an assemblage of photographs of England, titled *Canterbury. Salisbury. Stonehenge. Winchester. Oxford. Sept. 1891–August 1893–June 1892* (T11), clearly identifies three separate trips. The systematic spatialising grouping of pictures by place, into a slow and integrated single journey through the heart of England, suggests that the albums were not about actual travel as much as they were conceptual constructions, which, as I have suggested, retemporalised experience into focused narratives of place.

The geographical distribution of Tupper's photographs closely mirrors the popularity of specific tourist destinations, but their number seems to reflect levels of interest or novelty and perhaps the level of photographic intensity clustered around specific sites, rather than the length of time spent in a particular place. Thus, England, the base to which the Tuppers regularly returned during their stay abroad, is described in six volumes, while Egypt, where they spent less than three months, is treated in the same number. Eleven books are devoted to Italy, four each are dedicated to Spain and France, three show Germany, two each are of Holland, Austria, Belgium and Switzerland.

In contrast to many more formal assemblages of photographs made by other tourists (Nordström 2001), the Tupper volumes are truly scrapbooks (Figure 6.2). While standard-sized 7 × 9 inch albumen prints mounted one to a page predominate in their construction, the books also hold a wide variety of other material. Loose, unmounted prints are regularly tucked between the pages or inside a folded paper page itself (T3, T8, T17, T46). Other similarly included objects are a stiff pasteboard prayer card bearing an image of the Bambini di Aracelli, printed in garish chromolithography and gilt (T37), and two photographic advertisements for the Bonchurch Hotel, Isle of Wight (T23), printed on albumen paper. In a few cases, such ephemera are glued and positioned like the photographs. The last page of T1, *Algeria*, centres a crudely printed notice advertising 'A Good Occasion. A lion of the most beautiful races of Abyssinia aged one year is exposed to buyers near Alcazar Parisien'. Mounted in the same volume are two small deckle-edged rectangles of soft, rather luxurious paper bearing well-crafted engravings of costumed Algerians (T1: 20). In all 46 scrapbook volumes, Tupper's writing never appears directly on a mounted photograph, but on these prints he has pencilled the words 'Biskra April 1892' and 'On the Way to Town'. Otherwise these prints are treated like most of the photographs, mounted symmetrically on the page with Tupper's handwritten captions beneath them, here 'Dancing girl' and 'Bedouins'. Another, somewhat more crudely printed engraving, probably cut from a newspaper, appears in *Vienna* (T45). It is also treated somewhat anomalously, being the only instance where anything is mounted on an inside back cover. Tupper's short title 'Imperial Sepulchre' follows his usual practice, being handwritten in ink and centred beneath the centred print.

In *Zermatt Chamonix* (T46) Tupper includes six small round Kodak prints that show views of mountains, a glacier and a river, and two of the same party of ladies wearing straw boaters and mounted on horseback. Under one of these Tupper has written 'On the way to Riffelalp'. *Berne Canton Vaud* (T8), which probably marks a journey taken at the same time, also includes six round Kodak prints, mounted two to the page, and several other small images in rectangular format with technical flaws that suggest an amateur hand. None of the other Tupper books contains photographs of this kind. At the least, they indicate a traveller's encounter with a camera-bearing companion; from the vantage point of today, they prefigure the shift in tourist photographs from professional products to amateur inventions that was well under way before 1900 (Frizot 1998: 148–66).

The scrapbooks

Significantly, the Tupper scrapbooks are all handmade. This is relatively unusual as similar surviving productions more often used purchased albums with elaborately tooled, embossed, gilded or otherwise decorated covers and interior pages that took their form from that of rare or precious books (Edwards 1999: 228–30). Indeed, many of the nineteenth-century albums we know today may have survived precisely because of their substantiality, luxuriousness and beauty. Scrapbooks and albums as materially modest as the soft-covered Tupper constructions may have existed in greater numbers but would have been discarded or destroyed because they failed to be understood as objects of distinction. Each of Tupper's 46 volumes measures 13 inches at its spine by 15 inches; they vary from half an inch to almost two inches thick (Figure 6.2). This is somewhat larger than most albums of the period, though the images they hold are typically the 7 × 9 inch or 7 × 10 inch albumen prints found in smaller volumes. The larger margins permitted extensive captioning, suggesting, as does much of the picture placement, that this was planned from the beginning.

Each book is made of folded sheets of thick brown paper, between slightly heavier pasteboard covers, hole-punched and laced together with a loosely woven cotton ribbon. This binding does not permit the books to lie flat for writing on, suggesting that the pages were planned out, constructed and captioned before being assembled into their book form. About half the books are made of a hard and poreless, slightly glossy high-quality paper that has survived in good condition, while the rest are of a softer material that today has a tendency to crumbling and brittle fragility. Inside the scrapbooks most of the photographs are glued directly on to the pages. Two pieces of onionskin paper, found tucked between the pages of album 32, bear slits in four places for tipping in the corners of prints, as well as notes that are probably prices, suggesting how some unmounted photographs were sold and transported. Throughout the collection, many pages show pencil lines and notes that attest to the thoughtfulness and effort that went into the organisation of this collection.

As noted above, these books are difficult to handle and to store. They are too large to be easily handheld and too awkward to be laid out for perusal on a table. Because of their length and soft covers they cannot fit comfortably closed and upright on a shelf, and because of their size and quantity they cannot be stacked with any degree of stability into a single pile. It is hard to imagine the place or circumstances of their use once they were made, whether they were kept in a parlour or library for casual reference, or whether they were regularly consulted at all. The effort required to make these albums suggests that they could easily have been Tupper's principal occupation in the few years before his death, following his return to Brooklyn. The defining acts related to these books may have been those of their ambitious and time-consuming construction, literally re-enacting the travel experience through a kind of materially enacted taxonomy, rather than of any subsequent use. Once made, they become most

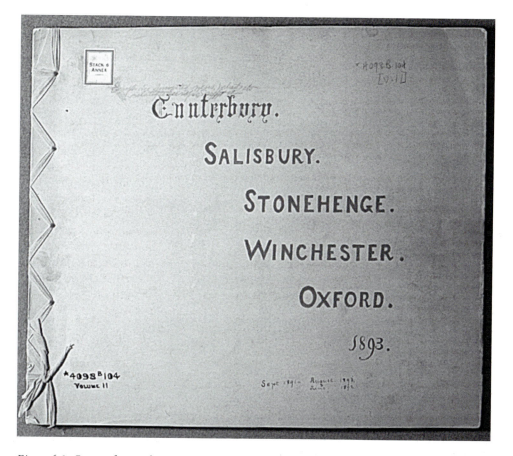

Figure 6.2 Cover of one of Tupper's albums; 'Canterbury. Salisbury. Stonehenge. Winchester. Oxford. 1893' (T11). (Courtesy of Boston Public Library, Print Department.)

important as an imposing material representation of an experience, as well as a means by which meaning and value are given to that experience. Their weight and the space they take up is significant; their very bulk grants them a kind of monumental quality. Tupper's travels are noted in his obituaries, and they were of such importance to him and his society that he is described there as 'an excellent narrator of his experiences . . . and one of our most instructive and entertaining public speakers' (*Daily Eagle* 1898). The scholarly organisation of experience that the scrapbooks represent may also have helped Tupper to prepare for his popular talks. It is not difficult to imagine the narrative of the album supporting the narrative of a lecture, or an album's extensive annotations as a speaker's notes. A comparison of the tone, itineraries and visual content of the Tupper work and that of such well known travel speakers as John L. Stoddard (1897) shows many similarities.

The covers of the scrapbooks materially separate one place from another as they mark the division and categorisation of Tupper's experience of abroad. They are, literally and figuratively, more substantial than the pages they enclose, being made of heavier paper in single sheets and being more intensively decorated with elaborately lettered place names as titles, and a placement of words that often serve to fill the page as much as to inform. They are titled with the name or names of the places depicted inside, usually with elaborately handdrawn letters several inches high. In addition, as noted above, some covers show dates. Fifteen covers show subtitles, sometimes in a different colour of ink from the main title, that identify an excursion's intermediary stops, so the cover of *London West and Environs* (T25) also lists Windsor, Stoke Pogis, Eton, Kew Gardens and Hampton Court; *Northern Italy* (T30) notes Como, Milan, Bologna and Pisa in a sequence that is replicated in the photographic contents of that volume. On the cover of *France* (T17) the subtitles 'Marseilles. Avignon. Bordeaux. Tours. Dijon' are informative, emphatic and decorative, being separated by periods, and elaborately drawn across the cover from corner to corner. On the cover of *Canterbury. Salisbury. Stonehenge. Winchester. Oxford. 1893* (T11) each place name is rendered in a different ornamental type style, with 'Canterbury' approximating Old English.

Eleven of the covers also carry extensive texts, usually quotations from authors as varied as Homer, Shelley, Herodotus and Oliver Wendell Holmes. Most are pithy epigrams like 'Everything fears time, but time fears the Pyramids – ABDELLATIF Arabian Physician' (*Lower Egypt and the Pyramids*, T26) and 'If we wish to see the life of Greece prolonging itself to our days it is to Sicily and the Bay of Naples that we must go. – Renan' (*Sicily*, T41), but *Scotland* (T39) carries an entire elaborately inked stanza by Arthur Hallam, and *Algeria* (T1) quotes extensively from a poem in French attributed to LeFevre. The one exception to the literary emphasis occurs on the cover of *Amsterdam* (T2), with notes, in the same elaborate script as the poems quoted on other covers, that may be Tupper's own or may be a summary of a guidebook description. The block of text reads: 'Amsterdam originated early in 13th Century. Gysbrech II, Lord of Amstel built a castle and dam here hence its name. The houses are all built on piles. The cost of keeping in order the canals and dykes is several thousand florins daily.' Regardless of its content, each of these texts serves to identify place, to position it in a set of historical or literary associations and to embellish the covers in a way that distinguishes them from the inner pages, where, even when elaborate captions and quotations occur, they are smaller and more simply written.

Photographic arrangement and narrative

The photographs in the Tupper scrapbooks typify, as I have noted, the commercial products available to tourists at the end of the nineteenth century. In roughly equal quantities, they include views and landscapes, depictions of buildings and monu- ments, images of people and reproductions of works of art. Most landscapes are standard-sized 7 × 9 inch horizontals, depicting images of mountains, rivers and other scenic attractions. Images of nature predominate in places like Switzerland where the natural world is the principal tourist draw, but in Egypt and Greece, where antiquity is the principal interest, most photographs are of buildings or artefacts. Tupper rarely writes captions for the photographs that emphasise scenery; at most he may append a two- or three-word translation of their photographer's caption. On the other hand, images related to history or art are usually elucidated by Tupper's ambitious identi- fications, quotations, drawings, family trees, statistics and personal opinions. Enmeshed in this mass of documentation, the photographs, one might argue, are effectively re-authored through an engagement with the mutability of photographic meaning that enables Tupper to stabilise his particular meanings through captions, a point to which I shall return.

The images of people in the Tupper scrapbooks, like those in other Gilded Age travel albums, are of several different kinds. Street and genre scenes are in the most standard 7 × 9 or 10 inch size, with photographers' titles like 'Groupe de pecheurs et pecheuses' (T2: 35) placing the image within the generalising discourses of 'the type'. Different in appearance but similar in intent are smaller *carte-de-visite* sized images, posed in the studio with conventionalised props and backgrounds. The quaint and exotic are paramount, so that Germany, for example, is represented by a bootblack (T45: 34a), a lottery ticket seller (T45: 34b), a rat catcher (T45: 39a) and a chimney sweep (T45: 39b). Others emphasise the romance of regional identity as marked by traditional garments such as 'Costume bernois (Suisse)' (T22: 36).

The other photographs of people in these albums are quite different in both appearance and placement from the generic types cited above. Five of Tupper's books include cabinet card images of royalty from Egypt (T26), Belgium (T5), Holland (T2), Italy (T37), Greece (T21) and England (T25). In each volume, the portrait is used as the book's opening picture, like a frontispiece, in contrast to the typological pictures that are invariably placed at the end of the book. In telling juxtaposition, the Italians' portraits are accompanied by an image of soldiers identified by the photographer as 'Corazziere guardia del Re' and the Greek monarchs are paired with a photograph of a troop of Greek soldiers (Figure 6.3). Queen Victoria's profile faces a rendering of Buckingham Palace, and is surrounded by likenesses of Prince Albert and Alexandra, Princess of Wales, and a detailed family tree drawn and labelled in Tupper's hand. Similarly, portraits of King Leopold and Queen Marie Henriette of Belgium open their volume on facing pages that embed the portraits in Tupper's lengthy handwritten history of their country, and, in *Lower Egypt and the Pyramids* (T26), a smaller image of

Figure 6.3 Greece: royalty guarded by Greek soldiers (T21: 1, 2). Unknown photographer. (Courtesy of Boston Public Library, Print Department.)

the Khedive of Egypt is shadowed by a same-sized block of Tupper's writing explicating the Albanian dynasty.

Fifteen of Tupper's scrapbooks include art reproductions or images of museum interiors and one, *Paris: The Louvre* (T34), contains only photographs of paintings. Tupper often interprets these images with authoritative quotations from John Ruskin and John Murray, or by his own emphatic judgements. Next to an image of Rubens's 'The Descent from the Cross', Tupper writes:

> It is difficult to conceive of greater artistic powers than those of Rubens. One's admiration for his genius continually increases and yet he seems to me to lack something which gives pictures their highest value. This is unquestionably his *masterpiece* and one of the few *really great* paintings in the world. Grouping natural yet full of movement. Coloring rich and powerful, drawing careful and true, expressions real and lifelike it is wonderful and impressive. But it seems to me to lack the religious sentiment found in many a poorer picture.
>
> (T6: 22)

In common with many contemporaneous albums of travel photographs, Tupper's scrapbooks usually begin with views and buildings, which are followed by art reproductions, and end with types, which are usually smaller prints mounted several to a page. When departures from this pattern occur they often seem like intentional contributions to the establishment of order and meaning. In France (T18) there are two images of the same size and type in which folk costumes predominate and which share the same painted studio backdrop. One (T18: 14) is of a peasant woman wearing sabot, carrying a bundle on her head and with several more bags hanging from a stick across her shoulder. The other (T18: 30) shows a man in stout shoes carrying an Alpenstock. Because of similarity in pose and size as well as backdrop, it would not be unusual to find images such as these side by side in a grid arrangement that reinforces the reading of the images as 'types' (Poole 1997: 133–4; also Langford 2001: 44–5). Yet here 16 pages separate them, and each image is isolated on an otherwise empty page. Here the placement of the images privileges content, as their contributions to the rhetorics of travel take precedence over format. Each image marks the beginning of a new phrase in the photographic sequence; for instance, the woman on her way to market is followed by several pages of market images. The man outfitted for mountain climbing marks the beginning of a series of images of mountains. Again we see the material placement of images as key to the establishment and pacing of the visual narrative and its meaning.

Iconic markers of geographical place such as The Matterhorn (T46: 1) or Vesuvius (T19: 1–2) appear as the first image in the respective volumes dedicated to the Alps and Southern Italy, while in *Canterbury. Salisbury. Stonehenge. Winchester. Oxford. 1893* (T11) the initial image is of Canterbury Cathedral, a signature building like the Tower of London that opens *London City and Westminster, 1891–92–93* (T24) and Pompey's Column at Alexandria that begins *Lower Egypt and the Pyramids* (T26). In several of his scrapbooks, Tupper identifies a beginning by introducing a marker of arriving: a port, harbour or distant view.

Within this general pattern, individual journeys are created. Tupper's journey to the Pyramids (T26) organises photographs that were probably purchased all at one time into a sequence that replicates his route. This album's first view is of what was most probably the Tuppers' entrance to Egypt at Alexandria. The small number of pictures from there may be explained by Tupper's urgent interest in Gizeh and his comment on an image of Pompey's Column: 'Except for an archaeologist there is little to delay a tourist at Alexandria' (T26: 2). Following this are a few glimpses of Cairo including street scenes labelled 'Date Sellers' (T26: 7) and 'Poultry Dealers' (T26: 8), followed by more than twenty images of the Pyramids and the Sphinx. It is in this section that we find an image that is anomalous because it was not mass-produced. It is labelled 'OUR PARTY DECEMBER 1892 FEBRUARY 1893' (T26: 24) and shows a group of nine, composed of Mr Tupper, his wife, daughters and three other ladies, who are identified by name in his caption, and accompanied by two men in Arab dress who are not. Significantly, this image appears at the literal centre of the album, as the twenty-fourth page in a book of 50 image-bearing pages. Its role in the linear narrative is to resonate through the photographs that follow, emphasising their equivalence to personal vision, underscored by such captions to subsequent photographs as 'we saw a similar review of English troops in this same spot' (T26: 28). Simultaneously, however, the album is transformed as a whole into an autobiographical object by the visual evidence of individual experience sited at its centre.

Tupper's volume on the Pyramids concludes his journey to Gizeh with a visit to the museum there that further underscores the sense of perambulation in the album structure. The first image of this section is of the museum's exterior (T26: 29) – in the language of narrative cinema, an establishing shot – and then the viewer turns the page to be taken inside with a series of photographs showing the building's contents. (T26: 30–43) This ordering of photographs occurs in other volumes too, not only in the treatment of museums, but in representations of churches, palaces, railway stations and hotels. Even cities are often presented in this way, so that Tupper first shows a view from a distance, then a closer view, then the gates or main entrance and finally shots of its streets or significant buildings. In *Athens* (T3) the Parthenon is shown in four images from four compass points, manifesting its importance and centrality, but also imitating its physical circumnavigation. The narrative structure here effectively embodies the viewer in the space of the photograph's narratives, stressing a virtual witnessing of travel, which, as I have argued, saturates these scrapbooks.

Tupper's albums are generally full, with one or more photographs mounted on each page. Empty pages appear to be intentional attempts to establish a viewing rhythm based on sub-categories, as in *Canterbury. Salisbury. Stonehenge. Winchester. Oxford. 1893* (T11), where a blank page acts as caesura between significant sites, but also stands for the places in between that are not worthy of notice or photography. The same pattern appears in *France. Marseilles. Avignon. Bordeaux. Tours. Dijon* (T17), where empty pages separate the stops identified in the volume's title.

The structure of the book as an organising system of photographs makes pairs of facing pages essential elements of photographic meaning. Sometimes Tupper seems to use this structure consciously, as when his images of royalty are faced by pages bearing photographs of their guards or palaces. Pairs are often formally symmetrical, so a picture of a man holding a teacup (T8: 36) faces one of a woman at a spinning wheel who appears to be recognising and returning his salute (T8: 37). In *Algeria* (T1) a group of camels shown facing front (T1: 21) stands opposite a group of camels photographed from the rear (T1: 22). In other instances, juxtaposition approaches collage, as

Figure 6.4 Egypt: climbing and 'constructing' the pyramids (T26: 20). Unknown photographers. (Courtesy of Boston Public Library, Print Department).

when Tupper builds a pyramid of his own in the pages of *Lower Egypt and the Pyramids* (T26). Here, on a single page (T26: 20), Tupper has pasted together two similar but mirror-image depictions of tourists ascending and descending pyramids, so the pictures form the familiar triangular shape that mirrors the other pyramid images on the pages that surround it (Figure 6.4).

Authoring the photographs

The Tupper albums are perhaps most unusual in the quantity and quality of their annotations. It is the annotations and captions here that 'author' the photographs, removing them from the generalised mass-produced image, and making them specific to personal experience, anchoring and performing personal memory and domesticating the iconic status of some of the images, such as those of the Pyramids. As Willumson has observed of a not dissimilar set of travel albums, D. M. Seaton's European Travel Albums of 1898–1902, 'The personal inscription of each image with a personal narrative and unique context served to narrow the interpretation of the selected images, effectively illustrating the writer's experience and authoring the meaning of the photograph' (Willumson 1998: 32). As on his covers, Tupper quotes extensively from varied sources ranging from Ruskin to Amelia Edwards to Herodotus, and he often adds elaborate informational drawings such as architectural plans of the Parthenon and copies of hieroglyphics. Sometimes even his texts embellish as well as inform, simultaneously extending the reading or image and anchoring it into his specific interests. For instance, he writes 'St. Mary Magdalen College 1457–1481. This college is possibly the most beautiful at Oxford. Among its students have been Wolsey, Hampden, Addison, Gibbon, Chas Reade, Collins' (T11: 37). The exalted names are written to cascade diagonally across the space beneath the photograph, so they stand out and fill the page.

From page to page, Tupper's notes ignore, contest, supplement or personalise the photographers' captions and intended meanings, and it is in these annotations that, as I have suggested, Tupper most strongly takes control of his journey. In the volume he calls *Lower Egypt and the Pyramids, December 21, 1892–March 8, 1893* (T26) Tupper redirects the photographer Sebah's direct caption 'Pont de Ghezireh', which is inscribed on the negative, with his own statement of priorities: 'An iron bridge across the Nile 1,260 feet long. It leads from Cairo to Gizeh. And to the Pyramids' (T26: 11). Following this, another Sebah image titled 'Bazar a Ghezireh' is given its personal importance by Tupper's handwritten caption 'Marketplace at Ghezireh on the way to the Pyramids' (T26: 13). Like a diary or a novel, the next pages reconstruct and replicate what Tupper saw, moving us out to the Pyramids, as they will later move us slowly up the Nile, the physical space of the album and the physical space of the land the photographs depict conflated by his narrative. Once at the Pyramids, we see again an instance of Tupper personalising the generic experiences represented by the photographs he bought. Thus, Legekian's 'Le Chef Bedu des Pyramides No. 17' is transformed by Tupper into 'the Sheick [*sic*] of the Pyramid who exacts "Backshish" for ascent or entrance to Pyramid' (T26: 26). This volume is one of the most enthusiastically annotated in the collection, and Tupper, as author, employs its numerous images of the Pyramids as sites for a variety of texts that utilise a wide range of voices. These include the romantic and literary:

> Few persons can be aware beforehand of the rich tawny hue that Egyptian limestone assumes after ages of exposure to the blaze of an Egyptian sky. Seen in certain lights the Pyramids look like piles of massy gold. Moonlight lends to their majesty the sense of mystery; and a strange loneliness to the desert.
>
> (T26: 16)

Tupper's captions also record botanical information, as in 'Route to the Pyramids Shaded by Lebbek trees' (T26: 13). In general, their voice is that of the scholarly, earnest and observant collector of facts: 'in regard to inscriptions not a single trace is found on the pyramids or in fragments near them although travellers' graffiti has been found' (T26: 14). Elsewhere, Tupper offers glimpses of his travels as fraught with annoyance, as in his labelling of an untitled image of a group of Bedouin men: 'The Pests of the Pyramids' (T26: 15). At times Tupper seems to echo the language of the guidebook, combining practical advice, geographical detail and the fulsome word picture, both to create an environment and to advise the viewer what to value in it:

> Two Bedouins are necessary and three are desirable for each person who climbs the Pyramid. The accompany [*sic*] pictures give some idea of the size of the blocks and the difficulty of surmounting them. At the top is a space about 30 feet square. The view is unique. In one direction are barren cliffs in another yellowish brown and glaring tracts of sand. Below is the SPHINX and the other two PYRAMIDS. Further away the PYRAMIDS of Abusur, Sakkara, and Dashur. Towards the east are the long avenues of Lebbek trees, the river NILE with luxuriant vegetation along the banks, fields intersected with canals bordered by stately palms shadowing fellah villages and far away Cairo with glittering mosques and minarets.
>
> (T26: 17)

Tupper's occasional departures from the pedantic to the personal are revealing. In one place on the journey his albums represent, we glimpse a footsore tourist in his caption of a photograph of Amsterdam's Ryksmuseum [*sic*]: 'A comfortable feature of the Museum is an attractive little cafe in the basement where an all day sight seer can rest himself and get his luncheon' (T2: 14). Elsewhere we see the pragmatic financier in Tupper's assessment of a Viennese cathedral: 'The shrine is very ugly but it has a ton and a half of silver in it' (T4: 12).

Some of Tupper's personal captions indicate interests and emphases quite different from the photographer's. An image by Pascal Sebah that foregrounds women carrying water jugs is labelled by Tupper only as 'Landscape near Cairo' (T26: 49). A large traditional boat that appears from its position in the frame to be the photographer's principal subject is de-emphasised by Tupper's caption 'View of Temple from River' (T27: 13). The relationship between image and caption is not always obvious: a picture of camels and columns is informed by several paragraphs on scarabs (T27: 15).

Conclusion

Tupper constructed his albums with forethought. Brief notes of place names in pencil, sometimes upside down, are still visible in one album (T18), and ruled guidelines, partially erased, outline the prints in several volumes. On Tupper's most heavily annotated pages, the photographs are mounted far to the right or left side of the page so as to leave space for writing, while the volumes with almost no writing at all display their photographs centred, further evidence that Tupper's project was planned, intentional and completed.

The photographs in Tupper's books began their trajectory when they left the photographers' shops, but the marks on the pages show that intervention and changes of use and meaning have continued to the present. As institutionalised objects, they bear the marks of continued engagements in different contexts. Notes and numbers on the scrapbooks' front covers mark their gift to the Boston Public Library, by 'donation of Mrs. T. Stevens' in 1948. Some fifty photographs, mostly of buildings and monuments, are identified with copy negative numbers indicating that they have been re-photographed in response to various research requests. In 2001, the Tupper scrapbooks were exhibited for the first time on a tour that included the Library, two museums and a photographic festival. The Library's preparatory conservation assessment determined that many pages, their paper grown brittle with age, were breaking at their ribbon binding, and, because of this, several albums were disassembled and their pages individually numbered.

The nearly 2000 photographs in the Tupper albums are individual paper objects, and should not be confused with the images they carry and display; instead they exist in an indissoluable relationship with one another. Each photograph has been uniquely manufactured, displayed, selected, purchased, moved, mounted, marked, captioned, viewed, numbered, stored, organised, exhibited and interpreted over time. The scrapbooks fix and preserve these actions by their first owner, and continue to accrue marks of their changing use as they subsequently pass through various institutional hands. Tupper's creative undertaking utilised a complex mix of sequence, size, number, image content and juxtapositions, to create a narrative by which he re-performed and thereby created, shaped and understood an actual journey, laying it out for his repeated gaze or as a site of discourse. The photographs that Tupper organised in this way thus have a much greater significance collectively than they do as individual things. Their meanings are constituted not simply as images but through the actions that have surrounded them, the structures that link them and the spaces between them.

Acknowledgements

I am grateful to Sinclair Hitchings and Aaron Schmidt of the Boston Public Library for their support of my research on the Tupper scrapbooks, to Michael Carlebach for his thoughts on this subject, to Janice Hart, and to Elizabeth Edwards for her interest, patience and friendship while this chapter was taking shape.

Note

1 The primary source for this chapter is the Tupper Scrapbooks, Boston Public Library, Department of Prints and Photographs. In this chapter they are identified by volume and page thus: (T24: 12) for Scrapbook 24, page 12. Following library practice, multiple photographs on a single page are identified by lower case letters from left to right, top to bottom. Volume numbers were assigned arbitrarily at accession in 1948. Page and photograph numbers and letters were added by library staff in 2000 and 2001.

7

PHOTOGRAPHIC PLAYING CARDS AND THE COLONIAL METAPHOR

Teaching the Dutch colonial culture

Susan Legêne

Shortly after the outbreak of the Second World War the Colonial Institute in Amsterdam was involved in the production of a pack of playing cards. The game comprises twelve sets of four cards each, illustrated with a photograph, a drawing and some keywords. The complete pack of 48 cards provides a thesaurus of what was regarded as traditional culture in the Indonesian archipelago. In this chapter I explore these cards as a dialogic relationship between the imaged and the material. They enable us to investigate how photographs that once were made in an equal act between a photographer and his subject during specific encounters in the Dutch East Indies are transformed through the material form of a set of playing cards into a series of timeless icons of otherness for children in the Netherlands. Designed to teach Dutch families a 'known-unknown world', this miniature image-world of Indonesia can be seen as an aspect of the social and discursive relations through which the Colonial Institute formulated and disseminated a 'home-colonialist culture' to Dutch families. Grounded in Dutch society, this home-colonialism endured beyond Indonesian independence and is indeed still an active force within Dutch society. After first focusing on the cards themselves and considering what happens when photographs became playing cards, I shall consider the meanings created in the cards as a series of images-objects and the material engagements in the very act of playing with them. Finally, I shall reflect briefly on the relationship of these cards to other classes of ethnographic objects and the shifts in their understanding in the discourse of 'authentic objects' within the museum.

From Indië to Insulinde

Let us begin with the 48 playing cards themselves. They are typical playing cards, measuring 10.4 × 6.9 cm, printed on a good quality matt lightweight card, slightly textured to the feel, their corners rounded off. The cards are housed in a solid cardboard box in which they fit exactly. A cotton ribbon folded around the pack of cards makes it easier to lift them from the box. A small instruction booklet explains how to play the game and how to read the images depicted. The folded instruction booklet opens out, making a sheet four times the size of the cards, on which is depicted a map of Indonesia. The photographs on the cards are photomechanical halftones, reproduced from black and white gelatin silver prints. Each card also carries a full colour drawing and a set of key words, some of them in Malay, others in Dutch. The drawings partially overlay the photographs, with the words in a list beneath them. The game was one of a series of 'Jumbo-play', which was (and is) the brand name of games distributed by Hausemann & Hötte, originally a German import and export firm, based in Amsterdam since 1853. It has been published in two almost identical editions. The first edition, called *Indië Kwartetspel* (published 'under the auspices of the Colonial Institute'), was issued during the Second World War, probably in or just before 1942, by Hausemann & Hötte NV Amsterdam and C. G. T. van Dorp & Co. NV in The Hague. Its selling price was Dfl. 1.50 (c. 0.70 euros). Schools placing orders for at least 36 games at one time also received, free of charge, a large map of the Dutch East Indies belonging to this edition. The second edition, called *Insulinde Kwartet*, was printed some time between 1947 and 1949, and sold for Dfl. 2.25 (c. 1 euro).[1] Insulinde (Indies Archipelago) was the poetical name that epitomised Dutch colonial consciousness, with all its ambiguities. It was coined in 1860 by Multatali (pen-name of the Dutch author Douwes Dekker) in his famous novel *Max Havelaar*, which was critical of this consciousness.[2] This second edition of the game, identical with the first in all but its name, was issued under the auspices of the Indies Institute, the name of the Colonial Institute from 1946 to 1950, the years of the Indonesian struggle for independence immediately after the Second World War.

Except for the references to the Colonial or Indies Institute, neither the box nor the cards bear any indication about the game's compiler. The compiler was probably Gerard L. Tichelman, a former civil servant in the Dutch East Indies colonial administration, who from 1938 onwards worked at the Colonial Institute's Department of Information and Education, for a concentration of representational activity coheres around the playing cards.[3] In 1940 he added some of the pictures used in the game to the Colonial Museum's collections and in 1948, contemporary with the second edition of the game, he also wrote a small booklet, *Indonesische bevolkingstypen* (Indonesian ethnic types), a publication that mirrors the cards in its systematic descriptive approach, as well as in its use of full colour drawings of the various people of the archipelago, their dress, attitude and appearance. I shall return to Tichelman presently. However, in order to understand the photographic playing cards and the institutional changes they embody, it is necessary first to look briefly at the Colonial Institute and its agendas.

Colonial Museum and the twilight of colonial culture

The Colonial Museum, which issued the pack of cards, was founded in 1864 in the Dutch city of Haarlem. Its mission was to strengthen knowledge of and research into the natural resources and products from the tropics, in particular those from the Dutch colonies in the Indonesian archipelago and Suriname (the East and the West Indies). Colonial trade products from the Dutch East Indies (tobacco, tea, coffee, sugar, rubber, petrol, but also batik, braiding and other crafts) were of a central concern to the museum. In 1910 this Colonial Museum became part of a new Colonial Institute that, from 1926 onwards, was housed in an impressive programmatic building in Amsterdam funded by the big colonial enterprises and private individuals, together with Dutch government and the City of Amsterdam. Today the Tropenmuseum is still situated in this building.[4] It was designed as a testimony of Dutch colonial greatness, and was intended to establish an environment in which enlightened colonialism (*ethische politiek*) could be fostered. The Colonial Institute and its museum prepared Dutch civil servants, scientists, businessmen, housewives, teachers, nurses and soldiers for overseas service. Its staff members were involved in physical anthropology, biomedical research, tropical agriculture and environmental sciences, ethnology, anthropology, ethnomusicology or linguistics. They advised the major Dutch colonial enterprises on wide ranging topics, from growing export crops to dealing with customary *adat* law, from improving public hygiene to understanding ethnic and cultural difference.[5]

It is obvious that to enlightened colonialists the museum was an important tool in creating the identity of Dutch society as a colonial power and engendering both pride in and knowledge of the well-being of the overseas colonies. Teaching on the essential characteristics of Indonesian culture was part of this process.[6] In this respect the museum activities of collecting and classifying ethnographic objects played a role in the formation of that special 'structure of attitude and reference' that became an integral part of metropolitan imperialist culture (Said 1993: xxiii). In the case of the Netherlands this implied the development of a supranational cultural sensitivity among a politically and economically powerful colonial elite that operated simultaneously rooted both in the Netherlands and overseas. At this period, Dutch culture in the Netherlands itself became increasingly segmented. Divisions, especially along religious-political lines, resulted in a deeply segregated society. In this polarised society Protestant and Roman Catholic children were not supposed to play together; likewise, social democrats and liberals moved within strictly separated networks. Conversely, in the colonial society of the Dutch East Indies these domestic religious and political segregations did not greatly matter. Overseas all Dutchmen were united in their being European, white and 'responsible' for the development of colonial society. As a result, the family members of this colonial elite, based in both the Dutch East Indies and the Netherlands, developed an 'imperialist' frame of reference that integrated the colonial experience, and escaped the narrow divisional lines of Dutch society. Indeed, Dutch identity was shaped in relation to its colonial backdrop. Within these contexts, and our concerns here, visual sources, like artefacts and photographs, became important tools in disseminating this colonial culture in the Netherlands.

The colonial card game, played during cosy family gatherings, brought colonialist experience into the heart of Dutch polarised society, the family, connected to the East Indies regardless of political or religious affiliations at home. As the 1949 Jumbo-play advertisement had it:

> As soon as Father has finished reading the newspaper, we play games . . . what family happiness is not implied in these simple words. In the twilight, the family gathers around the table and plays a game with the younger children. That is sociability at best and a valuable Dutch custom. Guided by Father or Mother, the children develop their intellectual capacities and learn to win or lose sportingly.[7]

On concentrating attention on fellow countrymen overseas, the game contributed to the development of a sense of colonial belonging, knowledge and control among the younger generation at home.

Colonialism as such, of course, was not a game, or, if seen so, the Dutch did not always play it in a sporting fashion. When the first edition of the playing cards was published, the Netherlands had been overrun by Nazi Germany, and the Dutch East Indies were soon after occupied by Japan. During this dark period, the publisher sent a promotional letter to almost 800 schools, which, after regretting the circumstances that forbade direct contact with the Dutch East Indies and extending 'special thoughts' to friends in the East Indies, recommended the game as a way of bringing the colonies psychologically closer. However, after the end of the Second World War, the Dutch East Indies appeared to be as far away as ever, and on 17 August 1945 Indonesia proclaimed its independence. The Netherlands government, which had been considering developing its colonial policy towards a kind of Commonwealth-like relationship under Dutch guidance, would not accept this unilateral declaration of independence. Convinced that the Indonesian majority would actively agree with continuing the common bonds, it prepared for war with the Indonesian nationalists under their leader Soekarno, who became the first President of Indonesia. The Colonial Institute supported the idea of a Dutch Commonwealth and accordingly between 1946 and 1949 changed its name to Indies Institute. However, after four years of armed struggle, the Dutch finally accepted the sovereignty of Indonesia in December 1949, and the Indies Institute again changed its name, this time to Royal Tropical Institute, the former Colonial Museum becoming Tropenmuseum.

This history is reflected in the two editions of the game: from *Indië-Kwartetspel* to *Insulinde-Kwartet*. Between 1942 and 1949 it was hoped that it would suffice just to change the game's name, not the game itself. However, with the colonial relationship between the Netherlands and Indonesia severed, the game no longer made sense either as a pastime for families or as an educational device. The cards became obsolete and eventually represented a departed 'home-colonialism', providing an 'objectification of a colonialist identity rooted in past time' (see Thomas 1991: 23, 25).[8]

Playing cards as a miniature image world

With this context in mind, one can now explore more closely these cards as material deposits of colonial culture. The game comprises twelve sets of four cards each, providing a miniature image world of the Indonesian archipelago. Each card has three elements: a colour drawing, a black and white photograph and four key words describing the category and subject matter of each card. The drawings are conventionalised and sometimes stereotypical representations of the subjects. Superimposed over the right hand corners of the photographs, these coloured drawings immediately attract attention. The photographs are printed in a soft, less than full black, which seems to reinforce the hierarchical order between drawing and photograph. They seem to have been selected in a rather eclectic way, mixing various genres, from studio portraits to snapshots, from panoramic views to narrow close-ups. All photographs are the same size and reproduced as a portrait format frame, regardless of their original format, a point to which I shall return. However, it is the photographs that create a 'reality effect' for the drawings.

Figure 7.1 The reverse of the *Indië Kwartetspel* cards based on a Balinese painting of the *Batuan* style. (Courtesy of Tropenmuseum, Amsterdam.)

The back of the cards states, repeated 48 times, that these cards are published under the auspices of the Colonial (or Indies) Institute, and depicts a detail from a Balinese painting in the characteristic Batuan style that in the 1930s had prompted Margaret Mead and Gregory Bateson's psychoanalytical interpretations of Balinese world views. The player of the game, holding a hand full of cards, displays to her opponents a lush tropical nature, full of symbolic animals, ghosts and spirits.[9] A mysterious Balinese spiritual world, with fragments of a clearly ordered society, faces the player (Figure 7.1).

The object of the game was not unlike that of the English game 'Happy Families'. Players had to collect whole sets of four cards to create a series. For instance, weapons or music. In a process strangely reminiscent of colonialism itself, 'The game is finished as soon as all sets of four have been collected, and the winner is the player who has acquired the largest number of sets', the instruction book for the game explains. Handling the cards – dealing, holding, swapping, rearranging in the hand – established a metaphorical or surrogate bodily relation with the beloved colony (see Edwards 2001: 47). The captions played an important mediating role, both on the cards and in the act of playing. Not only did the rules of the game demand this interaction, but they enabled the players, at home in the Netherlands, to talk to each other as well informed people who had mastered some Malay words and would perhaps feel at ease in daily life in the Dutch East Indies: 'Could I have your *màndau*, please?' Crucial to this embodied relationship with the cards as a series is their function as miniatured objects, a tangible image version of a distant world. Susan Stewart has described 'the secret life of things' that is hidden in the miniature. The miniature, she argues, presents a constant daydream 'that the world of things can open itself to reveal a secret life – indeed to reveal a set of actions and hence a narrativity and history outside the given field of perception' (Stewart 1993: 54). To Dutch home-colonialist families the cards, it might be argued, perhaps evoked a 'colonial daydream' of knowledge and control in the form of the material (a hand full of cards), the visual (the series of images they contain) and the verbal interaction of playing.

The movement of photographs through the game and Stewart's argument of the dreaming of knowing can be linked to Deborah Poole's concept of 'visual economy'. In this, photographs are approached as objects, the content of which is only one aspect of their meaning. The production of photographs, their circulation and their shifting use and exchange values have to be taken into account if we are to understand the complex processes of meaning making related to images (Poole 1997: 9–12). Here they embrace both the museum's institutional role in producing, circulating and validating images that contribute to the formation of colonial culture, and the Dutch families playing the game, in a mutually sustaining relationship. The idea of visual economy also accounts for the way in which so many different visual devices have been combined in the playing cards in order to create a convincing new whole. One of Poole's analytical categories for understanding the visual economy in which photographs function deals with 'the pleasures of looking' (Poole 1997: 17). The playing cards enable us to characterise these pleasures as an active 'game' that in itself has strong performative qualities (Edwards 2001: 17, 20), both as a social practice in Dutch families and as a metaphor.

Indonesian culture by the dozen

The game, as I have suggested, comprises the collecting of sets of image-bearing cards. It is to the implications of this that I now wish to turn, for arguably the conceptual and colonial order emerges only at the outcome of the game. Before the game starts and a player can question the others about the cards in their hands and build up series, the cards have to be shuffled and dealt out at random. However, to analyse further the series of images that make up this miniature panoramic view of Indonesian culture, it is necessary to explore here the underlying structure from which the game emerges. The twelve subject sets appear to have been conceived as an evolutionary history of Indonesian culture. The 'first' set of four cards deals with the natural environment: the *birds* in lush nature – among them the bird of paradise famous for its colourful feathers – followed by *undomesticated animals* – among them the crafty *kanchil* (a small deer) famous in Indonesian folktales – and the *flowers* that surround people's homesteads. After these three sets, people appear. First are people (*volkstypen*), then different buildings and houses (*woningen*), means of transportation (*vervoer*), ships (*schepen*), means of living (*middelen van bestaan*), crafts (*ambachten*), weapons (*wapens*), musical instruments (*muziek*) and, last but not least, games (*spelen*).

Each set of four cards comprises a self-contained taxonomic visual narrative that is pieced together through playing the game. In it can be recognised the ethnographic canon of museum scholarship. For instance, the four subdivisions of musical instruments are ideophones, chordophones, membranophones and aerophones.[10] More often, the set comprises two pairs: two men and two women, two ways of transport with animal traction, two with man power, a man with a pikulan (a yoke), a woman carrying a burden on her head (Figure 7.2); two plain prows and two more sophisticated boat types; two crafts associated with men (copperwork and braiding) and two with women (weaving and batik); two weapons for hunting (arrow with bow, and lance) and two ceremonial weapons, a Javanese *kriss* (dagger) and a Dajak *màndau* (knife); and so forth. These classifications constitute an essential summary of colonial knowledge and control, materially translated and performed through the act of playing the game.

In the game's evolutionary underpinning, based on the ethnographic and anthropological museum tradition of writing, collecting and presenting other cultures, we can recognise what Fabian (1991: xiii, 198) has termed allochronism – a detemporalising or 'temporal distancing'. The conceptual and rhetorical devices that were used in the work of the Colonial Museum to 'neutralise' time as a constitutive dimension in the changing relationship between Indonesian society and Dutch colonial rule were applied equally to the game.[11] Regardless of the historical specifics of the making of the photographs, on the cards they all conform to the same model juxtaposed with the drawings, with the same colour, tonal range and texture. The atemporal nature of the photographs accentuates the atemporality of representation. For even with close inspection it will not have been easy for the Dutch players to ascertain that the unchanging 'present' of the cards was in fact a past. There was no reference, in these photographs of contemporary traditional society, to the modernising colonial state. There are houses but no European plantation house, weapons but no gun, means of transport but no bicycle, boats but no steamer; nor are there any export crops, Chinese coolies or Javanese clerks. Thus, although the photographs in the game suggest a contemporary image of Indonesia, it is a present represented as apolitical and timeless. These mechanisms constructed and authenticated a stability and coevalness of this distancing overview of traditional Indonesian culture. It is a coevalness that is also expressed in the act of playing as such. Each time a family gathers in the twilight around the table with the pack of cards, passing them from one to another, physically reordering and cohering, traditional Indonesian culture is situated in a timeless undefined present and is recreated before their eyes through their own agency.

This temporal distancing was, as I have suggested, the very rhetoric that involved the players of the game in a miniature image world that could be seen, very literally, as their colony. In their hands the cards provided an endless variation, yet the images as such stayed the same. Holding a hand full of cards meant physical contact with a daydream of colonialism. This might be seen as the effect attributed by Stewart to the toy miniature in general, which, 'linked to nostalgic versions of childhood and history, presents a diminutive, and thereby manipulatable, version of experience, a version which is domesticated and protected from contamination. It marks the pure body, the inorganic body of the machine and its *repetition* of a death that is thereby not a death' (Stewart 1993: 69, original emphasis). Transposed to the card game, this suggests that each time players sat together, winning or losing, a society, well ordered and classified in twelve sets of four, was first constructed and then destroyed by a reshuffling of the cards. The cards, however, appealed not only to the 'childhood' of the players but also to traditional culture, not only to the 'machine' of rightly collected sets of four cards but also to an image of a well structured gender-based colonial society classified in pairs of two or sets of four, not only to a shared experience of family life at home but also to one of self and other. In a sense, this was also a way of teaching, by repetition,

Figure 7.2 The four cards making up the 'Transport' (*Vervoer*) series. (Courtesy of Tropenmuseum, Amsterdam.)

the subtleties and diversities of colonial knowledge and control that, perhaps, suggested the lived reality of the colonial experience.

In reading the cards in this way, the repeated formation of traditional society inherent in the game exemplified not only what Stewart calls the secret life of nostalgia and beauty, but also a secret fear for a dying colonialism. Locher-Scholten (2000: 34) suggests that the Dutch colonialists in the 1930s stressed traditional Indonesian culture (as in the playing cards) rather than the results of colonial progress, in order to counter their fear that weakening Indonesian culture through modernity would weaken political stability and ultimately bring about the end of colonialism. Playing the game metaphorically repeats this fear. The game's focus on traditional culture, reinforced by the reality effect of photographs, suggested an image world protected from (Western) contamination. But there was contamination in the game outside the grid in which the photographs on the card had been moulded. It can be traced in the very relationship between the photographer and his model (Pattynama 1998), inflections of which, once recognised, resonate through the playing cards.

Essentialism, ethnicity and race

In order to illustrate the allochronism of the game, I am going to examine the making of one set of four cards and consider how the objectified 'other' as an object is translated to play through the denial of co-temporaneity, the obscuring of colonial encounter through the selecting, framing and blanking out of images. The set of four *Volkstypen*, ethnic types (Figure 7.3), comprises a man from Java and a man from Aceh, a woman from Nias and a Dajak woman from Kalimantan. This *Volkstypen* set is pivotal in the game. The four cards enable us to investigate the full circle of a visual economy: those who produced the photographs, those who were willing to sit for the photographs, those who brought the images into circulation by editing them for the game through intervention in the original images and those who played with them.

To do this means, for a while, moving away from the cards as a series of images, and returning to the separate individual pictures, now archived in the Tropenmuseum photographic collection.[12] On the playing cards the four ethnic 'arche'-types are portrayed in a photographic style with a long established tradition in the discourses of physical anthropology and the delineation of racial difference (see Edwards 1992). In the archive, however, it becomes clear that this form of representation in the cards has been carefully constructed, not in the making of the image, but in the material translation into uniform demands of the cards. The four original photographs appear to depict four people acting independently in front of the camera, in different contexts that can be precisely dated and historicised. The 'Javanese' man of the cards, for instance, has been cropped to create a portrait format out of the original landscape format (Figure 7.4), in order to accommodate the material demands of the cards, but, further, according to the documentation accompanying the photograph, the subject is in fact not a Javanese man, but a Madurese head of a village in the department of Pamekasan on the island of Madura, and the photograph was taken before 1924. The full picture, showing him together with two other men, was taken by F. A. Droste, a colonial civil servant who was his superior in the colonial administration.[13] The woman from Nias, in the original photograph, is sitting relaxed in a rather informal pose on a European chair. From the original glass-negative (13 × 18 cm) we can see that,

Figure 7.3 The four cards making up the 'Types' (*Volkstypen*) series. All are created from cropping larger photographs. (Courtesy of Tropenmuseum, Amsterdam.)

Figure 7.4 The original photograph of men from Madura, *c*. 1924, from which the 'Javanese type' was created. Photographer: F. A. Droste. (Courtesy of Tropenmuseum, Amsterdam.)

on technical grounds alone, the picture must predate 1915. In 1925 it was donated to the Colonial Institute by C. W. Janssen, a former colonial Sumatra tobacco entrepreneur.[14] The apparently European setting of the photograph suggests that this 'Nias woman' was very possibly sitting in front of her own colonial house, belonging to one of the flourishing colonial companies of the period. The man from Aceh in this set of four *Volkstypen* is a farmer according to the historical documentation. The photograph was taken by G. L. Tichelman before 1937.[15] The farmer sits in front of what appears to be a European administrative building, as is indicated by the door handle. Finally, the Dajak woman from Kalimantan, according to the documentation, is in fact a Makoelit Kenja woman from the Apokajan region in the middle of Borneo, who was photographed in December 1919 by J. Jongejans, an enlightened colonial civil servant and ethnographer who met her during an expedition into the interior of Borneo.[16]

Consequently, the four people who, in the hands of Dutch card players, appeared as anonymous and inscrutable, at the moment of photographic encounter were, in all likelihood, a local member of the colonial administration (before 1924), the wife of a colonial entrepreneur (before 1915), a taxable farmer (before 1937) and a woman sitting for an ethnographer who was travelling through her region (in 1919). All four original photographs are individual portraits. Each sitter apparently had some rapprochement with his or her photographer and in looking to the camera looked at everyone who would see the picture, including himself or herself.[17] In the set of four cards, however, these complex photographic encounters are appropriated into the physiognomic and racial discourse of 'types'. Further, it was often material intervention, painting the background out of negatives, that was used to construct the timelessness of the 'type' and translate the individual into a generality (Edwards 2002: 72). While the photographers did not intend the photographs as 'types', their later institutionalisation in the Colonial Museum absorbed them into the institute's views and agendas on ethnic and racial diversity in the Indonesian archipelago. The selection of a Madurese village head to stand in for a Javanese *Volkstype* underlines and exemplifies this convergence of categories of ethnicity and race, and the translation of the specific to the general.

Nevertheless, all four photographers were, in Ann Stoler's words, 'administrators cum ethnographers', and worked both as civil servant or entrepreneur and as scientist on the concepts of 'population' and 'people' (Stoler 1995: 39). Their work was grounded both in the Dutch East Indies and in the Netherlands. The Colonial Institute institutionalised these links, while bridging time differences and framing individual experiences into an overall grid of classification that reflected those agendas. The photographers effectively endorsed this when they donated their photographs to the Colonial Institute.

The translation, through shifts in context and material form, of these four individual portraits into the set of *Volkstypen* seems to exemplify Poole's argument that vision and race are 'autonomous but related features of a broad epistemic field in which knowledge was organized around principles of typification, comparability, and equivalence' (Poole 1997: 15). Significantly, the rhetorics and processes of the visual economy would have been invisible to the average player of the game. The cards naturalised the visual economy and thus presented an apparently unmediated image of differences and distinctions in culture and ethnicity. Yet to Tichelman, most probably the compiler of the game, explaining the subtle distinctions between the two 'proto-Malay' dolichocephalic people (the Dajak and Nias women) and the two 'deutero-Malay' branchicephalic people (the men from Java, who for that purpose could easily be replaced by a Madurese, and from Aceh) to the broad public was particularly important. To this end he published the complementary illustrated booklet *Indonesische bevolkingstypen* (1948), mentioned earlier, in which he described the racial differences in the Indonesian archipelago in text, while showing cultural distinctions in drawings. In a remarkable historicising paragraph, Tichelman combined these two discourses by stating that the racial differences in Indonesia can be traced in age-old evolutionary and historical developments. Each different racial group had developed its own ethnic culture, rooted in distinct interpretations of 'a universal link between present and past, between the living and the deceased as an impressive organic whole' (Tichelman 1948: 19). It is in that sense that he succeeded in combining in the cards the allochronism of ethnography and the dynamics of colonialism.

Tichelman's implicit message in the pack of cards was that in colonialism, cultural differences were more significant than racial distinctions. Once the racial distinctions were known, the game valued culture over race. This reflected the Colonial Institute's overall policy. In many publications, such as the illustrated *Atlas of Indonesian Crafts* (Bezemer 1931), which includes some of the same photographs as in the pack of cards, and which was also aimed at the same Dutch purchasing public,[18] or in the textbooks for new colonial civil servants (van Eerde 1924; Kunst 1946), the Colonial Institute time and again stressed that racial differences among the indigenous people of Indonesia existed and were evident, but did not matter in colonial rule. What mattered was the ethnic and cultural diversity, united by the Dutch under one administrative umbrella.

Photographs, drawings and the museum

The game, as a miniature image world of Indonesia, contained a unity of ethnicity and culture within a small box of cards. Yet, like other miniatures, it was attached not to historical time but to 'the infinite time of reverie' (Stewart 1993: 65).[19] In obscuring the agency of photographer and sitter and matters of individual encounter and control,[20] the Dutch home-colonialists were free to let their imagination work through the colonial narratives produced through the juxtaposition of the photographic portraits of people with idealised expressive and colourful but generalising drawings. The link between the drawings and the black and white photographs also contributed to the atemporal discourse of the cards. To return to the *Volkstypen* example, the photograph of the 'Javanese' man is juxtaposed with ancient Javanese court culture represented through an accompanying drawing of the Javanese prince, with no suggestion of the colonial rule in which this Madurese village head participated. It is in this interaction between the indexical of the black and white photographs from Indonesia and the somewhat conventional line drawings made by the 'home-colonialist' institute that we can find the contemporary 'use value' in the visual economy of this idealised Indonesian image world, the indexical force of the photographs reinforcing the truth value of the more impressionistic yet stylistically conventional drawings.

These drawings place the pack of cards in the tradition of educational packs that developed from the early nineteenth century onwards, when educators started to advocate the importance of images as a learning device.[21] However, the photographs and drawings on the cards are complementary. Whereas, for instance, in the photographs the four people facing the card players as they are held in the player's hand appear passive and contained, the four drawn men superimposed over the photograph reflect dynamic and cultural distinction. In elegant full-length poses, and unlike the photographs not in direct frontal ones, these drawn figures show various markers of both difference and cultural identity, such as different dresses, different headwear and different weapons – a lance, a *màndau* with shield, a knife and a *kriss* (dagger). An experienced player would recognise these differences between the four cultures, having learned them through playing the game.

Further, the drawings of ethnographic objects, like the weapons, musical instruments, textiles and tools, can be recognised as representations of 'authentic' objects from the Colonial Museum; collected, classified, analysed and valued according to their materials, their function in society, their cultural and ritual meaning. This image world created a reading that could be extended to and reinforced by the ethnographic displays in the Colonial Museum as a public counterpart to the private playing of the game. It is in this very interaction between the family sphere and the public museum that the private colonial daydream was given metaphorical expression through the game of cards. For there is a sense in which the colonial education offered by the pack of cards and its categorisations and essential distinctions are not contained only within its own narratives, but must be seen as integral to those of the museum. The objects on display in the Colonial Museum confirmed the knowledge of peoples, objects and words represented through the cards, so a Javanese man has a *kriss*, a Dajak man a *màndau* (knife) and shield, a man from Aceh an Islamic cap, a Nias warrior a lance. Equally, the museum, in its displays of miniatures and models, enhanced the function of miniaturisation and containment, which, as I have suggested, characterises the cards.[22] Although not regarded as ethnographic objects as such, neither were they merely toys or souvenirs (Stewart 1993: 57, 135) but, like the photographs, colonial mediators, linking the ethnographic collection of the Colonial Museum in Amsterdam to a timeless world of everyday life in the Dutch East Indies. The cards brought them together into one miniature image world.

Conclusion

While I have concentrated especially on the four *Volkstypen* cards, the analysis applies equally to the other sets in the pack of cards. The photographs, drawings and key-words constitute a complex image world that is constituted through a material object: the pack of photographic playing cards. The ways in which the photographs were decontextualised, subject to interventions, cropped into a format change from land-scape to portrait, miniaturised and reformatted in new material performances reflect the ambiguities and contradictions inherent in both the Dutch colonial cultural tradi-tion of documenting and measuring differences and the colonial policy: people united in their diversity under a common Dutch rule. If the indexicality of images originat-ing in the light that once reflected off the bodies of Indonesian people on to the sensitised emulsion of the glass or film negative brought them nearer to Dutch fam-ilies, the material and thus contextual shifts also created distance, in that specific encounters and colonial experience were translated into generalised statements. While these processes are intrinsic to much colonial photography and its consumption, here they are given especial force through the material form in which the photographs are made to function: playing cards that are handled, shuffled, swapped, appropriated and ordered, a telling metaphor of the colonial relationship.

Notes

This chapter originated as a paper presented at the conference *Museum, Tradition, Ethnicity: XX–XXI Century*, dedicated to the centenary anniversary of the Russian Museum of Ethno-graphy in St Petersburg, 23–25 January 2002. It constitutes work in progress on the new semi-permanent exhibition on Dutch colonialism in the KIT Tropenmuseum (open in January 2003). Thus many ideas worked out here have been developed with my colleagues. I would like to thank Marieke Bloembergen, Mary Bouquet, Janneke van Dijk, David van Duuren, Itie van Hout, Jaap de Jonge, Ben Meulenbeld and Steven Vink. I also would like to thank Elizabeth Edwards, who, as a member of an international committee for the evaluation of the KIT Tropenmuseum collections (1998), and since then as guest speaker and referee, and as editor of this book, time and again has provided stimulating academic support that is not easy to find in the Netherlands, where 'museums' and 'universities' tend to be distinct worlds.

1 The cards were designed by 'Ateliers voor Grafische Vormgeving CO-OP 2, Amsterdam' and printed by 'NV Boek- en Steendrukkerij "De IJssel", vh R. Borst & Co, Deventer'. In the second *Insulinde* edition only C. G. T. van Dorp & Co. NV in The Hague is given as publisher. My research started with one privately owned pack which had no longer a box.

The Tropenmuseum holds one pack of the *Indië Kwartetspel* edition, collection number 3728–1045 a-yy. It was recently transferred from the library to the museum collection. I am grateful to Annemarie de Wildt, Amsterdams Historisch Museum, for her information on the publisher of the Jumbo-games, Hausemann & Hötte N. V. in Amsterdam (which holds the two editions of the game and advertising material).

2 *Max Havelaar of de Koffiveilingen der Nederlandsche Handelmaatschappij* (*Max Havelaar of the Coffee Auctions of the Dutch Trade Company*), first published in 1860 and in print ever since, is a beautifully expressed critique of Dutch colonial practice at home and in the Dutch East Indies during the mid-nineteenth century.

3 Gerard Louwrens Tichelman (1893–1962) went to the Dutch East Indies as an agriculturalist, becoming a member of the Indies Civil Service (*Binnenlands Bestuur*) in Sumatra and the Moluccas. He returned to the Netherlands in 1937.

4 The museum and institute now hold some 170,000 objects, textiles, paintings and drawings, 200,000 historical photographs, ethnomusicological archives and historical ciné film once commissioned by the Colonial Institute, as well as an impressive library with maps, books, manuscripts etc. During the German occupation in the Second World War, the Colonial Institute was effectively paralysed, with contact with the colony broken. However, during this period the many photographs collected in the museum were systematically classified and documented, the focus being of geographical region and content. This archive formation process is reflected in the pack of cards, where historical contexts of them were subordinated to place and content and eventually lost. See also Edwards's (2002: 71) analysis of the reordering and remodelling of many different forms of photographs into one uniform archive in the Cambridge University Museum of Archaeology and Anthropology and in the Photothèque at Musée de l'Homme in Paris. See also Edwards (2001: 15 and passim).

5 This coherence, in both the kinds of objects that have been collected and their provenance, exists in the multiple cross-references between the objects and the Dutch colonial elite that founded the Colonial Institute. See Newton (1998), and Edwards (2001: 29–30) on institutional networking. On the history of the Tropenmuseum, see van Duuren (1990), Woudsma (1990), Taselaar (1998) and Legêne (2000).

6 Together with B. Waaldijk I have tried to trace this didactic and essentialising process through the example of the *batik collections* (Legêne and Waaldijk 2001: 34). Photographs contributed to this process, both as collectables and as visual sources for the interpretation of other classes of objects (Edwards 2001).

7 The Jumbo brochure is undated but is probably from 1948. The *Insulinde Kwartet* is the only game linked to the Indies Institute to be listed in the brochure, but this suggests the date. In this brochure, the game is listed between the *Zwarte Piet Spel* (Black Peter) and the *KLM Kwartet*.

8 Memory of this role persists today. At a lecture on colonial culture, given in November 2002 in a small town near Eindhoven, six out of the 70 members of the audience either knew of the game or still owned it.

9 To date we have not been able to trace this specific Batuan drawing in the Tropenmuseum collection. The little instruction booklet for the game concludes with: 'Special attention is asked for the back of the cards, which is a piece of a *modern* Balinese painting on paper, in ink and colours' (emphasis added). The classification as a modern drawing is striking in contrast to the background of the image of traditional society on the reverse of the cards.

10 Representing the means of sound production: self-sounding instruments, stringed instruments, membrane-covered instruments and wind instruments respectively. In this respect, the cards follow the classification system taught by Jaap Kunst (1994), staff member of the Colonial Museum and in the first half of the twentieth century one of the founding fathers of ethnomusicology as a comparative research discipline.

11 I apply Fabian's critique of anthropology to the ethnographic practice of colonial rule as well. Although anthropological fieldwork and colonial data gathering are different (see Cohn 1996), many mechanisms at work in colonial ethnography resonate through anthropological practice.

12 Collection numbers: Borneo – 572.9 (992.27) N64; Nias – 572.9 (992.264) N28; Aceh – 572.9 (992.261) N31; Madoera – 572.9 (992.24) N7. In the near future these numbers will be replaced by a barcode; the pictures are available online.

13 In 1924 Droste donated 14 pictures of Madura to the Colonial Museum.

14 Janssen worked at the Senembah Tobacco Company, on Sumatra's east coast, between 1889 and 1914. In 1925 he donated 40 pictures of Nias. Back in the Netherlands, he became chairman of the Moluccas Institute, one of the supporting institutes of Dutch colonial enterprise that were represented in the Colonial Institute.

15 Between 1937 and 1960 Tichelman donated a large number of objects (many from Aceh) to the museum. His Aceh pictures were donated and documented in 1940, which strongly suggests that the cards were 'edited' during the early years of the Second World War.

16 In 1929 it was donated, together with 40 other pictures, at the initiative of Tichelman. In their relations with the Dutch East Indies, Jongejans and his wife C. J. Jongejans-van Ophuijsen adhered to the early twentieth-century principles of the Dutch 'ethical policy', which were dedicated to 'educating' the indigenous people. For Mrs Jongejans, strengthening 'emotional family bonds' and 'family tradition' was an essential element in the role Dutch and Indo-European women had to play in the formation of Indonesian society (Jongejans-van Ophuijsen 1947: 31–2).

17 This might even be the case with the woman representing the Dajak. Hers is the only portrait in the set of four *Volkstypen* that originally followed the ethnographic photographic tradition into which all four photographs in this set were transformed, through cropping, reformatting and blanking out. By inviting the Apokajan woman to stand in front of a backdrop that probably had been improvised in the open air, it was Jongejans himself who excluded all cultural context. In 1922 he published a book about his 1919 Borneo-expedition, *Out of Dajak Country: Impressions of the Life of the Headhunter and His Environment*. While the title of his book, in stressing the 'headhunter' image of the Dajak, was probably chosen to stir the Dutch reader's imagination, Jongejans wrote respectfully about the Dajak. He praised the people he met and the potential of the region. The role photographs played in Jongejans's expedition research is important for our understanding of the portrait of the Makoelit Kenja woman on the card. He took with him, for instance, books on earlier expeditions, in which some photographs of a former Dajak leader had been reproduced. Jongejans's hosts were moved when they saw these portraits of their deceased ruler. A picture of Jongejans's own wife and children, which he showed during meetings, was highly appreciated as well (Jongejans 1922: 163–4). Knowing this, and reading his very personal and caring accounts of his meeting with the Dajak, makes the portrait of the Makoelit Kenja woman less impersonal. It suggests a sense of agency on her part in her presentation, perhaps because she was aware of its possible use in Dutch publications.

18 This *Atlas* in many respects mirrors the pack of cards, explaining with many black and white pictures and few words the arts and crafts of the various people of Indonesia. It contains, for instance, the uncropped version of the batik-making women used in the game. Comparing these pictures provides another example of the way colonial pictures move in and out of various social and discursive relations. The original picture is part of a series in a carefully constructed album (no. 190 in the KIT Tropenmuseum collection), which deals with an exhibition of arts and crafts in Semarang in about 1925. In the cards, finally, this 'exhibition context' is no longer visible (Photonbr. 0001-8019).

19 'The reduction in scale which the miniature presents skews the time and space relations of the everyday life world, and as an object consumed, the miniature finds its "use value"

transformed into the infinite time of reverie.' Stewart's example in this case, a stamp album, based on the collections of the Metropolitan Museum of Art, New York, and allowing for 'an almost infinite set of possible arrangements and recontextualizations', might well be applied to the colonial cards here (Stewart 1993: 65).

20 This mirrored an Indonesian colonial society strictly segregated along racial lines, and a widening institutionalised distance between a white Dutch colonial elite and the various ethnic and culturally distinct groups on the Indonesian population. The playing cards reproduced this elite's perspective on Indonesian society (Clancy-Smith and Gouda 1998; Locher-Scholten 2000).

21 Educational cards had been used in Western Europe since the seventeenth century, becoming more wide ranging there and in the United States from the 1820s onwards. They were often devoted to geography, astronomy, national history, music, botany etc. (Tilley 1973: 149–52). In 1898 the German firm Wüst published a pack of playing cards for the Dutch market, with drawings that united East and West (with, for instance, the Queen of Spades a Javanese woman, the Queen of Hearts a Dutch virgin, the Jack of Spades a colonial soldier (Wiggers and Glerum 2001: 11). Pelita, an organisation for elderly Indies people who migrated (most of them forced) to the Netherlands, recently published *Indomemo-kwartetspel*, a pack of cards that is used therapeutically to activate the migrants' long-term memory, for which there are few anchor points in daily life in the Netherlands. The cards comprise drawings that refer to daily life – food, clothing, objects in the house and so forth – without any reference whatsoever to the 'ethnographic canon' that formulated the *Indië Kwartet* discussed here.

22 This is not the place to elaborate more on this hybrid aspect of the collection of models and miniatures but it should be noted that the KIT Tropenmuseum collection of models and miniatures contains almost every item depicted in the colonial cards. These models and miniatures embody a complex cross-cultural representational practice. The indigenous artists and craftsmen used the original raw materials and devoted much attention to depict exactly those details that confirmed the diversity among the people of the Indonesian archipelago (Grever and Waaldijk 1998; Bloembergen 2002).

8

'UNDER THE GAZE OF THE ANCESTORS'

Photographs and performance in colonial Angola

Nuno Porto

This chapter explores the specificity of photographic objects through an ethnographic example in which different biographies emerge from apparently similar photographs, leading them to perform different actions. It is argued that attention to the materiality of photographs enables one to understand more fully their roles as social agents, an idea that photographs might be said to share with other artefacts. It is also an idea that enables us to avoid what may be termed, after Latour (1991), 'the modern settlement trap' that scholarly critique of the medium has perpetuated a trap that brought about mutual exclusion of objects and image in the analysis of photography.[1]

I am drawing my alternative model to this modern settlement trap from work that has been developing in anthropology, bringing different approaches that propose that photographs might be analysed as being located somewhere along a continuum balanced between, at one end, the notion of image and, at the other, the notion of object.[2] The placing of photographs along this continuum is unstable, for they vary according to specific practices in which they are engaged. It is also dispersed in the sense that distinct agents attribute the same object to different places along this continuum according to their own interest, agency and subjectivity. This is so precisely because photographs are always, and for all users, both images and objects and, importantly, more often than not, it is because they are particular images that they are put to use as a specific kind of object. Because this is so, some photographs are better able than others to establish specific performances in specific situations, which, in turn, may require a material refiguration of the image in relation to the intended purposes of its use. Photographs, therefore, are always entangled in a web of social practice where they perform significant actions. If, within these practices, photographs become, as Gell (1998: 21) would have it, secondary agents, their analysis must recognise the historical situation in which a network of interests, purposes, expectations and intentions functions around them. The question then is not simply what photographs mean, but how they act, why they do whatever it is they do and to whom. For these reasons, analysis of photographs requires an ethnographic approach that can highlight the articulations between photographs' material systems and their biographical careers.

The concept of material system is drawn from Reynolds (1987: 157) who argues that any artefact comes to being, and exists, within a network of other objects, concepts and behaviours. These are dynamic elements and the analysis of any specific object, therefore, requires establishing how these elements articulate with one another, defining the specificity of each situation. The distinction between the object material system and the object biography (Kopytoff 1986) relates not only to different theoretical origins but also to different approaches to the material features of photographs. In fact, in the present context, the material system of photographs (their relation to other artefacts, conceptions governing their use and the organisation of procedures, knowledge, materials and agents engaged in their production, circulation and consumption) pervades their diverse biographical outcomes and their variation in value through their career as 'things'.

The following case study is concerned with the shifting actions of photographic objects and the dialogic relation between image and material performances. Because these objects constitute a particular entry of colonial photography genre, 'native portraiture',[3] concern has been confined to the analysis of style and colonial meaning. However, they can be not only revaluated but questioned from another direction. The portraits of natives discussed here were created as objects of knowledge. They became, later, central ceremonial exchange items, refigured as such within the colonial politics of the Portuguese in Angola. The expression 'native portraiture' is a contested and complex category, as is 'Portuguese in Angola', which seems to imply that this (or for that matter any colonial situation understood under such terms) was a unified field of practice. While a full exploration of these debates is beyond the scope of this chapter, my argument here demonstrates the limits of such categories. These photographs bring improvisation and experiment to the core of what Thomas (1994) has called 'colonialism's culture', supporting the idea that colonial cultures were characterised by a high degree of indeterminacy and social experimentation, rather than simply a prescribed agenda. This exploration of the use of photographs is thus also a way of addressing colonial culture through an ethnographic approach of its materiality and correlated practices.

Setting

The starting point for this exploration is the archive of the *Diamang* (*Diamond Company of Angola*), including its photographic archive. A Portuguese enterprise with multinational centres, the Diamang was devoted to the exploitation of diamonds in the north-east interior of Angola (the contemporary North and South Lunda provinces). It operated as a chartered company, incorporating in its obligations to the Portuguese colonial government the development and maintenance of the so-called 'civilising' infrastructures, such as roads, settlements, agricultural, educational and health services, as well as any kind of industry related infrastructures. Between its inception in 1918 and the 1950s the company became, its opponents claimed, a 'state within the state'. From the initial 130 'white employees' it grew, by the 1950s, to nearly 2,500 white employees and their families, and about 25,000 'native workers'. The numbers grew steadily until 1975, when Angola gained independence and the company was nationalised.

The management philosophy of the company, and the hallmark of its external relations, was based on knowledge and high technology. This included a reliable communication network between the local headquarters at the Lunda and higher decision-making processes located in Luanda, the capital of the colony where the General Direction in Angola was based, Lisbon, the administrative headquarters, and Brussels, home of the Technical Direction. Photography was widely used within these bureaucratic channels as a technical tool for management and decision-making and, among the technical personnel employed by the company (geologists, civil engineers, mechanical engineers, agronomists, veterinarians, medical doctors, nurses etc.) there was also the office of the photographer.

With the strengthening of the nationalist dictatorship at the political centre, especially from the 1930s on, the company engaged in a 'nationalising policy' of its white employees. The claim that the company was the Portuguese outpost in the heart of black Africa, the last boundary of the empire, aligned it with the metropolitan discourse. In the 1940s, the German occupation of Belgium led to the transfer of all administrative services to Lisbon, which further encouraged the nationalising policy. It is within this internal refiguration of the colonial enterprise as a national mission that a museum was developed in the Lunda province, located at the Dundo, a village founded in 1920 solely for the purpose of establishing the company's local headquarters. Cultural salvage was key to the concept of the museum. Since 'material expressions of native life and art tended to disappear, saving them was urgent' (Machado 1995: 13). In time, the Dundo Museum became the most important museum of the Portuguese Third Empire, publicising the Diamang practice of 'scientific colonialism' and providing a model to other museum projects, including the National Overseas Museum in Lisbon (which only opened in 1976 under the name National Museum of Ethnology). It was within museum-related work that photography became something other than a technical tool.

At the company photography was a work-related instrument, or more precisely, a diamond production-related instrument. Inside the concession area, photographic practice was generally forbidden, the unauthorised possession of a camera being a sufficient cause for dismissal.[4] Photographic recording was a privilege granted to only a few top positions in the company's hierarchical structure, and, obviously, to the photographer, whose work was tightly controlled by the higher management. The concern for a representational accuracy that accorded with the company's view was the reason for this monopoly on image production. Photographic images, therefore, were seen as key elements of its bureaucratic structure. They circulated through its networks as part of the technical reports sent monthly from the Dundo to Luanda and from there to Lisbon, demonstrating how the work of the different departments of the company had progressed since the previous reports.

Museum work had another use for photography, which was to record and collect that which was threatened with disappearance in the area: native culture. Photographs complemented the collection of objects for the museum, producing ethnographic documentation. These functions were combined as photography was integrated with the collection of objects, and produced a wide range of photographic documents as part of a broader category of graphic documentation, materialising the notion of 'collection by inscription'. Among such documents was the collection of 'native types'. Commenting on the start of this project, the museum curator wrote:

> This project should bring very interesting results. Not only because these
> chiefs appreciate being photographed and because of the historical importance

of the matter, but also for the following reason: these gentile chiefs (by blood) are the most exact representatives of the anthropological type of their races, either because they descend from the central line, or because they are elected by the most pure groups of their tribes.

(Annual Report 1943: 5, author's translation)

From his perspective, therefore, the photographic collection of native types came to double as a collection of local chiefs. This removed the project from the exclusive realm of scientific knowledge, articulating it with colonial policy. In fact, the curator does not mention that these 'pure representatives' of their races were also the mediators between colonial administration and local population. Under Portuguese colonial law, native chiefs were assigned the status of *Regedores*, a position that was the basic link in the colonial administrative chain between the metropolitan government and the native population. One of their main tasks was periodically to update the local colonial authorities on the available contingent of individuals fit for working purposes. The implementation of industrialised work relations (frequently by forced labour) also involved tax collecting, and the *Regedores* were made responsible for its payment according to the population under their jurisdiction. Consequently, this photographic project embeds scientific endeavour (collection of native types) with modes of colonial surveillance (portraiture of specific subjects). This dual purpose is given material expression in the Gallery of Native Chiefs, a photographic portrait installation included in the museum History Room. It is to this that I now turn.

The History Room

While the museum itself was founded in 1936, and the building finished in 1949, from 1942 its collections were displayed in a house at the Dundo. Only then was the curator's programme for the exhibition of 'native culture' executed. This programme had been negotiated with the delegate-administrator of the company, who had realised that a tolerant attitude towards 'native culture' improved colonial peace.[5] By the time the museum opened its doors it had already become part of colonial culture. Members of the native population had participated in collecting campaigns conducted throughout Lunda and neighbouring districts. They had been actively engaged in decorating the museum walls with 'local motifs', and supported the development of the museum native village, where there dwelt people classified as 'tribal masters': blacksmiths, sculptors, weavers, painters, musicians, dancers and so forth. They were employed as skilled workers and subject to the rules of industrial production, and formed folkloric groups who were called to perform 'native culture' dance and song at the regular company festivals or whenever 'distinguished guests' dropped by. Through these practices the museum had come to define what 'true' native culture was, establishing the division between its representatives and agents, 'tribal natives', who usually also worked with the museum, and 'detribalised natives', known for their contempt of tradition, the museum and, concomitantly, their own chiefs, and thus colonial authority.

Museum collections were, therefore, only one part of the museological complex of cross-cultural relationships. Inside the building, objects were displayed in a progression from 'material' to 'spiritual life'.[6] The exceptions to the rule were the two 'noble rooms' of the museum: the Honour Room that welcomed visitors with a collection of

Figure 8.1 The History Room of the Lunda and the Diamang. (Photographic Archive of the Ex-Diamang (box *Exterior and Rooms*) negative no. 8.280/1958. Courtesy of Museu Antropológico, University of Coimbra.)

rank objects (arms, 'thrones' and so forth) and the History Room, which was located between the 'material life' and 'spiritual life' galleries. Its full designation was the 'History of the Lunda and Diamang Room'. The company's colonial setting was positioned as a direct outcome of the turn of the century explorations of Henrique de Carvalho.[7] These, in turn, were positioned as the natural result of the 'discovery' of Angola by the Portuguese in the fifteenth century. The Gallery of Native Chiefs was a wall mounted portrait gallery that occupied the exit wall of this room. A full-length portrait of the explorer, placed above the doorway, was flanked by 16 portraits on each side, an arrangement that probably reflects the curator's sense of aesthetic symmetry (Figure 8.1).

The first relevant aspect of these portraits is their museographical installation. It implies their production, selection and purposeful placing at a specific stage of the visiting 'script' of the museum, and their relation with other objects whose ensemble materialises the past, whether remote or recent, where native and Portuguese history merged. Photographs appear to be appropriate objects for this sort of justification of the past, for they inevitably refer to an actual event. Significantly, photographs were the first objects sent from Lisbon for display in the History Room: a collection of the album of the *Portuguese Expedition to the Muatianvua*, led by Henrique de Carvalho in 1884–8, was sent by the delegate-administrator in 1938.

Nowhere could this collection find better home than in the headquarters of the explorations of this company that carries on, under other forms and aspects, the work of penetration, study and valuing of the region initiated by that explorer and his companions.

(Annual Report 1938: 4, author's translation)

Photographs such as these, because they were historical, testified to the antiquity of the Portuguese presence in the area, for the longevity of the Portuguese presence in Angola was a central theme at the History Room. This historical relation was monumentalised in the display of a map showing the routes followed by the several Portuguese travellers and explorers from the fifteenth century. A replica of the stone marker left by the fifteenth-century travellers on the shore of the Congo River, ancient maps and photographs attesting to the Portuguese role in 'pacifying' the area constituted the remaining objects with which these contemporary portraits paired. None the less, they could not but stand for a history previous to the foundation of time by the Portuguese presence and the Diamang operations.

According to the records, the material presentation of the Gallery of Native Chiefs was extremely successful among visitors. As it is reported: 'This is one of the aspects that most impresses European visitors and causes true admiration among native visitors who feel honoured by seeing their chiefs distinguished in such a manner' (Annual Report 1952: 21, author's translation). A second effect emerged among 'native' visitors as a consequence of time and the play of power in the colonial divide. Once it was realised that the use of portraits in the museum operated as a marker of distinction among native population, the display became a form of dynamic colonial surveillance and control. For the administration instigated a practice of installation or removal of portraits in accordance with the particular relationships between the company and chiefs, at any given moment, especially in connection with the provision of the labour force.

The physical removal of a chief's portrait from the gallery was a direct consequence of his failure to provide agreed or expected labour contingents from his respective area and as such constituted a severe symbolic sanction. Conversely, those who met the expectations of the company, and therefore had a stabilised presence in the gallery, came to stand metonymically for the traditional Lunda and Cokwé chiefs of the area, erasing, through physical removal, past opponents of the colonial enterprise from collective tribute performed in museum visiting. Ultimately, the Gallery of Native Chiefs mirrored the effectiveness of colonial authority, the shifting material encounter with the photograph-objects, charting the network of cooperative colonial subjects and establishing the colonial venture as a common goal. In time, however, the gallery came to represent only deceased subjects. As a solution to this default exclusion of the contemporary collaborators, the portraits were instead transformed into ceremonial gifts, reframed in new celebratory performances of the colonial community by the end of the 1950s, a practice to which I shall return later in this chapter.

The Gallery of Native Chiefs is effectively key to the development of the History Room project at the new museum building. The idea for the History Room was present at least from 1938 (when the photographs of the Portuguese Expedition to the Muatianvua were sent to the Dundo by the delegate administrator), when the collection of types was already under way, but with very few results.[8] In 1946, the company's photographer was replaced and, with this replacement, major technical and bureau-cratic changes took place: on the one hand, the new photographer managed to establish much more up-to-date working conditions; on the other, taking into account its growth, the museum was equipped with cameras but dependent on the photographic laboratory for developing and printing its photographs.[9] When the Gallery of Native Chiefs was put together, the material system of photographs changed, being distributed between the laboratory and the museum. The curator's view of the potential of chief portraits had also changed, since he now had a much deeper knowledge of the area and a greater intimacy with several of them.

In 1946, commenting on the project, he wrote: 'Very few things impress them as much as contemplating portraits of the important members of their race after they have died' (Annual Report 1946: 8). Some of the photographs produced as types, but whose subject the curator had come to know as a person rather than as only a 'representative of the race', were used in the gallery. This extended the biography of the photograph into another material system. Eventually, this interest in portraiture coincided with the photographer's own subjective interests. Unlike his predecessor, he volunteered to make these portraits using the Linhoff Technica camera (producing 12 × 9 cm negatives) instead of his usual camera (a 6 × 6 cm Contaflex). Portraiture of the chiefs was usually done at the native village, posing them in traditional attire suggesting the colonial image of pre-colonial times. In the late 1940s and early 1950s what mattered for the curator was to have not 'representatives of the races' from each area, but the actual image of *Regedores* of each administrative district. This not only distinguished museum collaborators and fuelled local rivalry in a way likely to favour the recruiting of new collaborators, but also, following the golden rule of maximising associations with the company's interests, displayed the company's colonial achievement.

In the gallery, contemporary chiefs were paired with deceased chiefs. The portraits were printed on matt 'Gevalux coal paper'[10] and framed in glass and wood 60 × 50 cm frames, and hung in rows on the six metre tall museum walls. They were revered by native visitors and referred to as 'older ones', until they too became included among the ancestors with the deceased chiefs. With the exception of the lowest row of portraits at eye level, the chiefs were seen from below, as the visitor looks up. Viewing the portraits in this way reproduces the bodily performance required in Tshokwé and Lunda etiquette, where a person's head should always be below that of a chief. Further, this presence of the ancestors, despite the colonial context, would appear to account for the native classification of the museum as *mutenje ua cijingo*, the 'house of powers'.

The biography of the photographs engaged with in the Gallery of Native Chiefs annuls their former value as types, for their association to a new material system enables them to act differently. This new material system articulates three different elements. First, there is a new technical environment in which a cooperative technician, the photographer, is called to interpret the curator's intentions; second, these portraits are supposed to dignify the subject depicted, implying willingness of the subject in being depicted, trust in the photographer and in his apparels and a previous social relationship with the museum; third, and more relevant, it implied the making of a museum object and its inception in the museological environment, as an object of visual interest related not only to other similar objects in the same room, but also to the rest of museum collections. During the museum tour, after having passed the Honour Room, Domestic Life, Hunting and Fishing, and Indigenous Industries, and immediately before entering the 'Spiritual Life' Galleries devoted to Native Religion, Folklore and, finally, Sculpture, the chiefs, together with Portuguese ancestors, are displayed, merging local past with the company's history through material juxtapositions.

Visitors, especially those on 'ritual visits' (such as those of the Grand Feast Day), were tutored during the visiting process to see 'properly' what stood before them. Thus, unlike a museum visit by an unaccompanied visitor – who would, as Carol Duncan (1995) puts it, officiate his or her own experience of museum visiting – a visit to the Dundo Museum implied engaging in a highly circumscribed, colonially determined, way of seeing, because neither photographs nor other objects have intrinsic meaning that can be communicated unproblematically. Chief's portraits placed visitors, literally, as we have seen, under the gaze of the ancestors, whose wills were now voiced by museum employees.

Such material effect cannot be undervalued. As the museum curator wrote in 1956:

> The chiefs' gallery has become really popular among the indigenous. It has been recorded that some chiefs, not yet honoured in the collection, have claimed the presence of their portrait in the gallery. The fact that their absence may be remarked in the set of the portrayed chiefs is taken as offence to their esteem.
>
> (Annual Report 1956: 17, author's translation)

The material system of chiefs' portraits refers not only to the physical portrait but to the environment, technical proceedings and social relations in which it is engaged. The importance is vested not simply in having the portrait taken, but in having it enlarged, mounted, framed and displayed inside the museum; to be included as a member of a group, the subject of a dignifying action of the subject. Materiality of the image, in other words, goes beyond the photographic object to imply a whole social setting in which it acts, differently, for the agents engaged. In fact, the chiefs' portraits allow for the performance of at least two kinds of agency. In Gell's (1998: 21) terms the portrait is index both of the prototype (the chief) and of the company (the author or artist). Depending on the situation it may act as either an empowering device for the chiefs (transforming them in ancestor-to-be) or material evidence of the accomplishment of the company's civilising mission. But as had happened before, the effects of the gallery were unpredictable and the portraits subject to a third shift in the material system.

Portraiture and the colonial persona

To appreciate the material performances more fully we must look briefly at the shifting nature of the images themselves. The portraits in the Gallery of Native Chiefs had emerged from the evolving photographic practices of the Diamang setting. Because of these changes, the initial performance of identity through portraiture that equated natives with colonial past progressively shifted to an identification with colonial future. Distinguishing three different concepts of the colonial person performed in this photographic portraiture, attention must be paid to their differential articulations with the crystallisations of colonial culture they imply. Such a model covers the framing of 'native types' during a period of survey of the area: the replacement of this concern by the inventory of exemplary 'true characters' of 'tribal' culture that was invested in the native subjects who personified the tribal past in the colonial present. Finally, with the spread of the practice of portraiture articulated with the recognition of the authority of local chiefs within the colonial situation, it is the 'assimilated native' that is materialised in the portraits. Although the general tendency is for these concepts to have a chronological succession, these different styles of portraiture coexisted at some point, but had different objectives. The idea of type, and its correlate idea of a native deprived of agency, departed from portraiture with the latter's concern for the individual, in that it recorded physical detail. It simultaneously provided photographic documentation on 'hair dressing', 'body scarification' or 'dental mutilation', within the formal characteristics of 'type' photographs. The image composition of 'tribal natives', on the other hand, tended to be arranged at the museum native village. In these photographs, the formal aesthetic of 'the type', neutral background and front and profile views were replaced by a more informal photograph produced within the contained space of a colonially framed 'native culture'. Thus, colonial modernity was excluded from the frame, allowing the portraits to stand for pre-colonial times. Finally, there were the photographs of the chiefs as *Regedores*, often more recent, wearing the identifying Portuguese colonial officer's uniform. Many of these portraits were intended as gifts, and materialise yet another moment in the colonial process by framing, literally through the style of image and presentation, the incorporation of native authority into the colonial administration and, in this sense, a normalisation of the colonial situation. In substituting for those of chiefs wearing traditional clothing in the Gallery of Native Chiefs, these photographs directed local history away from the past and into the colonial present. Thus the representation made visible only two registers of colonial persona: the 'tribal' native of a regulated past and the 'assimilated' native of an expected future. It is precisely because such a perspective is contested by everyday practice in the Diamang context that the gallery was crucially relevant in the museum project as an axial element of colonial agency.

Colonial culture categories regarding 'natives' may, thus, be understood as being co-constituted through these photographic practices. These photographs and the way in which they were performed through display established a visual, identifiable pattern of what was what in the colonially constituted native human landscape. Clearly, the main differences in this process lie in the division between type and portrait, and in the latter, between those chosen to be used as ceremonial gifts to the subjects and those not. Crucially, then, it is not form alone or mainly that distinguishes type style from portrait, but circulation and consumption.

While circulation of 'native type' photographs was restricted to the company services and interweaving interests of labour management, health services and the charting of physical anthropology that I have outlined, portraiture implied public circulation, with the consumer integral to the production process of specific object forms of images. The portraits were thus intended to inculcate the native population with colonial views of order, by honorifically displaying colonially defined moral examples in the Gallery of Native Chiefs as a sanctioning device.

Gifts

The entanglement of the photographic portraits with gift exchange practices establishes another material system of photographs, and another biographical element. It is to this that I now wish to turn. The use of photographic portraits as gifts, and their absorption in ceremonial forms, appears to have developed from a specific form of field work: the historical survey mission. In the process of establishing a national colonial hagiography, one of the tasks assigned to the museum was to chart scientifically, and to correct, previous information about the area that had been gathered during travels by Portuguese explorers in the Lunda. The most important of these museum endeavours was the *Campaign for the Recognition of the Route of the Portuguese Expedition to the Muatianvua* of 1942, during which the company's 'employee' (not yet museum curator) followed in the footsteps of Henrique de Carvalho, updating and correcting his annotations regarding geographical data, population distribution, natural resources and so forth. This campaign re-enacted not only the original mode of travel, on foot, with a train of guides, hunters and porters, but also local collaborative and exchange relationships vested in the provision of food supplies and local knowledge.

Chief Satxissenga was one such collaborator. Descended from one of Henrique de Carvalho's allies, he guided the museum mission through his territories along the 'stations' established during the original route. Among the rewards for his efforts, the chief was presented with his framed portrait in a special ceremony held at the Dundo (Figure 8.2):

> The offering of a portrait to Chief Satxissenga
>
> The following pictures show Chief Satxissenga and his attendants at the Museum courtyard after he had received from the Director himself, a frame with his own portrait.
>
> The photograph was given a caption, quoted below, which explains was said:
>
> 'To chief Satxissenga,
> Presented by Commander Ernesto de Vilhena, Delegate Administrator of
>   the Diamang
> Dundo 31/10/43
> Ethnological Museum'
>
> It was a happy day, maybe the happiest in his life, to chief Satxissenga!
>   (Annual Report 1943: 164, author's translation)

This portrait, like many other photographic images, has several concomitant biographies in a number of object forms, which should be seen as multiple originals.[11] The print presented to the chief at the ceremony was similar to that in the Gallery of Native Chiefs but larger, comprising a photographic enlargement in a 50 × 60 cm glass and wood frame. It was taken home by him, where, one can conjecture, it formed a material focus for positive relations with the Portuguese. The fact that Chief Satxissenga descended from people who had actually met Henrique de Carvalho endowed him with some sort of continuity between the past and the birth of the Diamang project. He was therefore someone who should, for different good reasons, be co-opted to the company's allies by being enrolled as a museum collaborator. This relationship was

Dois aspectos da
entrega de um qua-
dro com o seu re-
trato, ao Soba
Satxissenga

Figure 8.2 The presentation of the framed portrait to Satxissenga. Annual Report of Dundo
Museum, 1943, page 164. (Courtesy of Museu Antropológico, University of Coimbra).

given material expression through the two linked objects, one being a ceremonial presentation and the other placed in the Gallery of Native Chiefs.

Gift exchange practices, and the use of portraits within these practices, had become well established in the museum. In its second phase of development in 1946, the museum extended its ethnographic research to biology and archaeology, publishing its own scientific journal and developing an academic network of museum collaborators and correspondents from museums and academies worldwide. In this context, an informal gift exchange system, involving native field assistants who worked for goods, had developed.[12] In order to maintain good relations with museum collaborators the administration established the routine of giving them with Christmas gifts.[13]

The ceremonial presentation of portraits in the museum's History Room established yet another material system of the photographs. In this context, they are intended as ceremonial objects playing a central role in a tight ceremonial script, which served to celebrate the company's colonial achievement. This ceremony made its debut at the Diamang concession in 1958. The date is significant, for colonial Africa could no longer be taken for granted. Neighbouring Belgian Congo was involved in negotiations for independence. This situation perhaps suggested diplomatic action rather than a show of muscle in the company's relationships with the native population. This new ceremony might be seen as part of the company's policy shifts in this direction, and likewise the institution of the Annual Indigenous Feast in 1950.

Unlike the portraits intended to be displayed at the gallery, the intention in making these portraits was specifically to give them away. While the proposed use of the photo-objects determined their technical specifics in size and framing, they were also linked to the specifics of the company's management strategies. Almost no portraits had been made during that year yet the availability of the photographer for this particular task suggests its importance to the company. It would also appear that a sort of census was carried out, maximising on the photographer's work. The 1958 gift portraits were thus obtained following several administrative directives, using the more practical 6×6 cm format camera, instead of the 9×12 cm Linhoff. Most of the chiefs were photographed against a neutral background, wearing not native outfits, but the Portuguese uniform that immediately identified them as *Regedores*, which distanced them from traditional authority, and thus reference to pre-colonial times. Unlike most of the earlier chief portraits, the 1958 photographs depicted the subject half-length, not unlike an identity card photograph. While also mounted and framed in wood and glass, the resulting photographs were smaller in size, measuring 13×18 cm.

Although, in terms of materials and techniques, these photographs are not dissimilar to others, it is that they are intended as ceremonial gifts that locates them in an entirely new material system – that of gifts for natives in the contexts of a collective rather than personal ceremony. In fact, besides the gift to Chief Satxissenga of his own portrait discussed above, the practice of offering gifts to the native chiefs within the contexts of the company seems to have been formally constituted in 1945. While on a study trip in Lisbon, the curator personally selected a series of objects for museum collaborators with the agreement of the delegate administrator. Hair combs, razor blades, tobacco and traditional chief mantles especially produced in Lisbon, according to the curators' instructions, were then sent to 14 chiefs who had been cooperating with the museum. In the letter explaining to whom these gifts were to be offered, the administrator of the company specifies that: 'It goes without saying that none go to him or those who, in the meanwhile, for any reason, including the provision of native labour, have not demonstrated themselves to be worthy of receiving a gift from the company' (Annual Report 1945: 23, author's translation).

Gift exchange established certain subjects as privileged partners of the company. But these chiefs had to apply for the honour by proving their acquiescence. Inclusion in gift exchange relations with the company, therefore, acted as a reinforcement of colonial authority. Prizes offered by the company to 'distinguished workers' – distributed in a public ceremony at the end of the Grand Feast Day, before the Indigenous Feast – further underline the political character of these gifts. Unlike work prizes – in money or merit medals – the award of which was clearly delineated and within the reach of any compliant worker, company gifts were apparently haphazard and personalised, establishing the public recognition of an individual by the company. With the institution, in 1950, of the Grand Feast ceremonies, the *Regedores* were included as recipients of these sorts of gifts. Initially these were limited to a Portuguese flag and a medal, presented early in the morning of the Diamang Day, following the singing of the Portuguese anthem. The combination of this sort of distinguishing ceremony with the clear influence on the native population of the Gallery of Native Chiefs led to the production of these 1958 portraits. Although they shared most of the characteristics of the former portraits, accentuated to great effect in their material presentation in the History Room, they in fact belonged to the category of ceremonial gifts. Their material system, specifically the other objects with which they articulated directly – the flag and the medals – does not involve the permanence, publicity, reverence or 'power' of the portraits hanging in the Gallery of Native Chiefs. The gift photographs are marked as other things.

These other things, however, were presented in the museum's History Room, as part of a tight ceremonial script, serving to celebrate the company's colonial achievement, mainly that of contemporary colonial administrative agents. Consequently these photo-objects recover their efficacy by borrowing it from the material system in which they appear to be operating. They acted as one thing, while, in fact, they were quite another. These portraits and their presentation represent the company's recognition of the changing times and an attempt to overcome them by publicly demonstrating, with this novel ceremonial script and the gift of objects, that nothing had changed. At a political moment when coercive measures seemed possible, to choose to do the opposite was a performance of power meant to disorientate, confuse or blur contesting agendas.

Finally, and although this is obvious, it remains to highlight a pedestrian relationship between the use of photographs for these different purposes and the company's 'rationality'. As has already been suggested, the internal maximisation of alliances through the use of photographs within bureaucratic structures was an effective means of getting photographs made in the first place. It should be noted that they were also, in terms of the company's budget, extremely cheap. This 'low cost' of production makes them appropriate for the purposes used, especially in the light of the local scarcity of photographs. Since photography was a prohibited practice, photographic portraits were rare for everyone, and even more so for non-Europeans. Apparently unattainable for the native population, but costing close to nothing to the company, photographs were also an icon of the modernity that colonialism was supposed to bring. Turned into a ceremonial gift and acting as a marker of distinction, they are placed, as an object, into a final form of consumption, never leaving the sphere of sumptuary goods for those to whom they were presented. At this level, portraits not only objectified natives as subjects in different manners, but did so by technological means that, because they were powerful and incomprehensible objects, were iconic of the company.

Visiting the museum

These gifts were made in the context of museum visiting. Visiting the Dundo Museum became an established routine both for the native population ('locals', 'from outer areas' or 'visitors') and for colonials, tourists, scientists or visitors to whom the company accorded the status of 'distinguished guests' (Figure 8.3). In a way that has very modern resonances, the museological process incorporated the analysis of the exhibits' reception by the public. These two main categories of public (natives and Europeans) were guided by museum staff who carefully noted visitors' remarks, preferences and dislikes. 'Native visitors' were also, in the course of these visits, asked to contribute to the museum collections. Native self-representation at the museum by donation became common practice and was frequently coloured by previously existing local rivalries.

Museum policy in a way countered the fierce colonial state policy of erasure of local material culture. Offering of objects to the museum, was, for the native population, a secure means of preventing objects from being confiscated or destroyed. Furthermore, in donations of this sort, the museum constituted itself as keeper, rather than as owner of the objects, allowing for the use of objects by their proprietors under certain conditions. In some cases, a visit to the museum was directly to pay tribute to artefacts, belonging to an individual or group.

It was in these contexts that the museum incorporated the presentation of portraits into the company's festival, which was initiated in 1950, under the name of the Grand Indigenous Annual Feast. The Grand Feast was the climax of a cycle of celebrations, including a sports competition held in the four main urban centres of the company and a contest for the best village, designed to distinguish the native village that conformed best to colonial precepts of hygiene and decorum. This culminating feast took place at the Dundo, and one of its structuring moments consisted in a collective visit to the museum. The presentation of the portraits was incorporated in the mid-1950s. In 1958 the ceremony was preceded by a long speech delivered by the museum curator, which, like other public speeches, was broadcast by the local Radio Diamang. He describes the affective tone of the photographs:

> We are now on the ninth edition of the grand collective visit to the Dundo Museum, held by the company's native guests to the Diamang's Grand Feast. This visit, in a way a pilgrimage, is clearly a tribal visit. More than one hundred chiefs and people from their lands, from every corner of the Lunda, were organised in a cheerful parade of thousands of individuals who have been walking, solemnly, along the museum galleries. There are exclamations of surprise at every moment and for very different reasons. Satisfaction, curiosity and engagement are obviously present in each one's face, be they Lundas, Cokwé, Matabels, KaCongos, Lubas or from other ethnic groups of this area.
>
> In the large History Room . . . the flow of visitors pauses and wonders, looking around with emotion. The reason is simple: from the top of the walls

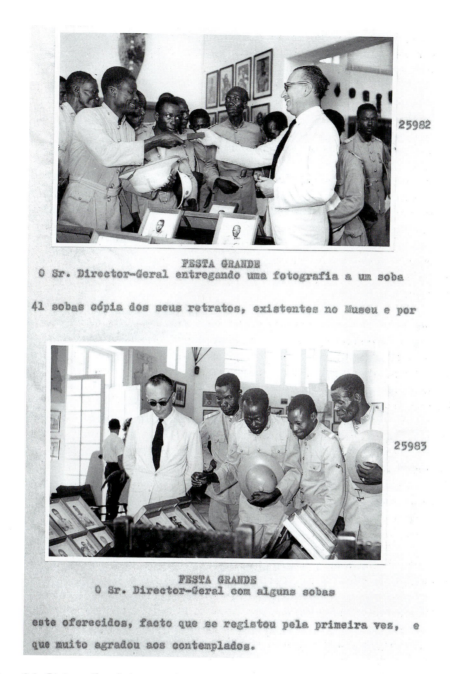

Figure 8.3 Giving gifts of photographs to distinguished visitors. Report of the Grand Annual Indigenous Feast, 1960, page 52. (Courtesy of Museu Antropológico, University of Coimbra.)

of this noble room, visitors are under the gaze of dozens of their elders, several of them already deceased, yet perpetuated here as a tribute to the chiefs of the Lunda, as determined by the company's administrator.

Some of their names are voiced by the people: Sangime . . . Nachir . . . Samacaca . . . Satxombo . . . Txilumba . . . It even seems that they have joined the crowd. The portraits of the deceased native chiefs, in a people still marked by traditional beliefs, is above all an animist belief. The parade goes on, less directed by those who are ahead than forced to move on by those who are still arriving, attracted by the evocation of names familiar to everybody.

(MR September 1958: 11–13, author's translation)

The curator's comments on 'native belief' are a clear indication that the probable effects of these portraits were known or, at least, previously imagined, devised and intended. The whole experience of encountering the photographs was orchestrated to show them as technologies of enchantment, with apparent success. The whole 'pilgrimage' to the museum was a massive piece of organisation, involving the transport and feeding of thousands of people, followed by the impressive ceremonies of the Grand Feast themselves: the hoisting of the national (that is, Portuguese) flag, the collective chanting of the national anthem, the award of medals and flags to local chiefs and an open-air mass. Everyone then moved on to the museum, native festivities at the Folklore Ground of the Native Village lasting until dawn.

Inside the liminal space of the museum, they received a guided tour with tutorial purposes, which directed the visitors' attention and prevented them from viewing and experiencing otherwise. The climax was prepared in the History Room, where the portraits, as photo-objects, worked as they should: bringing the dead into the present and, with it, banishing 'nativeness' into the past. The presentation of portraits then took place in the room, entangling the living chiefs the dead chiefs and their photographs in one material system, one further intensified by the political environment of African decolonisation. Issues of legitimacy and power are heavily entangled in this seductive transformation of the portraits into ceremonial gifts in a way that is impossible to disregard.

The work of materiality

For all these reasons the material system of the portrait as ceremonial gift is to be located outside of photography itself and directly placed in relation to the Portuguese flag and merit medals awarded to the same chiefs earlier in the morning. Indeed, despite the museum curator's pretensions on the racial purity of chiefs, the colonial administration simply nominated anyone to the job to work to its administrative agendas.[14] Most of these chiefs were only recognised as such by their subjects in very restricted fields. Their legitimacy was highly problematic and they were frequently subjected to violence and interference by the colonial administration. The presentation of portraits was specifically intended to endorse these colonially-made chiefs with the tribal authority evoked by the museum curator, either by placing them side by side with ancestors, thus according them that same status, or by presenting them with their own portrait inside the very room where the ancestors were present in a comparable material form. Dignifying these colonially made chiefs with the honours of the ancestors empowers them as much as legitimises them in relation to their subjects, in that they are presented as the contemporary ancestors-to-be in the colonially fractured world. From the company perspective these were times, not for a show of force, but for concealment beneath seductive ceremonies that could define it as keeper of traditions, in contrast to the colonial state administration. This is why, paradoxically, these photographs do not really mean anything, but (as if to compensate for this lack) they work very well.

This being said, it must be noticed that they do not work in the same way for everyone, their potential mutability being extremely efficacious within a colonial culture that was essentially unsure, circumstantial and experimental. Thus I would argue that the way in which these photographic objects express this processual character of colonial culture may be better grasped by exploring the different material systems that they entangle, and that, according to this argument, establish provisional understandings about these objects, and from which different actions can be defined and articulated. The issue of time and mutability of historical configuration regarding colonialism in Africa is therefore crucial, for it frames the relevance and purposes that photographic objects are called upon to operate at the Diamang. Instead of different portraiture styles, three different material systems of photographs should be distinguished: type photographs, chief portraits as museum items and portraits as gifts. They cannot be reduced to styles of image content, for each of them implies distinct fields of practice and a specific value of the materiality of photographs.

Conclusion

It has been suggested that the search for meaning in the analysis of photographs, which has been understood as a means of representation, is an equivocal endeavour that may productively be diverted to the analysis of photographs as objects, questioning how they act in specific situations. To inquire into photographs as objects makes it possible to address the issues of circulation and consumption ethnographically. Through exploration of the uses of these photographs, native portraits, with superficial similarities of image, are revealed to be quite different objects, a difference that articulates with the indeterminacies, experiments and improvisations of colonial culture process. Types gained their specificity from their internal circulation and consumption during a brief moment of construction of colonial knowledge. Tentatively, they paved the way for 'native portraiture', where the enactment of pre-colonial times through portraiture engaged with a policy of seduction of the native subjects. Unlike the previous records, early portraits were made into museum objects, intended to construct the past visually and to be experienced within highly ritualised forms. They were empowering both of the depicted subjects and of colonial rule and an order that positioned itself as keeper of traditions and of their disappearing world. In the late 1950s, portraiture, intended as ceremonial gift objects, worked in distinct ways, emerging as an experiment to divert contemporary social and political contestations and create the temporary illusion of control over a broad history. None of these actions is to be seen in the images alone. Operating as mediators of social relations, portraits are activated within networks of interaction, in specific situations, relating agency and agents with separate agendas, at concrete places, at particular timings, under specified motives. If, in the process, they seem to gain control over their own motives it is because their role as image-objects fulfils, for everyone involved, unsettled affairs of colonial culture.

Notes

1 Latour does not phrase 'modern settlement' as a trap in quite this way. One of its characteristics is its elusive presence, which, he argues, must be made re-presentable (Latour 1991: 12) ceasing, from then on, to be a trap (which also happens with traps properly speaking). This 'modern settlement' is based on two types of operations: those of translation and mediation and those of purification. These are, for him, contradictory since the first tends to the production of hybrids that the second denies. Because they are contradictory, modernity has never been a fulfilled programme. The obsession with *the medium* in photographic analysis of the 1980s (for example, Slater 1980; Walker 1980; Green 1984) falls – for obvious reasons – into this trap, even if some of these efforts (for example, Sekula 1986; Tagg 1988) have been highly productive for current anthropological analysis of photographs.

2 Throughout this chapter the term 'native' is used when speaking of the local Angolan population. This is a historical usage that defines the relations between the Diamang and Portuguese Colonial Administration. The term 'native' operated to differentiate from 'indigenous', which is the legal designation of colonial subjects who were to be 'civilised', among other practices, by being forced to work. 'Native' as used in the company's reports aims at distinguishing the cultural entity from the 'legal persona'. Hence, their use of the term 'native' is reproduced here because such language is part of the colonial discourse that stressed the civilisation gap rather than affirming a specific culture. The photographs were integrally entangled in this discourse.

3 The methodological shift to a more ethnographically oriented analysis of photographs is at the core of this alternative. To my knowledge, no previous engagements in this shift have phrased it this way (for example, Faris 1996; Edwards 1997; Gordon 1997; Pinney 1997). Nevertheless, this view embraces work emerging from the classical anthropological endeavour of placing things in their social and cultural context. It has also engaged in useful dialogue with recent developments in anthropologically based studies of material culture.

4 Article 22 of the standard working contract states: 'It is forbidden for the employee to introduce and use, within the area of the company, photographic or film cameras as it is also forbidden to reproduce by drawings or painting of any aspect, scene or fact related with the services of mining works. Whenever the company instructs the employee to obtain photographs, films, paintings or drawings of any sort, those works will be of exclusive property of the company and cannot be used in any manner by the employee, neither in their original form, nor in any kind of reproduction.'

5 Such 'tolerance' was a distinctive feature of the Diamang's colonial project and came to be inscribed in the concept of 'scientific colonialism'. Frequently the company contested colonial law regarding 'native's habits and costumes', especially from the 1950s, when an increasing official assimilationist colonial policy tried to eradicate what were seen as 'tribal costumes'.

6 In the absence of specific rules for museums, the Annual Report of 1949 outlined a plan for the museum to reflect local character. The Dundo Museum was to engage with the population, both colonial and native. As a regional museum, it deliberately linked science with aesthetics, a convenient compromise between the two crucial elements: the local character of collections and its main public (native people), and the general appeal of scientific displays. Thus the museum was to be a lived space where both natives and colonials could encounter native culture, not 'a graveyard' [sic].

7 Henrique de Carvalho was appointed by the Geographical Society of Lisbon to chart the area and establish agreements with local rulers. His survey and the alliances constituted the basis for Portuguese claims to the area in the Berlin Conference 1884–5.

8 Until 1948, and some bureaucratic changes, the curator frequently complained that the photographic laboratory did not cooperate with the museum.

9 The new photographer demanded a new dark room, studio and archive at the museum. New magnifiers were installed and new cameras, namely a Linhoff Technica (12 × 9 cm), a Contaflex (6 × 6 cm) and one unspecified 35 mm camera, replaced the old glass plate camera.

10 The tones of this printing paper are softer, perhaps placing the subject in a suggested pre-photographic time.

11 One version was hung in the Gallery of Native Chiefs, surviving its subject. Another was published in a popular history journal in 1946, facing the portrait of Henrique de Carvalho. Finally, there were archive prints with their many applications, including the reports.

12 This applied to field assistants recruited locally. Within the museum, native employees were classed as 'specialised workers' of the company. But once in the field, monetary payments were not authorised and almost anything (food, clothes, empty bottles, medicine etc.) could be involved in these transactions.

13 In the 1950s this network covered about 200 persons from different villages near the Dundo. Christmas gifts usually comprised cloth for women and tools for men. Other gifts such as food, wine and tobacco were part of an informal payment to 'artists' for folkloric performances.

14 Such characters were commonly referred to as the 'beating up chief', in that these chiefs were doomed from both sides of the colonial divide. Their subjects saw them as puppets of Portuguese administration who in their turn replaced the chiefs if they failed to comply (Margarido 1975).

9

THE PHOTOGRAPH REINCARNATE

The dynamics of Tibetan
relationships with photography

Clare Harris

Since 1950, when China began its takeover of Tibet, the socio-political contexts of Tibetan material and visual culture have been radically dislocated. All pre-existing activities of a religious, social or cultural nature have had to be reinvented either by Tibetan refugees in the alien conditions of host nations or by those who remained 'at home' in a country that has been renamed the Tibet Autonomous Region (TAR) of the People's Republic of China (PRC). Whether as exiles or members of a *minzu* (national minority) of a colonising communist state, Tibetans have been engaged in processes of cultural retrieval and reconfiguration in which the photograph has been an active co-participant. This chapter explores the ways in which Tibetans use, adapt and create photographs, with an emphasis on their presence in the physical world. A cross-cultural perspective allows us to investigate the specificities of shifting relationships between Tibetan bodily practice in the domain of photographs, while also suggesting ways in which a global technology like photography (and the theories attached to it) can be adapted for a contemporary Asian setting. As a physically tangible thing with an indexical link to persons deceased or places vacated, the Tibetan photograph is more than just a 'certificate of presence' (Barthes 1984: 87), it is a socially salient object that literally embodies and enacts relationships with the past, present and even the future. This is possible due to the specifically local Tibetan concept of reincarnation, in which the human body is seen as a receptacle, fleetingly occupied by a person or deity, but when apprehended in sensory and haptic registers, these values are literally incarnated in photographs. Following from this, when consumed by refugees as part of an 'artefactual diaspora', photographs become the temporary physical location for the transmigration of ideas about identity and belonging in both local and global contexts.

Locating 'Tibet' in exile

The ethnographic focus of this chapter is primarily drawn from observations made in Tibetan communities in northern India, particularly in Dharamsala (Himachal Pradesh), where the project of reconstructing Tibet in exile is led by the Fourteenth Dalai Lama Tenzin Gyatso, his government and monastic institutions. Here the sense of loss and displacement that accompanies what de Vos (1981: 32) calls the 'virtual social identity' of refugees is at its most acute but more than 100,000 Tibetans dispersed across the globe also share this experience. Creating exilic Tibet was initially a matter of dealing with the brute facts of economic and physical survival in host countries, particularly India, but it rapidly transformed into a process of making Tibet anew: rebuilding monasteries and other key cultural organisations on alien soil. The concept of the vacated homeland unifies Tibetans and is a key element in the construction of the neo-nation in exile. It is essential that exiles remember (and depict) the 'Tibet' that was taken over by the Chinese, beginning in 1950 and fully effected by 1959, and continue, despite the ravages of Chinese colonialism, to imagine it in a state of unity and boundedness. This is the nation they hope to reclaim but in the meantime are forced to reinvent in other locations. An exilic elite of religious figures and artists, writers, performers and musicians have been at the forefront of the promotion of an 'invented tradition' of what it means to be Tibetan after 1959; an invention defined in terms of the imagined communities (Anderson 1983) of Tibetan Buddhism and neo-nationalism. Within and without the elite, Tibetan exiles refer to themselves as *nangpa* or Buddhist 'insiders', a term that emphasises their membership of a community of Tibetan Buddhists in which pre-exilic regional and sectarian identities have been subsumed for the sake of social and political survival. This *nangpa* sense of Tibetaness is articulated through a 'preservation-in-practice' ethos wherein the connection between the Tibetan homeland and the global community into which the refugees have been displaced must be mediated through the Buddha and Buddhist cultural markers; that is, a religio-cultural definition of what it is to be Tibetan has been privileged.

In the institutional environment of exile, such as monasteries and *lha khang* (image chambers), painted and sculpted images of Buddha and bodhisattvas perform a key function in the 'presentation' of a specifically Tibetan cultural style to be consumed by an internal (*nangpa*) audience and an external group that consists of tourists and an intermediate category of non-Tibetan Buddhist practitioners. Although it is the intention of the exilic elite that the social contexts for such idolatry should remain static, in practice such 'traditionalist' icons are often beyond the economic means of ordinary refugees. Hence, beyond the elite and public image nexus, it is the Dalai Lama photo-icon that is most visible, present and active in *nangpa* lives rather than the consecrated Buddha index. This is due, in large part, to the combination of facets of the personality of the Fourteenth Dalai Lama, who is both god-like (he is the incarnation of the Buddha of Compassion, *Chenrezig*) and an individual (Tenzin Gyatso) whose thoughts, actions and biography are received as a narrative of a nation in exile. His departure from Tibet in 1959 triggered the exodus of thousands of ordinary Tibetans who sought to follow their religious leader wherever he went. For the majority this meant setting up home on the Indian side of the Himalayas and sharing in what Appiah (1994: 159) terms the 'scripted identity' of migration. However, the dispersal of Tibetan bodies (ultimately to diverse locations around the globe) has also generated what we might call an artefactual diaspora in which a shared sense of what it means to be Tibetan after 1959 is produced through the circulation of goods – particularly photographically generated ones.

The portability of photographic objects makes them ideally suited for spreading networks of cohesion between people separated by great distance both within and beyond national boundaries. When acquired by refugees, photographs are supremely transnational objects that, like their owners, may begin life in one place (or nation) but are forced to travel through space and time to new destinations. They may be marked by this passage through alien territories and drastically altered by the influence of host nations, a point to which I shall return. However, throughout this experience they retain a primary role as a signifier of home and an aspiration to return to Tibet. Photographs of the Dalai Lama in particular have been deployed to mark a bald political fact: the Dalai Lama is abroad in the world, literally and pictorially, due to his ejection from Tibet. For *nangpa* this is a bitter memory that dominates the quotidian experience of life in exile; hence the display of the Dalai Lama icon is part of a strategy of cultural solidarity in the face of loss.

This message of connectedness is communicated in part by the content of a photograph – that is, through the representation of a reincarnate body – but the relationship between leader and followers is also made evident in the performative acts of persons in the vicinity of image-objects. This observation accords with the theoretical drive towards a more explicitly material culture focus in the analysis of photographs and a move away from the 'ocularity' of much previous work. Material forms enter human consciousness through a variety of pathways – through individual senses – so that they may be, as Stoller (1989) suggests, quite literally 'tasted' (or heard, seen, touched, smelt), but there is also a total haptic response, which involves the collective input of all sensory mechanisms coupled with a knowledge of the most intimate physical space we inhabit, the body. Our 'being in the world' (Bourdieu 1990) is therefore frequently orientated towards and around objects, to the extent that we can argue that just as objects can be said to construct persons so they construct places and spaces; that is, there is a mutually constituative relationship between us and them, persons and objects. Moreover, in adopting a series of choreographed positions from which we may most readily mobilise our faculties (sitting, standing etc.), our relationship with objects becomes highly performative. Importantly, these acts are subject to cross-cultural variability (as the Tibetan examples below demonstrate) but when considering the question of materiality and photography in a Tibetan setting, I want to begin by acknowledging that photographs are part of a circulatory system of purchase and exchange wherein they accrue value and their objectness is emphasised.[1]

Circulation

If photographs are to be treated analytically as they are experienced (that is, as objects), then they must be considered as part of the mass circulation of goods moving between people. That objects follow 'social trails' (Parkin 1999) and circulate in networks where they may gain or lose various types of value (ranging from economic to 'symbolic' capital) has been well established by Appadurai (1986) and others. That they may also create identity and even extend the dimensions of individual personhood in a manner akin to a prothesis (moving beyond the individual's biological body) has been explored most effectively by Gell (1998) and Strathern (1988), responding to the classic work of Marcel Mauss. For Tibetans, photographs are undoubtedly commodities and as such are purchased at roadside stalls or in specialist shops, but they simultaneously function within domestic gift giving ceremonies. The most popular type of photographs acquired by Tibetans for these purposes depicts religious leaders, ranging from the Dalai Lama downwards through a hierarchy of reincarnates (*tulku*)

Figure 9.1 Dalai Lama photo-icon in the home of a Tibetan refugee, Ladakh, India, 1991.
Photographer: Clare Harris.

and teachers (Figure 9.1). When passed between people such photographs are understood to possess merit. Merit accrues to both donor and the recipient of images and
subsequently increases when the object is treated with respect; that is, the status of the
person is enhanced by his or her behaviour in the presence of such objects. In these
transactions merit appears to flow between bodies and objects in a manner similar to
that in which sacred substances are encountered by Buddhist individuals, particularly
during pilgrimage or visits to high lamas in monasteries. Within Tibetan culture
certain persons, places and things are thought to be animated by powers that derive
from either the spirit world or the influence of Buddhist deities. Sometimes the sight
of an object (or person) of great sanctity is the goal of the pilgrimage. In other cases
the entire body is pressed against the earth of a *ngas* (power site) as in full length

prostrations around sacred mountains, or the soil is literally ingested in order to acquire the cleansing, curative and meritorious benefits of its sacred materiality.[2] Frequently a photographic memento of this engagement is acquired and taken back to the home to be added to the family shrine.

All of these acts increase an individual's stock of merit, without which the chances of a good rebirth in a future incarnation are doubtful. Hence, when a photograph acquires the physical traces of merit, whether in the form of the touch of a sanctified person or in the act of exchange itself, it generates the added value that determines the future state of persons as bodies passing through a series of reincarnated states.[3] This value is not to be thought of as merely metaphoric but is intrinsic to the photographic object as it moves between locations. Hence, when the black and white image of the current Dalai Lama is presented to a fourteenth-century clay representation of the Buddha (alongside offerings of cash), the power (and value) of each is augmented, demonstrating that there can be animated relationships between two objects as much as between persons and things.[4] Just how Tibetan photographs are seen to be invested with such power, whether it be via the veracity of indexicality or perceptions of the force of the religious personae depicted, is discussed below, but we must return to the question of their positioning in space.[5]

Spatial hierarchies

There are numerous ways in which Tibetan bodily praxis connotes respect for objects or persons and in which a hierarchy of relationships between the mundane and supra-mundane worlds are delineated. Circumambulation (*khorra*), for example, is a codified activity in which a place (or object) of sanctity is circled in a clockwise direction (for Tibetan Buddhists; or anti-clockwise for Tibetan followers of Bön), preferably in full-length prostrations. In the domestic context seating positions signify the social stature of those assembled, with visiting religious figures accorded the highest honour of a seat by the hearth or even a chair. From the nineteenth century Tibetan aristocrats such as the Ragashar family of Lhasa demonstrated their wealth and superiority by adopting Western-style furniture, as illustrated in photographs from the collection of Sir Charles Bell, where both the women of the household and their sons sit on chairs while their servants stand or sit on the floor. In general, the higher the status of the person or object the higher it (they) should stand in the world – hence when photographs of religious leaders began to enter the homes of high-ranking Tibetans in the 1930s they were hung at the top of walls in a traditional gesture of respect.[6]

The hierarchy of height extends to other contexts in which the materiality of photography is of the essence. Most Tibetan homes contain, if not a dedicated shrine room, then at least a shelf or cabinet where the most precious family possessions are kept. In the past, the shrine room would have been positioned at the top of the house (nearer the gods), but among exiles living in refugee camps in India, this kind of construction is often not possible, so the family shrine may be a simple wooden plinth in the living room. This can function effectively as long as it is well above the level of ordinary domestic activities. For most refugees the 'precious goods' displayed there will be photographs of religious figures. Under no circumstances should they be placed on the floor (risking the defilement of the dirt and feet) and certain activities (drinking, smoking, sex) must not be carried out in their presence. Framed and unframed colour prints of the Dalai Lama, 'root gurus' and other teachers are collected together on these improvised altars alongside photographs of painted deities. Each morning an offering of eight bowls filled with water is made for the refreshment of the gods, as it would be in a monastery or temple. In these shrine assemblages, photo-icons of key Tibetan Buddhists are not just reminders of specific individuals but relate to a lineage of other religious masters and ultimately to the god they embody. Hence they are positioned to reflect the relationships between different schools of Tibetan Buddhism or different regions of Tibet, since many refugees continue to follow the root guru of their 'home' monastery even if they will never visit the place again. A narrative of the exile situation can thus be discerned in the organisation of a refugee shrine. With his multiple roles, as incarnation, leader and protector, the Dalai Lama always assumes paramountcy, usually in both height and scale, in that his photograph is often substantially enlarged. On the other hand, monks from regional monasteries are present in smaller prints, reduced in scale and visibility. In many ways, this photographic grouping functions as a kind of family album, with portraits arranged in frames of connectedness.

Bourdieu draws a useful comparison between the album of ancestors and funerary rites, remarking that their role is similar in 'recalling the memory of the departed, the memory of their passing, recalling that they lived, that they are dead and buried and that they continue on in the living' (Bourdieu 1990: 31). However, for Tibetan Buddhists it is not family members who are recalled in photographic objects but members of a lineage of religious leaders. The twin concepts of lineage and reincarnation mean that their identity is always imagined to flow beyond the current living body. Hence photographs are not just 'of' the present subject but conjure the remembered image of others (as in Tibetan meditational practice where the mind is channelled to recall the extraordinary physical characteristics of deities) and gesture towards their future incarnations. Had Roland Barthes found himself in a Buddhist environment, we might ask if he would have experienced quite the same level of anxiety when faced with the image of his mother (Barthes 1984: 63–71), since for Tibetans the body is merely a receptacle fleetingly occupied by a person. The photographic record of that body therefore becomes a positive affirmation of an ongoing stream of presence rather than a memorial to absence.

We might also argue from the evidence above that in many Tibetan contexts positioning the body correctly in relationship to objects is not simply a matter of preparing it for vision. This is not about the production of 'the gaze' in any conventional Western sense, nor even directly comparable to the Hindu concept of *darshan*, in which devotees prepare themselves to see and be seen by a deity (in object-like form) in a temple. These actions are designed to bring the person into the orbit of an object through total bodily contact, or what Christopher Pinney (1997: 171) calls 'proximal empowerment'. Achieving proximity with powerful objects, like photographs of sacred individuals, is a positive act for Tibetans, akin to gift-giving, but in this case the object donated is the entire body. In such bodily praxis the tangibility of photographs is constantly reiterated by a series of physical acts in the domain of objects. However, in the Tibetan case this proactive relationship also frequently hints at intangibility. As one of the reincarnatory cultures, Tibetan Buddhism (like Hinduism) emphasises the way in which objects and bodies pass through a series of life cycles where substances can become insubstantial only to return reformulated. Hence, in the

137

case of Tibetan photo-icons, where the content of the photograph is entirely enmeshed with its materiality, the photograph has become a reincarnation of its subject.

The body politic

So far we have concentrated on cultural norms within Tibetan society that have been reinvented for the new conditions of post-1959 Tibet rather than investigating radical or novel solutions to the politics of colonisation and exile. Two such innovations arose in direct response to the threat posed by the aggression of China. Significantly, they both involve an intimate bodily engagement with photographs. These actions must be seen in relation to wider issues arising from what I have termed 'representational fields', wherein competing depictions of Tibetan culture have been mobilised for the sake of political agendas (Harris 1999). The three primary agents responsible for the production of conflicting representations since 1959 are the Chinese state, the inventors of Western mass-produced images (ranging from travel books to news photography) and Tibetans themselves.[7] Photography began to play a particularly explicit role in these representational battles in the context of the Cultural Revolution (1966–76) and its impact on Tibet when Socialist Realist portraits of Mao, People's Liberation Army generals and other propagandistic mythologies were forcibly inserted into the lives of Tibetans back home in the TAR. Following the murder and starvation of hundreds of thousands in the homeland, the destruction of monasteries and all Buddhist imagery (which was particularly rigorously implemented during the Cultural Revolutionary period) inflicted another searing wound across the body of Tibet. As Norbu reports 'Before, the sacred mantra "Om Mani Padme Hum" was carved on rocks; the Red Guards now inscribed quotations from Mao's Red Book. In short, Mao replaced the Buddha in every respect during the Cultural Revolution' (Norbu 1987: 263). The Tibetan reaction to the destruction of the image of the Buddha was to replace his form with that of the Dalai Lama. In conditions of cultural obliteration and Maoist 'organised forgetting' (Connerton 1989) it was he who could provide the agency to fight back.

During the 1960s and 1970s guerrilla fighters from the Eastern region of Tibet (Kham) attempted to do battle with the People's Liberation Army. Alongside guns and knives they wore *gau* (amulets) containing photographs of the Dalai Lama. Prior to the Chinese takeover Buddha amulets had been worn in war time, as the icon was believed to deflect arrows and bullets, just as the Buddha himself had diverted the weapons of his enemy Mara, but in the battle to reclaim the land he had been forced to abandon, the Dalai Lama was enlisted for service. As a bodhisattva the Dalai Lama exhibits a dual personality: he is both god of *Chenrezig* (god of compassion) and fierce protector of *tam drin* (Buddhism). Khampa guerrillas sought to embody the agency of a *tam drin*, transforming the photo-icon into an ensign of the battle for the independence of Tibet, merging it, in its material form, with traditional *gau*. The portability and potency of the Dalai Lama photograph enabled his image to be radically reconfigured as a kind of photographic shield protecting Tibetan bodies against an onslaught of both weaponry and alien imagery. It has continued to perform a similar function ever since, for following the Cultural Revolution the possession and display of Dalai Lama icons has been repeatedly banned by the Chinese authorities in the TAR, though Tibetans continue to risk arrest by secreting the icon of their absent leader about their person. For them his personhood is intimately incorporated into their sense of self but must be concealed from view. Slipped inside monastic robes or the folds of a *chuba* (secular Tibetan dress), the Dalai Lama photo-icon is attached to the body like a second skin, reiterating the sense in which the materiality of the photograph enables its consumption through senses other than the eye. Positioned close to the heart, it can literally be embraced.

During the Cultural Revolution Tibetans also used their bodies as political weapons in an undercover battle against Maoist demolition of their preferred images. Alongside the wholesale destruction of many religious buildings and artefacts, the PLA inserted posters of Chairman Mao into Tibetan homes and workplaces as part of a policy designed to eradicate Buddhist and, arguably, thus nationalist sentiment. To remove, deface or protest against these images was a dangerous act that could lead to the perpetrator appearing at a *tam dzing* or denunciation session or worse. Instead, Tibetans deployed a culture-specific bodily tactic of disrespect and slept with their feet facing Mao's photograph. Since the foot is both the lowest element of the body and closest to earthly impurities, it can be used to defile or degrade. Without even touching the image of Mao, Tibetans expressed their disgust at his photograph and consciously inverted a traditional practice in which images of particular deities, including photographically generated ones, are touched with the head (not the hand) in a gesture of respect that enables the transmission of merit between object and devotee.

The life and death of the photograph

In both the radical and the traditionalist contexts we have explored above, the Tibetan photograph has performed a prosthetic function, augmenting the body and articulating aspects of identity formations construed in religious terms (such as the acquisition of merit) or politicised notions of Tibetaness. How is it that photography has been allowed to assume this role when Tibetan culture is replete with examples of powerful objects, from sacred *mani* stones inscribed with prayers to three-storey high sculpted Buddhas? I would argue that a series of conceptual paradigms established centuries before the invention of photography have been transferred from one set of material forms to another. Much recent material culture theory asserts that objects have 'lives' and that we can write biographical portraits of things as they circulate in use (see, for example, Appadurai 1986; Miller 1989; MacKenzie 1991; Hoskins 1998). For Tibetans, the lifelikeness of objects is so frequently articulated through quotidian acts, as I have shown, that we can demonstrate that photographs are often not just of bodies (having lives) but treated as bodies that can be born, become ill and die. Objects are encountered as if they had been animated by a life force (in the case of architectural structures the wooden pillar at the centre or heart of a building is literally referred to as such) that is acquired during the birthing process or *rab ngas* ceremony when the eyes of a religious statue are ritually opened by a monk. During its life, such an object will be dressed in fine clothes and kept clean. Should it become damaged or tarnished in any way this is taken as a sign of a sickness that could infect all those living in the vicinity of the image. That is, the object can become active in a negative sense and behave like an infective agent, rather as Tibetans perceived Mao photographs during the Cultural Revolution. At this point the object must be replaced by a new version of itself – another, cleansed, incarnation. The old model must be safely disposed of (though some of its component parts may be transplanted and reincorporated into the replacement) and is subject to the treatment meted out to the dead; that is, it may be incinerated and the ash retained in the form of a *tsa tsa* (clay votive tablets). In recent decades photographically generated images of religious figures have been accorded similar last rites and just as ash from the bodies of cremated monks is mixed with clay to make *tsa tsa*, so the photograph retains the particles of personhood that upon the death of the subject must be recirculated in an appropriate manner.

Tibetan attitudes to materiality stem from a cosmological scheme in which the world is composed of innumerable particles that are assembled into bodies, objects, spaces and places with varying degrees of closeness to the perfected nature of the supra-mundane.[8] The perfect body is construed as a dead one that has previously been inhabited by an incarnate being. Hence the corpse of a monk who was able to die in an exceptional mental or physical state (such as the lotus-position) is embalmed and displayed to the public. The body is left to stand as testimony to a worthy life but importantly the material stuff that remains on view – the skin, flesh and bones – is not thought to contain the 'identity' of the individual concerned, but is seen as a memorial to their achievements. Until the early twentieth century, drawings or other kinds of effigies were used to represent the dead in Tibetan funeral ceremonies, a practice that may explain why any attempt at mimetic reproduction of the living body drew responses of fear or disapproval and artists were discouraged from making portraits from life. Tibetans then operated in what Hans Belting (1994: 471) calls the 'era before art' when 'the image had been assigned a special reality and taken literally as a visible manifestation of the sacred person'. Belting compares this period with the development of Renaissance perspectival realism and a move towards 'likeness' rather than 'presence'. Current attitudes among Tibetans suggest that the technology of photography, and especially its material products, somehow combines both of these tendencies. When photographs are used to invoke the authority of an exceptional individual, such as the Dalai Lama, they function like an embalmed corpse and simultaneously a highly lifelike being. The mechanical reproduction of the Dalai Lama photo-icon means that when he is physically absent from communal gatherings his portrait can be present. The photographic object is treated as a living body, seated on a throne, shielded by a canopy and blessed with a silk scarf of greeting. Activities are conducted as if he were present because the particles of personhood have been reassembled and redistributed in the material form of photography (Figure 9.2). But how has this dramatic shift in attitudes to indexical imagery become possible?

Historically, Tibetan accounts of the production of images frequently underplayed the agency of human beings in the representation of divine bodies. As was the case in early Christian conceptions of icon-making, the uncircumscribable nature of divinity led to great unease about the role of artists. Tibetans solved this problem through the use of strict iconometric codes and by promoting a general diffidence about portraiture or any kind of realism. However, the Thirteenth Dalai Lama set a precedent by allowing the camera to undertake the dangerous process of copying from life. As an object mediating between the 'real world' and the image, the camera created a simulated reality that was acknowledged as such in the photo-icons of the Thirteenth and his successors. Here the monochrome photograph of a specific body is left exposed, while everything else – clothing, furnishing, landscape – is over-painted in the style of *thangka* (scroll paintings). In these objects, the photographic component is left to

Figure 9.2 Dalai Lama photo-icon in use in a Tibetan monastic building. Photographer: Clare Harris.

stand as testimony to the actual body of a Dalai Lama or other high-ranking monk. Those parts of the anatomy that most clearly reveal the physiological characteristics of an individual – the head, and sometimes the hands, of a monk – are left untouched by the artist's brush. In this way the photograph has eclipsed the role of iconometry, which for centuries had determined the visual portrayal of incarnates. The camera had assumed a special status as the re-producer of identity, while the material interventions of the paintbrush were devoted to the portrayal of imagined Tibetan-style worlds.

The acquisition of aura

In 1910 the Thirteenth Dalai Lama had taken refuge in Darjeeling, India, after the Chinese sent four hundred troops to Lhasa (the capital of Tibet), an act he and his government interpreted as the beginnings of a mission to kidnap him. While in temporary exile in British-run India he established a relationship with Sir Charles Bell, British Representative to Tibet, Bhutan and Sikkim. Under Bell's guidance the Thirteenth was the first Tibetan to encounter some of the more sophisticated technologies of Empire, including photography. He even asked Bell to take his photograph. For a Christian European, recording the impression of a living body was an acceptable part of the process by which an image functioned in the 'cult of remembrance of loved ones, absent or dead' (Benjamin 1992: 219); hence, at the Thirteenth's instigation Bell overturned a Tibetan taboo. In pre-1959 Tibet a picture of the deceased was used by

141

Tibetan families during *bardo* ceremonies over the 49-day period when the spirit of the corpse was encouraged to move to its next incarnation. Hence Tibetans had good reason to express concern about the production of a photograph, as Bell (1946: 383) recalls: 'In November, 1933, the Dalai Lama, summoned one of the Nepalese photographers in Lhasa to take his photograph. This alarmed the people of Lhasa, who took it as a sign that he intended to die soon.' Unfortunately their collective premonition proved true. By mid-December the Thirteenth was dead. However, he had been having his picture taken since 1910 and according to Sir Charles Bell the Dalai Lama's portrait had quickly been converted into an object of veneration. 'This was, I believe, the first photograph of him seated in the Tibetan style. I gave him a large number of copies, and these proved useful to him; he used to give them to monasteries and to deserving people. These all used the photograph instead of an image, rendering to it the worship they gave to images of Buddhas and deities' (Bell 1946: 114). Bell comments that thereafter he saw thousands of these photo-icons in circulation throughout the Tibetan communities of the Himalayas. But how had the taboo been overcome, allowing a photographic portrait of the living Dalai Lama to become an object of sanctity? It might be said to be the result of collaborative work by three agents: the Thirteenth Dalai Lama, Sir Charles Bell and an anonymous Tibetan painter.[9]

From presence to likeness

Bell's account of his relationship with the Thirteenth (appropriately entitled *Portrait of the Dalai Lama*) includes a copy of the photograph he had taken, but with material accretions. His picture was re-presented to him with both the seal and signature of the Thirteenth, emphasising the sense of direct – indexical – contact with its subject, and had been tinted by a member of the Thirteenth's retinue in Darjeeling. Bell notes that the artist had used 'the appropriate colours for his hat, his robes, his throne, the religious implements . . . and the silk pictures of Buddha which formed the suitable background of it all' (Bell 1946: 114). That is, the areas surrounding the Thirteenth had been Tibetanised through the agency of a Tibetan artist. However, Bell fails to mention that the undressed parts of the Thirteenth's body, his head, arms and hands, remained in unt(a)inted monochrome. That is, the primary features that expose an individual identity were left undisturbed by pigment. The Tibetan painter, still wary of proscriptions against portraiture, allowed the camera to produce the simulacra of a religious body, just as, according to Tibetan accounts, the living Buddha could only be depicted from a reflection in water or an imprint in cloth. (Looking closely into the eyes of the divine therefore remains an occupational hazard that Tibetan artists must avoid at all costs.) Importantly it is the camera that captures the 'aura' of an exceptional individual in a way that blatantly contradicts Walter Benjamin's famous complaint that mechanical reproduction would destroy the aura of the authentic and the original art work in the West. The Thirteenth Dalai Lama seems to have deliberately encouraged an 'ideology of the charismatic individual' (Cardinal 1992: 6) and selected Bell to be his Felix Nadar. For him the photo-icon provided the possibility of making Barthesian 'certificates of presence', attesting that what is seen has existed, and that his very particular body had housed the incarnate godliness of a bodhisattva. Bell's photographs would also allow the aura of his personality to spread far beyond the immediate confines of his physical circumstances. It is worth noting that the

Thirteenth took this step at a point when he was in exile in British India. In the lifetime of his next incarnation (the Fourteenth, Tenzin Gyatso), the power of the photograph (both still and moving) would perform the even mightier task of communicating the narrative of Tibetan exile, from its base in independent India, to a massive global audience.

In the decades following the collaboration between Bell, the Thirteenth and his painter, the tinted zone surrounding the photographic 'certificate' became an area in which the agency of artists could be asserted. Exiled artists took this model and expanded the referential possibilities of material additions even further to acknowledge the social and political facts of relocation. Incorporating the Dalai Lama's index into a wider field they began to use photography within an aesthetic dialogue that, *contra* Barthes (1984: 82), could 'restore what has been abolished (by time and distance)'. In the West, Belting reminds us that the move towards art meant that the image became 'a simulated window in which either a saint or a family member would appear in a portrait. In addition, the new image was handed over to artists, who were expected to create from their own fantasy' (Belting 1994: 471). Tibetan exilic artists are not yet at liberty to create worlds of pure fantasy, particularly when they reference a religious prototype. There remains a degree to which, as in the era of iconometry and the use of stencils, human agency must be underplayed in the representation of a divine body. However, since the actions of the Thirteenth, the technology of camera enacts this principle and frees the artist to approach subjects without entering into the dangerous process of copying from life. However, while the indexicality of the camera recreates the bodies of reincarnate beings, emphasising their ongoing presence (and denying human agency), the 'likeness' of the homeland can only be imagined and artistically recreated. The landscape of Tibet has become a painted diorama or studio backdrop to a life lived in exile. It cannot become incarnate except when Tibetans return to the soil of their birth. Due to the political and psychological realities of the condition of exile it is the 'artness' of these images that enables a Benjaminian 'cult of remembrance' of a 'loved one' (such as the Dalai Lama) but especially of a 'beloved place absented' (Tibet).

However, Tibetan exilic identity should not be defined only in terms of nostalgia. The 'likeness' of other images reflects adaptation to the reinvented social and political boundaries of *nangpa* life. When representing the environment of the host country India, landscape appears to fall into the domain of photographic indexicality. In a 1990s photo-icon, the Fourteenth Dalai Lama is shown to occupy the same time and space as his followers (Figure 9.3). Like them he can stand in Indian locations such as Bodh Gaya (a favoured exile pilgrimage site and scene of Kalachakra initiations given by him), though his status as a sacred person is demonstrated by the image-maker in lines of irradiating light (emitted from his body as they had from the Buddha-body). In these photo-montages, photography and painting combine in a manner that destabilises the conventional 'realism' of indexical images as the sacred hierarchies of height are once again employed. Proportion, which presents the Dalai Lama as larger than the photographed life around him, also suggests that he eclipses the architectonic embodiments of the Buddha and those who perform *pradakshina* around the base of the Bodhi stupa. Here the Dalai Lama's status as bodhisattva of compassion (rather than *tam drin* or protector) and representative of pan-Asian Buddhism is privileged, acknowledging that he and his followers take solace in the fact that their 'home from

Figure 9.3 The Fourteenth Dalai Lama depicted at Bodh Gaya India. Street stall photo-icon purchased in Dharamsala, India, 1992. Maker unknown.

home' locates them in a wider community of Buddhists. In contrast to the imagined space of Tibet, this 'home' is observable and subject to different systems of viewing and representing.

Fundamentally, the possession and viewing of such images also relates to a condition of aspiration and expectation that both the Dalai Lama and the independent nation of Tibet will be reincarnated. This principle has been activated by monks at the monastery of Likir (Ladakh, India), where the Thirteenth Dalai Lama photo-icon hangs in the *du khang* (assembly hall) as an object of veneration but also a record of history and future expectations. They reference the reincarnatory lineage of Dalai Lamas by attaching two images of Tenzin Gyatso outside the Potala, surrounded by a crowd displaying the Tibetan flag to the image of his predecessor. The Thirteenth had designed this flag, the first ensign of the Tibetan nation, and predicted the calamitous events that would occur in the lifetime of the Fourteenth, though he did not foresee that both the flag and icon of the Fourteenth would be banned on Tibetan soil. For Tibetans the vulnerability and ephemerality of images and bodies is counteracted by the indestructible concept of transmigration of 'souls'.

This politicised conception of reincarnation is also powerful within the TAR and in recent years photo-icons have been utilised in a restorative process in which absent persons are returned to their rightful places. Young reincarnates, discovered in exile, are imagined at their monastery in the 'homeland'. The Dalai Lama revisits his seat of power, the Potala Palace, accompanied by an iconic representation of *Chenrezig* and the Tenth Panchen Lama, and the Potala (formerly the Dalai Lama's palace) is located in a landscapeless blue void: the tourist facilities, parades of shops, karaoke bars and other monuments to Deng-style consumerism, which currently surround it, are obliterated. This image was available in Lhasa in 1993 at a period when the prohibition of the production and sale of images was 'relaxed'. In the summer of that year the Barkhor, the ancient trading centre of the Tibetan capital and a circumambulation zone around the Jokhang (the most important temple in Tibet), was filled with stalls selling photo-icons. Such images were bought by pilgrims, many of whom were en route to Tashilunpo, the Panchen's monastery 30 miles south-east of Lhasa, where his remains were to be placed in a commemorative stupa. As the second highest ranking figure in Tibetan Buddhism, the Panchen Lama had not followed the Dalai Lama into exile but stayed on during the Chinese takeover to attempt to negotiate with PRC leaders. For his pains he spent much of his life in prison, and it was undoubtedly politic that his death (which some suspected was not from natural causes) should not lead to unrest. It should also be noted that the point of sale for his image, the Barkhor, had also been the primary zone for expressions of dissent during the 1989 riots in which monks and nuns were shot and killed by Chinese police.

Hence, for a brief period in the TAR, Tibetans were allowed to remember their dead and perhaps to dream of a different future in which the impact of China has been erased. Given the history of battles fought over images in Chinese occupied Tibet, it appears rather surprising that this activity was condoned by the Chinese authorities in Lhasa. I would suggest that this was possible due to contrasting systems of viewing between Chinese and Tibetans. PRC officials apparently saw no danger in Panchen photo-icons because for them they were mere memorials to the dead – certificates of presence without ongoing personhood – whereas for Tibetans such icons imply a lineage of individuals and a larger communal identity.

Another Barkhor photo-icon of the same year illustrates this point (Figure 9.4). It depicts three figures who no longer had physical presence in the TAR: the Dalai Lama (absent), the Panchen Lama (deceased) and the Buddha (long deceased). Here all three are re-presented photographically: the two monks by portraits taken in different locations (India and Tibet) and the Buddha by a photographed *thangka*. The montaged image condenses large expanses of time and geography in order for all three to appear in the same space that they occupy in the minds of Tibetans; that is, as part of a lineage of Buddhist teachers whose physical forms may alter but whose spirit transmigrates to an imagined place that currently does not exist, an independent Tibetan Buddhist nation. Only the photographic object with its power to reincarnate can currently distribute such a concept.

Conclusion

Today photography is one of the most powerful globalising technologies and, like television, is virtually ubiquitous, but as this case study has suggested we must not assume that universal coverage implies a universally consistent response. Tibetans engage with photographs in dynamic and productive ways that allow them to articulate culture-specific attitudes both ancient and modern. An anthropological approach to material and visual cultures enables us to engage with the novel forms emerging from such encounters between the global and the local, as Veena Das has observed when examining Indian soap opera. She stresses the importance of ethnography in

Figure 9.4 The Fourteenth Dalai Lama, the Tenth Panchen Lama and the Buddha. Street stall photo-icon purchased in Lhasa, Tibet, 1993. Maker unknown.

acknowledging the fact that 'local cultures do not simply kneel down in abject supplication before the onslaughts of global culture' (Das 1995: 170), identifies ways in which Indian television viewers are by no means passive recipients of images and shows how the narratives of TV programmes extend into everyday life. Her description of 'performative interaction' with the sacred tales of Hinduism as they appear in televised form has useful echoes for our analysis of Tibetan photographic engagement. For Hindu television viewers an episode in which Rama and Sita are married can inspire acts of devotion such as the distribution of sweets to friends and neighbours and 'in this sense the time of gods and the time of men is made synchronous' (Das 1995: 182). In the same way, then, the pious acts of Tibetans in the presence of photography have a similar aim in mind, to create the sense that they are coterminous with the gods and other perfected beings such as Dalai Lamas. Perhaps even more importantly there is also a desire to be coextensive with them (to share the same space and place) but, for refugees, any determination of rootedness in space is complicated by the fact that the homeland is a space denied. It is only in the artefactual domain in which photographs circulate that Tibetan bodies can reconnect with the aura of Tibet.

Notes

1 See Deborah Poole (1997) for further discussion of the ways in which the possession, circulation and exchange of photographs enhances their value.

2 Daniel Smith (1995: 35) notes that 'in the Tamil Nadu pilgrim town of Palni (where one of the foremost shrines to the popular South Indian deity, Murugan, is located) pilgrims return home with wallet-sized god posters of the deity, to be ingested as a curative later by members of the family who are ill'. In this Hindu context photographic objects are consumed like *prashad* (sanctified food). Though Tibetan Buddhists also consume the sanctified particles from 'sand' mandalas for the sake of their health, I have yet to come across an example of Tibetans ingesting photographs. For further analysis of Tibetan activities at pilgrimage sites see Huber (1999).

3 Tibetan paintings (*thangka*) of high-ranking religious figures sometimes include their hand or footprints on the reverse, and these, like photographs, are of course indexical traces. In the past they were also inscribed with the seed syllables of a relevant mantra (depending on which deity is depicted) by a monk rather than an artist, emphasising the importance of sacred touch. Today many photographically generated religious images have these letters printed on the back.

4 For discussion of human bodies being treated like things and vice versa see Gell (1998). His analysis of the pre-pubescent girl who performs the role of Kumari (a Hindu goddess in Nepal) bears comparison with the way in which Tibetan religious figures also become art-like or object-like when revered by devotees.

5 In Tibetan Buddhist philosophy the distinction between persons and things is not as sharply defined as in Judaeo-Christian cultures. Since the material world is made up of particles that recirculate into forms (through reincarnation), all things and persons are part of the same infinitely recurring cycle of movement between different states of being. Hence there is the possibility of returning to the world as an animal having previously lived as a person, for example. A thing (such as Buddha image) can become personlike (or more specifically godlike) when it is animated by a 'life force' during consecration ceremonies, just as, in the contrary direction, when a person dies his or her body becomes a mere thing.

6 This is probably coupled with a desire to emulate the display style of the clubs and residences of the British Raj.

7 Space precludes further discussion of these 'fields', but see Harris (1999).

8 It has not escaped the notice of the current Dalai Lama that this concept of 'particles' has parallels with the atomic building blocks of Western science. And he has held a colloquium with eminent physicists to explore the similarity. For a record of one such discussion see Chöyang (1991: 152–68).

9 I have discussed these issues at length in Harris (2001).

10

'PHOTO-CROSS'

The political and devotional lives of a
Romanian Orthodox photograph

Gabriel Hanganu

Introduction

In this chapter I explore how a visual object and the 'social lives' associated with it provide an entry point for analysing the relationship between Romanian Orthodox Christian religious practices and post-Second World War communist politics. My theoretical and methodological perspective is that of a visual anthropologist. Following Banks and Morphy (1997), I argue, on the one hand, that the conceptual worlds, sensorial experience and religious and political practices of the social groups involved in the production and use of that object are structured in mutually interdependent spheres. Drawing on recent fieldwork, my case study demonstrates how the Orthodox theological concepts associated with icon veneration are brought into relationship with the visual and material expectations of Orthodox Christians about photographically reproduced pilgrimage cards, and with the Stalinist political practices reinforced in Romania by local communists after the retreat of the Soviet Army.

On the other hand, I employ this case study to argue that both material and visual qualities are equally accountable for the 'social salience' acquired by certain objects, and therefore a common theoretical and methodological framework should be employed to study both material culture items and the 'visual systems' associated with the groups producing and employing them (Banks and Morphy 1997: 15–17). Here I suggest that if we ignore the material qualities of the object discussed, and the particular role ascribed to matter in Orthodox icon veneration, its devotional use in a domestic icon shrine as a photograph with the capability of physically embodying the sanctity of icons, cannot be properly assessed and understood.

The broader aim of this chapter is to address some of the theoretical issues raised by the anthropological study of photographic visual objects. Following Pinney (1997) and Edwards (2001), I use the photographic object discussed here as a way of relating the social worlds of its producers, assessors and users by paying attention to the particular ways in which the photographic medium and the associated photographic practices affect the construction of social values. Drawing on Gosden and Marshall (1999), I sketch out a 'cultural biography' of the object as it unfolds at the interplay between the Romanian political and religious backgrounds, and the biography of the photographer who created it five decades ago. More specifically, by elaborating the distinction emphasised by Edwards (2002: 68), between 'social biography of image content' and 'social biography of a particular photograph', I show how on several occasions during the object's 'life' its photographic support became crucial, determining the organisation of social relations in particular ways.

Finally, I address the issue of performativity of visual objects (Ginzburg 1983: 82), with a particular reference to photographic objects. Of the various forms of 'internal' and 'external' performativity, I focus on the interplay between what has been termed 'performance of the image through the spatial dynamic of its framing' and 'performance of reception' (Edwards 2001: 20). The successive stages in the production of the photographic object, influenced by the producers' assumptions about the users' visual and devotional experience of Orthodox icons, are placed in relationship with its presence in a domestic icon shrine. In addition, socialist economic and cultural impositions determined the ways in which independent artists used their domestic religious displays for exhibiting their work.

I.R. and the 'photo-cross'

The object through which I am exploring these relationships among religiosity, materiality and photography is a photograph of a photo-collage, produced by I.R., a photographer who had been active both before and after the Second World War, and who is a committed Orthodox Christian. The significance of this object emerged during my wider study of the 'social lives' of Orthodox Christian icons, in the context of the modification of local visual systems in Romania during the 40 years of socialism and after the political transformations of 1989.[1]

I.R., aged 86, and now in poor health, was very happy to talk about his long professional activity. He had started as an apprentice to a local photographer more than 70 years earlier, and had been a photographer all his life. He still had in his possession, and was willing to show me, various images, including original paintings by him, photographs he took for various clients in his studio, others that had won prizes in national competitions, as well as more complex visual objects he had created by cutting and pasting photographs, over-painting them and writing captions next to the images. Among those he showed me was the 'photo-cross' (as I shall refer to it), a postcard-sized photograph displaying a set of small photographs of the nunnery of Vladimiresti, arranged in the shape of a cross and surrounded by several religious images. I.R. had made this photo-montage in 1952, during the period of the harshest anti-religious persecution under the Romanian communist regime. As a result he was arrested and sentenced to ten years in prison.

This visual object emerged as an embodiment of the relationship between the political and religious spheres that entered into collision as soon as the communists seized political power in Romania. It also sheds light on the ways in which the relationship between the religious and artistic, respectively public and private domains, have been modified as a result of these political changes. I return below to the ways in which the material presentation of the photographs and their shifting performances made them so dangerous politically. First, it is necessary to describe the object itself.

The 'photo-cross' (Figure 10.1) is a complex visual object. One could be tempted to read it as an old black-and-white postcard of a Christian-related subject. Indeed, even

Figure 10.1 The 'photo-cross', a black-and-white photograph of the original photomontage by I.R., 1952.

to those unable to read the Romanian captions, the Christian connotation of the iconographic representations, religious symbols and cross-shaped display of the photographs is clearly evident. However, the familiar postcard format indicates a communication-oriented function of the object. Nothing is written on its back, and the printed gridlines usually found on the back of the postcards are also missing. However those familiar with Christian pilgrimage religious practices, and the visual objects circulated on these occasions, could assume, correctly, that the 'photo-cross' is in fact a pilgrimage card: a visual representational object acquired from, or on the road to, a location considered sacred by the pilgrims, and carried back home as an affective and spiritually significant reminder of the journey. To an audience acquainted with the Romanian Orthodox visual context, the 'photo-cross' is likely to look fairly unusual due to its material support (photograph) and its relatively elaborate structure. Unlike other images circulated at the Orthodox pilgrimage sites in both pre-socialist and socialist Romania, which were mainly prints rather than photographs, and which reproduced famous 'performing-miracles' icons or relics, the 'photo-cross' is a sophisticated multi-layered visual nexus, accomplished through a sequence of graphic, photographic, painting and collating processes.

The 'photo-cross' is a 5 × 7 inch black-and-white postcard-size photograph of an original photo-collage. The photo-collage itself comprised seven numbered black-and-white photographs pasted on a painted and ornamented cross-shaped frame. It is positioned with three painted religious images (two divine characters and a symbolic representation) and a set of handwritten titles and captions.

The captions associated with the seven numbered photographs read as follows:

1 *Crucea din porumb. Locul primei vedenii dumnezeiesti* (The cross in the corn field. The place of the first divine revelation)
2 *Bordeiul. Inceputul vietii calugaresti* (The hut. The beginning of the monastic life)
3 *Paraclisul. Primul locas de inchinare* (The small church. The first veneration site)
4 *Biserica Mare. Vedere interior* (The big church. Interior view)
5 *M. Stareta Veronica Intemeietoarea Manastirii* (Mother Veronica, superior and founder of the nunnery)
6 *M. Veronica in mijlocul soborului* (Mother Veronica amongst the monastic community)
7 *M. Veronica vorbind credinciosilor* (Mother Veronica preaching to the faithful).

Two smaller captions identify the painted figures above the cross as *Mantuitorul* (The Saviour) and *Maica Domnului* (Mother of God). A first heading, handwritten in capital letters at the very top of the image, reads *Locasul minunilor lui Dumnezeu* (The abode of God's miracles). A second title, in slightly bigger letters, placed at the bottom of the image, reads *Manastirea Maicii Domnului dela Vladimiresti* (The Vladimiresti nunnery of Mother of God). Finally, a thin black hand-drawn contour frames the image, and floral motifs drawn from folk decoration adorn its four corners.

I return to the significance of these images as images and the significance of their material presentation below, but in order to understand how such a seemingly innocuous object could become politically and devotionally active, one must describe both the political and theological environments in which it came to acquire meaning.

The political context

The coming to power of the Soviet-backed communists after the Second World War brought fundamental changes to the economic and political situation in Romania. The annihilation of the political opposition and the gradual emergence of the Communist

Party as the dominant and single political force in society went hand in hand with radical economic reforms, especially the nationalisation of industry and the collectivisation of agriculture. This brought about radical social shifts as Romania was saturated with a stringent communist ideology, which operated a climate of repression and denunciation to suppress monarchists, conservatives, liberals, and the intellectual and religious elite. Undesirables were labelled 'enemies of the socialist order' and were subject to show trials, the verdicts of which were predetermined.

As a former sympathiser of a radically anti-communist political group, I.R. did not have a safe position and he risked denunciation, which would have added his name to the blacklist of the increasingly powerful repressive system. When he was finally arrested in 1960, a key element in the accusation of 'plotting against the socialist order' was that, in addition to helping the impoverished families of priests imprisoned for their opposition to the regime. In the early 1950s he had illegally contributed to the production and distribution of the photographic pilgrimage card that praised the newly founded Orthodox nunnery of Vladimiresti, a stronghold of opposition to the state imposition of atheism in all spheres of activity.

The nunnery itself had been founded by Vasilica, an illiterate orphan peasant girl born in the village of Tudor Vladimirescu in southern Moldavia, who, in the summer of 1937, said she had seen a vision of Christ and the Mother of God in a beam of light on a hill near the village. Christ had commanded her to found a nunnery dedicated to the Mother of God for the redemption of Romania. Work began that very week, carving a cross from the wood of the old tree from beside which Christ had spoken to Vasilica. In 1941 Vasilica took the veil to become *maica* (Mother) Veronica. She continued to work side by side with the other novices, and in 1943 the church and the surrounding rows of cells and annexes built on the place of revelation were complete.[2]

The flourishing nunnery attracted the attention of the communist authorities. In 1948 the Romanian Communist Party Secretary paid a visit to Vladimiresti, unsuccessfully trying to persuade Mother Veronica to turn the model community of Vladimiresti into a commune ruled under the directives of the Central Committee. The convent had become an embarrassment to government and politburo, not least because it had long been suspected, correctly, that it had been used to shelter 'enemies' of the state. Moreover, it had become an increasingly popular pilgrimage site that attracted millions of pilgrims annually. Miracles were reported, and the nunnery also gave spiritual advice and moral comfort in the context of extreme political and economic difficulties, faced with post-war reparations and the Soviet Red Army billeted in the country.

These pilgrims were the intended audience for the 'photo-cross'. The impetus for the card came from Father Ioan, an Orthodox priest attached to the monastery since 1947. His intention was to produce a sort of religious souvenir that could be disseminated among the pilgrims, focusing attention on the miraculous foundation, and hence the special religious vocation, of the nunnery. He knew I.R., who had previously visited the nunnery, and asked for his support in producing the desired object.

The nunnery's stance against religious persecution, and especially the anti-state preaching of Father Ioan, culminated in 1955, when he addressed a personal letter to the government, in which he accused the socialist state of gross intervention within the religious beliefs of the people, and the officials of the Orthodox Church of collaboration with the atheist government. As a result, he and Mother Veronica were arrested and charged as 'enemies of the people', and one year later the nunnery was requisitioned. Although released in an amnesty of political prisoners in 1964, Father Ioan, Mother Veronica and the nuns were subjected variously to a brutal regime of beatings, torture, hard labour, systematic ridicule and public humiliation.

The closing down of Vladimiresti was the beginning of one of the harshest periods of religious persecution in Romania. If initially, within the general climate of under-ground opposition to the foreign occupation, the Romanian communist elite and Orthodox Church hierarchy had often backed up each other against the Soviets, by the end of the 1950s the political power relationships were being renegotiated. The withdrawal of the Soviet-appointed politburo and the retreat of the Red Army in 1958 found the local communist leaders anxious to exercise their new power. This resulted in a new series of purges targeted at the alleged 'enemies of the socialist order', including many members of religious institutions and monastic communities.[3]

I.R. himself was a 'beneficiary' of these purges. Although the authorities knew of his role in producing the 'photo-cross', he had escaped being interrogated when Father Ioan was arrested in 1955. However, the purges of the late 1950s activated his poten-tial 'enemy' status, and his former collaboration with Father Ioan and other clergymen who had opposed the regime was seen as incriminating.

The status of the 'photo-cross' itself was modified as a result of the political changes. From a religious souvenir and a foundational account of Vladimiresti it turned into an ideologically loaded and politically dangerous object. The meaning assigned by its makers was modified and reappropriated according to the understanding and shifting interests of the Romanian communist leaders. If until 1955 Vladimiresti, as a poten-tially rebellions community, was tolerated, Father Ioan's letter accusing both local communists and the Orthodox hierarchy resulted in the activation of the potential 'enemy' status of the nunnery, and consequently its social and political stigmatisation. However, only those directly involved were repressed. No concerted action was taken against the alleged 'collaborators', or frequent visitors to the place. At that stage the 'photo-cross' itself did not represent a direct threat to political power, as proved by the fact that I.R., who co-produced the object, was not involved in Father Ioan's trial. Like I.R. himself, the 'photo-cross' was ideologically only a 'virtual enemy', and it was probably possible for the pilgrims to keep it at home as long as it was not publicly displayed or circulated.

However, by 1959, following the power shift in favour of the local communists, not only the open protesters against the regime became punishable, but all those suspected of having been connected with politically stigmatised people or events. I.R.'s arrest emphasised that by that date the 'photo-cross' had become ideologically an 'active enemy' in the eyes of the regime, and arguably even the simple possession of a copy could become incriminatory for its owner.

In addition to its image content, the materiality of the 'photo-cross' as a photo-graphic object was an important element in the reappropriation of its social meaning by various groups at different moments in time. One must bear in mind that the 'photo-cross' was both a photographically produced and a photographically reproduced object. I point out below that in the particular case of a photographic object the alteration of the status of one copy affects all existing and subsequent generations of copies. Now I turn to the producers' intentions in creating the 'photo-cross', and analyse the degree to which its materiality, in addition to its image content, was taken into consideration and influenced the producers' decisions, as well as the audiences' responses.

Religious contexts of production

I.R. knew that the photographs he took at Vladimiresti in 1952 were to be used for a photo-montage postcard, but he could not imagine, at the time of photographing, either the visual or the textual contexts of which they would eventually be part. Selecting the images, adjusting their size and shape, ordering them in a number-associated sequence, assigning them a place on the painted cross, captioning them, placing them next to the painted religious images and within the adorned frame of the photo-montage and finally rephotographing the maquette and reproducing it, in multiple copies, in the postcard-sized format, were all subsequent processes to which he made a limited contribution and over which he had little control, as it was Father Ioan and, to a lesser extent, Mother Veronica who determined the final form of the 'photo-cross'.[4]

In producing the photo-cross Father Ioan required an object that was *portable* (in that it was thin, small and light), one that was *replicable* through mass production and thus replaceable, as well as *accessible*, in that it was cheap both to produce and to buy. While many objects sold on pilgrimage sites displayed these material qualities, the visual object he needed had to be an item specially designed for Vladimiresti, as he was convinced of the particular religious vocation of the place. Therefore, supplementary *narrative* and *biographical* qualities were required from the planned pilgrimage card, which was to act as a sort of visual identity card of the monastery. To that end, photography proved to be the most appropriate medium. Through the complex solution of the photo-collage, the 'photo-cross' was able to accommodate both the indexicality of the seven photographs and the symbolic and iconic values 'injected' by the painted religious images. Thus it met both the general requirements for pilgrimage objects and the particular features meant to highlight the special status of Vladimiresti.

Unlike other photographic postcards of pilgrimage sites displaying famous icons or relics preserved on the site, which are still produced and disseminated in contemporary monasteries (Figure 10.2), the 'photo-cross' was more concerned with what could be labelled 'the objectification of a miraculous biography' (Hanganu, forthcoming). Veronica's revelation was a biographical, rather than objectual, 'anchor', and in order to emphasise this the photographs had been arranged in the 'photo-cross' in a particular manner. Their individual indexically based visual narratives had been deliberately altered through cropping, numbering and miniaturisation in order to fit a *biographical* order anchored by the captions.[5] Sometimes these complemented, and at other times they subverted, an *iconographical* order suggested by the shape of the cross, painted images of Christ and Mother of God.

While a detailed account and analysis of icon production is beyond the scope of this chapter (see, for example, Nicolescu 1971; Stefanescu 1973; Evdokimov 1990; Ouspensky 1992), it can be said that in the case of the 'photo-cross' two distinct scenes of traditional Orthodox iconography, employed as models, had been adapted and displayed around the cross-shaped photo-collage in order to build up a new meaning. A votive scene, comprising the founders, the Mother of God interceding for them, the

Figure 10.2 Colour postcard of the Monastery of Bisericani. In the centre is the locally vener-
ated icon of the Mother of God. Unlike other Moldavian Orthodox monasteries
preserving famous old icons of Byzantine origin, the Monastery of Bisericani has
reshaped its identity around a newer icon, locally revered for working miracles.
Postcard published by Trinitas, 1999. Purchased 2000.

maquette of the newly built church and Christ receiving and blessing it, had been
placed next to a 'protection veil' representation, showing the Mother of God praying
with outstretched arms and covering the church at her feet with her veil. As a result,
through a complex process of meaning translation and adaptation, the cross bearing

the seven photographs had become associated with the newly built church offered by the founders to Christ for blessing, bringing the church under the protection of the Mother of God's veil. Read in the general context of the two sets of captions and the symbolic image, the general meaning of the cross, which in Orthodoxy has always been associated with the Resurrection to which the Crucifixion leads, was integrated through the pasting of the seven photographs with the individualising topos of special election by revelation, thus investing Veronica and the community with the exemplary status of martyrdom.

The image content and the materiality of the medium were therefore equally important issues addressed by the producers of the 'photo-cross' during the process of the construction of its 'internal' meaning. But on a less visible level, the production process also involved a fine tuning of the object's intended use to the cultural and religious expectations of the pilgrims who came to Vladimiresti. Father Ioan's project employed familiar iconographic and symbolic images, such as the shape of the cross and its relationship with other images, as I have just suggested. They resonated both culturally and sensorially with the pilgrims' visual and material experience of the religious images employed in Orthodox devotion, and in particular the religious cards circulated at pilgrimage places.

In Orthodox Christianity pilgrimage is closely connected with icon and relic veneration, and therefore the cards acquired on such occasions often reproduce the 'wonder-working' icons, or the images of the saints whose relics are preserved on the site. Unlike Latin Christianity, which, following the teachings of Aquinas and Bonaventura, ascribed a mainly instrumental and representational role to religious images (Freedberg 1989: 166),[6] Orthodoxy has often emphasised that icons are devotional objects meant to convey spiritual energies between the visible humans and the invisible divine characters. In order to be activated, they require the veneration of devotees. The devotional character of icons is based on the particular Orthodox understanding of the relationship between religious image and divine prototype, according to which the rightful veneration of an icon by a devotee will pass on to the depicted prototype;[7] conversely, the spiritual energies released by a divine person will be forwarded through the icon down to an appropriately receiving devotee. But, importantly for my argument here, it is equally rooted in the particular understanding of matter itself in Orthodoxy, as a worthy complement of the Spirit, equally necessary for the deification of man and the transfiguration of the created cosmos. Matter is not evil or impure, and it does not deter man's soul from acquiring salvation; on the contrary, it was originally made good by God, and even after the Fall it was deemed worthy of bearing Spirit, as proved by God's Incarnation.[8]

This belief that matter can bear a spiritual charge explains the relationship between image and matter in Orthodox devotion. Icons themselves are seen not as images only, but as indivisible compounds of religious images and material supports. Consequently, the devotional practices associated with their veneration consist of a mixture of verbal, mental and bodily devotion, such as kneeling, crossing, prostrating and eventually kissing them, thus involving a crucial embodied relationship with images.

Seen from this perspective, the pilgrimage to a sacred place is an activity meant to facilitate the aim of Christian life, which in the memorable formulation attributed to St Seraphim of Sarov is the acquisition of the Holy Spirit while still in a human body. During a pilgrimage this is attempted by addressing particular divine persons through their icons or relics displayed for veneration on the site, by seeing renowned elders known as 'Spirit bearers' residing in the neighbourhood, or by simply interacting physically with an environment imbued with spiritual presence. The objects acquired from pilgrimage sites themselves are thought to be imbued with spiritual energy, and their presence in the domestic icon shrines is thought to facilitate individual prayer and protect the household. Therefore, the practice of taking pilgrimage cards home has always been strongly associated in the pilgrims' minds with religious devotion. Cards so imbued with sanctity were often pinned up in domestic icon shrines, and included in the devotional acts associated with daily prayers.

It can be argued, therefore, that the pilgrims who visited Vladimiresti in the early 1950s understood the 'photo-cross' as a devotionally employable visual object. Despite the card's title, referring to the pilgrimage place rather than any particular icon or relic preserved there, the familiar size, format and system of distribution of the 'photo-cross', as well as the visual religious 'triggers' of the cross and the painted Christ and Mother of God, must have acted in favour of a reading along the same lines as the other pilgrimage cards circulated on such occasions.

It is not known how many of the 5,000 or so copies of the 'photo-cross' distributed at Vladimiresti were actually used along with other religious paraphernalia effectively employed in daily devotion, but arguably one can assume that some had been employed in that way, at least until the closing down of the nunnery in 1955, but possibly also at a later stage, during the less repressive periods of the socialist regime. As I discuss in the next section, for a limited period of time I.R. himself used a copy of the 'photo-cross' in that way. His case was obviously very particular, since he had both participated in, and suffered the consequences of, producing the object. Yet, as a practising Christian, he shared with the other pilgrims a common visual and material experience of religious images, and particularly important for my argument here, the practical habit of displaying them in domestic shrines as elements that could be devotionally 'activated'. This was slightly different from the intentions of the producers, who mainly wanted to convey the particular martyric status of Vladimiresti, although not as different as was its reading as 'enemy' by the communist leaders. In the following section I address this issue of the shifting biography of the 'photo-cross' by emphasising a distinction suggested by Edwards (2002: 68) between the biography of a particular photographic object and the biography of its image content. In doing so I look at the way in which the 'photo-cross' survived, and is entangled with I.R.'s own history.

Contexts of display and use

Materiality is key for the understanding of the different photographic copies as objects with their own distinct biographies. I.R. issued various sets of copies of the 'photo-cross' after 1952.[9] Having reproduced the original batch in his studio, he kept a few exemplars for himself and sent the rest to Vladimiresti. Of the preserved copies, some were offered to trusted friends and clients in Piatra Neamt, and the others were confiscated by the authorities when he was arrested in 1960. Back from prison, I.R. worked for several years in his former studio, which in the meantime had turned into a socialist photographic cooperative. Then in 1973, taking advantage of a short-lived easing of control by the regime, he opened a photographic studio in his house, in association with one of his daughters. Although part of the same building, the studio employed a room with a separate entrance, which allowed I.R. to meet clients, take photographs and process negatives as if he worked in a completely separate location. On the walls of the room he displayed a range of work samples, mainly studio portraits, but also occasionally reproductions of icons and other religion-related projects. The relative religious liberties of the period also allowed him to display in his icon shrine images that for many years had been exposed to the risk of being denounced as a political undesirable. Among these icons there was a copy of the 'photo-cross', which had miraculously escaped the communist purges by having been kept in a different location. Although it was not used effectively in devotion as such, the simple fact of its being present in the shrine provided I.R. with a particular feeling, which he described as 'beneficial to praying'.

A few years later, when the cultural and religious liberties were again restricted,[10] and the small family business became illegal once more, the commissioning of independently produced photographic work could only be done unofficially, through networks of friends, relatives and professional connections. I.R. continued to use his studio in a semi-official manner, but the religious commissions, which had become his speciality, could not be displayed officially anymore, so he pinned some of them up in his icon shrine. Occasionally he invited trusted clients who visited him to see these images as models for potential commissions. It would appear that they were removed from the shrine quite often and passed to the visitors for closer inspection, for they still bear the physical marks of repeated handling. Thus these religious projects, including the 'photo-cross', gradually became engaged in a supplementary visual context, within which they were shown and commented upon not only symbolically and theologically, but also materially and technologically.

The separate location of the studio had allowed I.R. to keep the religious images displayed in his shrine away from the photographic samples displayed for the general public, and thus to select the work shown to the clients who visited him. However, this became impossible during the last period of his professional activity. As a result of the gargantuan socialist plan under Ceauşescu, aimed at reshaping both the Romanian architectural landscape and the citizens' individual identity, I.R.'s house was demolished in 1986. I.R. and his wife were relocated in the two-bedroom apartment of a newly built socialist block. There he continued to do some work as a retired 'independent' photographer, although the high taxation rate prescribed for this professional status, the difficulties in getting access to materials and the challenge of the better located state-run photographic studios drastically limited his production capacity.[11]

In addition, the impossibility of employing a separate space as a studio affected the social strategies necessary in order for his work to be advertised. Since I.R. was not a member of the national Party-controlled Association of Artist Photographers, and therefore could not publicly exhibit his work, he realised that in the cramped space of the apartment block, the only suitable space for displaying samples of his religious-based work was the icon shrine. Any visitor could see these images as they were pinned up there for I.R.'s own religious and aesthetic enjoyment, and thus he could not be accused of illegally advertising independently produced work. Without being prompted by the host, such occasional visitors passed their impressions about the photographs to friends and connections, thus carrying out in a more or less conscious manner what could be termed an *apophatic*, or negative style of advertisement, consisting – very much in the Orthodox style of conveying information – in silently seducing the religious and aesthetic sensibility of a random audience, rather than attempting to persuade a targeted set of individuals.

Giving gifts to the potential clients was also part of the practice. I.R. pointed out that there had been situations when visitors particularly liked certain images displayed in his 'icon shrine', and he offered them as gifts, then replaced them either with similar copies or with other images. This 'compositional elasticity' of the shrine did not seem to affect its devotional quality. Despite the variable identity and number of the icons, the shrine continued to function for I.R. as a devotional visual interface, in front of which he addressed prayers, burnt his oil lamp and smeared his forehead with myrrh. I.R.'s case was not singular. The icon shrines of many other visual artists (including painters, sculptors, textile weavers) who produced religion-related objects during the late socialist period became multilayered visual contexts adapted to fulfil this kind of 'soft' advertising task without impending on their devotional quality.

Having moved into the new block, I.R. had to rethink the structure of his icon shrine due to the lower ceiling level and smaller surface of the bedroom. Some of the large icons were replaced either with smaller ones or with over-painted black-and-white photographic reproductions made by himself (Figure 10.3). But with I.R.'s increasing involvement in the unofficial photographic networks, the composition of his icon shrine became even more subject to external conditions, influenced as it was by the tastes and interests of his religious commissioners. By the late 1980s the 'photo-cross' itself became a 'victim' of this externally driven selection process. Due to its subject's lack of appeal, and the relatively complex production process, it was removed from the icon shrine and stored safely in I.R's personal archive next to some other photographic projects. Instead, a less sophisticated Vladimiresti-related photograph became a favourite, and was accommodated in the structure of the shrine.

For that project I.R. had inserted a reduced-size photograph of the Vladimiresti church within a larger photograph of a protection veil mural scene (Figure 10.4). The resulting photo-collage had been rephotographed, then over-painted and framed in order to enhance its icon-like appearance. The use of the photo-collage, as well as the caption attached, individualised the iconographic scene by creating the impression that it was the Vladimiresti church in particular, rather than just any Orthodox church, that benefited from the special gift of Mother of God.

However, it was possible to change the name of the monastery displayed in the title without affecting the overall meaning of the 'photo-cross'. That made the photographic object less obviously connected with a particular time and place, thus increasing its value as a potentially broader Orthodox visual scheme. Unlike the 'photo-cross', which was related structurally at a much deeper level with the biography of Vladimiresti, the more elastic composition, and simpler religious message, of the other project appealed to many visitors, who commissioned similar cards, either for themselves or to have them sold in church shops in and around Piatra Neamt.

Nevertheless, for the potential clients interested in the miraculous foundation of Vladimiresti, I.R. issued a new set of copies from the original 'photo-cross' negative, which had also escaped the communist checks of his studio. The new copies were processed in the dark room improvised in I.R.'s bathroom, using cheap chemicals and the only photographic paper available locally, and they conveyed a higher contrast

Figure 10.3 I.R.'s icon shrine, Piatra Neamt. The mixture of styles, materials and production techniques is supplemented by the various provenances of the displayed items: purchased, gifted or produced by I.R. himself. A hand-painted copy of I.R.'s protection veil montage (see Figure 10.4) hangs to the centre left. Photograph: Gabriel Hanganu, 2000.

grey toning and slightly broader format in order to allow the captions and the seven tiny photographs to be more easily read.

It was precisely one of these recent copies that I.R showed me when I first met him. Later, when I was able to compare it with I.R.'s 1952 copy, I was struck by the

Figure 10.4 The protection veil cast above the monastery of Vladimiresti: black-and-white postcard-sized photograph of an original photomontage by I.R., 1952.

different formation of the marks of handling. The more recent copy had clearly never been pinned up in the icon shrine, although it was occasionally shown to visitors. During the previous ten years it was preserved in easily accessible storage in an ordinary A4 envelope, and therefore its dog-eared corners and bent surface witnessed an evident three-dimensional deformation. On the contrary, the general look of the older copy was incredibly flat. Despite the clearly visible manipulation marks – two pin holes in its upper edges, rounded corners and dirt traces on its lower and left edges – the print did not have the curvature or rough surface one might have expected. That was precisely because the old copy had spent the previous decade compressed in one of I.R.'s albums, and as a result the handling marks were reduced to two-dimensionality. The tenacity of the 'photo-cross' as an object that remained covertly active and was cared for as a print, especially given that the negative was still available, again points to the way in which materiality was integral to its power.

This material-based comparison is crucial to the understanding of the two copies as different photographic objects with separate biographies. It allows us to reflect on the entire and multiple biographies of the 'photo-cross', and become fully aware that the relationship between the various photographic objects sharing the same visual content is not fixed. On the contrary, it is active, and the status of each copy ultimately depends on the status of the others. When, at the end of my fieldwork, I.R. gave me his old copy of the 'photo-cross', releasing it from his personal archive, its potential as a socially salient object was suddenly reactivated. With the publication of a printed image of the 'photo-cross' in this book, its status, and indeed the status of any other 'dormant' copy that might exist in personal or institutional archives, has already acquired the potential to be resuscitated and re-evaluated.

Similarly, I.R.'s imprisonment had affected the status not only of the copy of the 'photo-cross' attached to his incriminating file, but also of all the copies preserved in his studio and distributed at Vladimiresti, and each owner of a copy became virtually associated with an 'enemy' status. Even after I.R. was released from prison, throughout the whole socialist regime, the stigmata associated with the nunnery continued to affect the status of other copies that might have survived, as well as that of their owners. This may explain my unsuccessful attempts to identify further copies in Piatra Neamt during my fieldwork. Even people whom I knew, from other sources, had been to Vladimiresti in the early 1950s told me that they had not seen the 'photo-cross' before. Although in some cases that might have been true, it was still very probable that some had acquired copies of the 'photo-cross' from Vladimiresti, but then either destroyed them for fear of becoming victims of the communist purges or kept them secretly, still avoiding talking about them.

Conclusion

This case study adds to the increasing body of work that argues for the study of 'socially salient' visual objects from a theoretical and methodological perspective drawing from both visual anthropology and material culture studies (such as Banks and Morphy 1997). The shifting status of the first-generation copy of the 'photo-cross' makes up an extremely rich cultural biography of the object, built at the interplay between the initial agenda of the producers, the sensorial and spiritual experience of the devotees and the conceptual and devotional frameworks of Orthodox Christianity, all set against the shifting background of social, economic and political practices enforced during the past five decades of Romanian history. My argument has been that only by paying attention to both the visual and material qualities of the 'photo-cross' can the relationships between these intertwined worlds be properly addressed. For instance, had I only addressed the image content of the 'photo-cross', and analysed exclusively the more recent copy I was shown when I first met I.R., I would have missed the relevant 'detail' that an older incarnation of the same image had been pinned up in I.R.'s shrine, as revealed in the material traces. That would have prevented me from considering the hypothesis that some of the Vladimiresti pilgrims had employed their own 'photo-cross' cards in a similar manner. Additionally, I would have failed to understand that the contemporary lack of visibility of these copies did not necessarily mean that they had become unimportant for their owners.

This case study also emphasises how the particularities of the photographic medium influence the structuring of the social relationships in ways that would be differently articulated had another medium been employed. For instance, had the 'photo-cross' been a printed image, rather than a photographically reproduced one, the social and political implications of its production would have been quite different. The greater dissemination potential of a printing press would have been likely to have alarmed the communist authorities more than a manually produced set of photographs, and such 'sabotage' would have been punished exemplarily, instead of being tolerated as a mere inoffensive religious project. The cultural biography of photographic objects, and in particular the distinction between the biography of a particular copy and the biography of its image content (Edwards 2002: 68), is a useful analysis tool that can be successfully employed in the study of religious objects, in this case photographically reproduced religious cards. This distinction helpfully emphasises the materiality of the photographic images employed in religious devotion, and reorients researchers' interest from the mere symbolic interpretation of the image content to the ways in which the objects themselves are being socialised among the people who produce and employ them. As I have demonstrated through this discussion of a photographic object integrally entangled with active religious and devotional practices of Romanian Orthodox Christianity, the unilateral interpretation and dichotomy of key concepts, such as 'image' and 'materiality', is inadequate to understand the complexity and social use of such image-objects. Engagement with the particular meaning of such concepts and the associated religious practices that socially embody the interplay between the respective religious concepts and objects are essential for a fuller understanding.

This chapter also addresses, by implication, the issue of the researcher's access to pre-existing objectual evidence, in addition to textual and visual data that are being recorded during fieldwork. In the context of my case study, a question that still persists is whether the copies of the 'photo-cross' that had been distributed at Vladimiresti are lost or merely socially invisible. More than a decade after the end of the totalitarian political regime in Romania people are still unwilling to disclose links with previously 'stigmatised' persons and events. This should represent an important methodological warning for researchers studying social biographies of objects in societies that have recently experienced traumatic social treatment. Such scholars should be ready to challenge one of the main biases engrained in contemporary Western scholarship, which tends to associate the existence of these 'socially salient' objects exclusively with their social visibility.

Notes

1 Between 1999 and 2001 I spent 18 months undertaking field research in Piatra Neamt, a small town in north western Moldavia, Romania, as part of my doctoral work in anthropology.

2 One story tells how Vasilica toured the country seeking finance. One day she found herself at Peles Castle at Sinaia, where she approached a man in overalls working on a motorcar.

He told her to wait, went inside and returned with a casket of jewels. Later, further donations of cement and wood for construction were made, and the beneficiary turned out to be King Mihai of Romania.

3 For instance, the promulgation of Decree 410, effective from 1959 to 1965, resulted in a halving of the number of theological seminaries and monastic communities (most of the smaller convents were closed altogether), and the interdiction for lay persons to become monks or nuns before the age of 60.

4 Unlike Mother Veronica, who only completed her education later in life, Father Ioan was highly educated, having carried out postgraduate theological studies prior to his arrival at Vladimiresti. To some extent the theological ideas conveyed through the 'photo-cross', and their visual and material embodiment, must have been influenced by the type of approach and scholarship available in the theological academic training of the period.

5 For instance, the invisibility of Mother Veronica from the photographs numbered 6 and 7 is contradicted by the captions that affirm her presence.

6 Latin Christianity maintained a circumspect view on the ontological transparency of the visual connection realised by means of religious images. According to Aquinas, Christian images could be used for the instruction of the unlettered, who might learn from them as from books. They could also be successfully used as reminders of the important historical events of Christianity. For Bonaventura, the need for images came from our human shortcomings: the ignorance of our mind, the sluggishness of our emotions, the lability of our memory. Religious images 'stood for' the 'heavenly kingdom', but no relation of resemblance was required between the represented image and its referent. Both Aquinas and Bonaventura located religious images within a 'semiotic aesthetics' (Freedberg 1989: 162–6). Unlike Christian Orthodox practice, which followed the Byzantine tradition and integrated icon veneration within the Liturgy, Catholicism removed the images from the spiritual core of the Church, and assigned them an instrumental and representational role.

7 The Seventh Ecumenical Council in Nicaea (AD 787), which concluded the eighth-century iconoclast debates, stated that it was in accordance with the Christian theological doctrine to represent and venerate Christ, the Mother of God and the saints through the intermediary of their icons: 'the honour which is paid to the icon passes on to that which the icon represents, and he who reveres the icon reveres in it the person who is represented'. See English translations of the main sources in St John of Damascus (1980) and St Theodore the Studite (1981).

8 The Incarnation is key for the understanding of the status of matter in Orthodoxy. In addition to having demonstrated that God can be visually represented, Christ also constituted the proof that matter can acquire spirit, and be thus 'transfigured': 'If flesh became a vehicle of the spirit, then so – though in a different way – can wood and paint' (Ware 1997: 42). This optimistic view of Orthodoxy on the transfigurative potential of matter is rooted in the Book of the Genesis, according to which the world was made good by God. This theme of the original 'sacredness of the world' is further expanded by certain Christian Fathers, such as the seventh-century St Maxim the Confessor, who maintains that the Creator endowed each created thing with a *logos*, or inner principle, that makes each thing uniquely and distinctively that which it is, and at the same time connects it with God in an essential yet invisible manner. It is through these subtle cosmic links, nourished by the divine energies, that the world is being preserved and developed. Within this context, and crucially for the argument here concerning the photo-cross, matter is not just 'inert stuff', but a living, energetically driven element of Creation.

9 Some other copies might have been done by others, by photographing, photocopying, scanning etc. exemplars from the initial batch of cards that had been distributed at Vladimiresti, those gifted by I.R., and confiscated by the communist authorities, or those

issued by I.R. later on. The limited space of the chapter allows me to discuss here only the series of copies reproduced by I.R. himself.

10 Significant for the desperate attempts of Ceauşescu's late socialist regime to preserve some external positive image against the appalling Western reports about the human and cultural rights violations in Romania was the commissioning of I.R. by the regional ecclesiastical authorities for what ironically turned out to be one of the largest projects of his professional career. For about four weeks he was offered a car with a driver, and all the quality materials and technology necessary to photograph about 100 important monasteries and churches in Moldavia. The images illustrated an album designed for international distribution, which emphasised 'the care of the Romanian socialist regime for the national historical and religious heritage'.

11 In order to survive professionally I.R. had to perform little services for people working in the photographic units of the state-run institutions, who helped him with materials and technology, and with maintaining contacts with the local Orthodox hierarchy, which had the ability to distribute photographically reproduced postcards through the internal commercial system of church shops.

11

PRINT CLUB PHOTOGRAPHY IN JAPAN

Framing social relationships

Richard Chalfen and Mai Murui

The more [photo] stickers I have, the more comfortable I feel about my relations with others . . . This notebook [photo-sticker album] is proof I have lots of friends.

(Teenage female interviewed in a Tokyo arcade, June 1996; Naito 1996)

Students can not imagine school life without Print Club.

(Voigt 1998: 15)

[The] purikura phenomenon is more than just a short-term fad and . . . may be turning into an established part of Japanese culture.

(http://tomen.co.jo/we/we29/mosaic/mosaic.html)

Introduction

Japan has offered the world an example of pictorial communication that has seemingly escaped scholarly[1] and even, for many, general attention. Readers of this book and related scholarly publications may not be aware of an immensely popular form of Japanese vernacular imagery known as Print Club. The purpose of this chapter is to introduce Print Club to visual social scientists by first describing this phenomenon and then placing its significance within the rich fabric of Japanese visual culture. In doing so, we discuss several emergent themes that help us connect our Print Club data to key features of Japanese society and culture, namely important issues of consumerism, youth culture and gender as related to the social order. Most non-Japanese people are not familiar with a form of photography that since 1995 has proved to be enormously popular in Japan, and that has begun to spread across the world. Conversely, it would be very hard to find a Japanese person who had not heard of Print Club. To Western ears, 'Print Club' is an awkward phrase of problematic meaning. In Japan, Print Club is also known as *Purinto Kurabu* or, in its most popular abbreviation and colloquial version, *Purikura*. *Purikura* refers to a combination of technology and photography, specifically a digital photo booth that within moments produces a small page of colour photo stickers. Though considerable variation now exists, originally these machines delivered a page of 16 small, 20 × 25 mm colour photographs for

300 yen. Details of these postage stamp-sized pictures and recent developments are given below. The machine has been described as an 'innovative revamping of the old instant photo booth'[2] and appears like a cross between an automatic passport/licence photo machine and a video game. This booth contains a computer connected to a colour video camera and a colour printer. In the most basic terms, the machine provides users with a fast and cheap way to get multiple small images of themselves. Were there not much more to *Purikura* than this, we would not have much to say, but such is not the case. Given the continued popularity of *Purikura* well into the twenty-first century, one suspects that something else is going on. Clearly Print Club represents something different, and seems to provoke new and popular habits of personal representation, social affiliation and, perhaps, identity.

Why do we find such popularity of these photographs at this time in Japan? Ultimately we want to speculate on why Japanese people and Japanese culture have welcomed and heartily endorsed the practice of Print Club. Can we identify features of a vibrant Japanese visual culture that might be responsible for Purikura popularity? Is Print Club another product in a succession of short-lived fads? How might *Purikura* represent something trendy – that is, something new and modern – while still conforming to the old and traditional? What are Print Club users saying about themselves and their identities as members of Japanese culture? Is there a particular connection of culture and visual communication that might be easily overlooked by Western observers?

Technical development and growing popularity

The original concept for Print Club came from Sasaki Miho, a 30-year-old employee of the Tokyo-based Atlus Co. Ltd, who proposed and developed the idea. She thought that having photo-stickers of herself and her friends would be lots of fun. In July 1995, Atlus, the original developer of Print Club, joined forces with the well known video game manufacturer Sega Enterprises Ltd to produce and distribute Print Club machines throughout Japan. Primary locations included game arcades, fast food shops, train stations, karaoke shops, bowling alleys and other popular culture locations.

This type of photograph was first introduced in Japan in February 1995, and Atlus expected it to be very popular with families as an inexpensive addition to family photograph collections. Miho said: 'I kind of expected that older couples and families would take Print Club pictures during dates and family trips' (Anonymous 1998a). But, initially, the older generation did not accept this innovative pictorial form with any sense of enthusiasm.[3] When the machines were put into game arcades in June 1995, they were met with similar lack of interest.

In short, Print Club practice spread very quickly and virtually exploded.[4] Just one year later, by June 1996, 3,500 photo booths were available mostly in the bigger Japanese cities, and by March 1998, 25,000 were in operation. The enormous popularity of Print Club in 1997 is documented, with reports of one location in Harajuku, Tokyo, having 25 photo booths, with as many as 2,000 customers on Saturdays and Sundays and as many as 1,000 on weekdays. Friends have reported to us that it was not unusual to see people standing on sidewalks, lined up around city blocks, waiting to use Print Club. In one 1998 article we read that 'each machine in Japan averages 100 "plays" a day' (Voigt 1998: 15).

Photo booths and picture content

Photo booths essentially produce informal portraits of between one and five people (seven might be the record) – two or three are the norm. One enters a Print Club booth by stepping behind a vinyl curtain to stand in front of the machine. One looks into a video monitor displaying the user's image and offering a choice of backgrounds. A user can select a background (or 'frame'), then deposit 300 yen (approximately US $2.70 as of mid-1999), strike several self-monitored preferred poses for an unseen video camera attached to the monitor, select the best pose, wait a minute and then receive a sheet of photo stickers. Patrons can then use a pair of scissors attached to the machine to divide the sheet among themselves.

Each photo sticker image comprises two components, namely people and backgrounds. First and foremost, the photo stickers show people, usually heads and shoulders; the backgrounds create a frame surrounding people in the picture. We learned that changing one's choice of photo-partners is as important as changing the choice of surrounding background, making Print Club very hard to 'do' just once.[5] Relationships of both social and visual factors, responsible for 'repeat business', as connected to issues of evidence of personal and social affiliation, are discussed below.

The other key factor focuses on changing the non-human content of the images. Print Club is often spoken of in terms of 'frames'. Frame refers to the decorations that surround the rectangular horizontal image format. In conjunction, such decorations might be seasonal or feature other thematic features. Frames might include celebrity faces; for instance, popular cartoon and *manga* (comic book) characters such as Doraemon, Miffy, Atom Boy, Snoopy, Cupid, Snowman, Harvey, Winnie the Pooh, Tweety Bird, Hello Kitty or a Disney character such as Mickey or Minnie Mouse (Figure 11.1).

There are also frames that feature popular media stars: idol singers and groups such as Puffy, Amuro Namie, KinKi-Kids, Tokio and V6; foreign movie stars such as Keanu Reeves and singers like Mariah Carey, Celine Dion and Michael Jackson; and well known fictional characters from Pepsi Man to Poo, from *Men in Black* to *Betty Boop* (Figure 11.2). In these cases the object is to get oneself into a group picture with a person or group of people of celebrity status. More recently, important political figures began to accompany the heroes of the entertainment industry. *Focus* magazine pointed out that the former Prime Minister Ryutaro Hashimoto had his own frame, 'Ryu-chan Purikura' (Anonymous 1998b), so young women could get themselves into a Hashimoto frame (Anonymous 1997a, 1998b). One of our interviewees pointed out the importance of being handsome; she doubted, for instance, that either former Prime Minister Tomiichi Murayama or the late Prime Minister Keizo Obuchi would have their own frames. In short, we found that the majority of frame designs are directed towards attracting female users.[6]

Clearly Print Club is still very popular and even evolving in several ways. In all cases, we notice an increase in variety and choice for consumers, and, in turn, an increased penetration into Japanese daily life. We have noticed three types of changes. First, we found changes in picture shape and sticker forms. Patrons are now offered images varying in shape (e.g. full body portraits), size of image (small and large on the same sheet), number of pictures on the same page (as many as 300 in one case), with a choice of printing (e.g. black-and-white, sepia-toned) and a broader range of frame choice: as many as 240 in the same machine, including holiday-specific frames

Figure 11.1 Vinyl curtains in front of cameras and monitors, featuring cartoon characters Doraemon, Poo-san (Winnie the Pooh), Minnie Mouse and the very popular Hello Kitty. They advertise the particular features of individual Print Club machines. (Authors' photographs.)

Figure 11.2 One of many machines featuring photo-sticker frames of popular music idols such as the KinKi Kids, 1999. (Authors' photograph.)

(Valentines, Christmas), seasonally varying frames and changing life-stage frames (birthdays). We also found an increased number of formats, including calendar pages, picture postcards, picture puzzles, wanted posters, business cards and covers of popular magazines, e.g. *Cosmo* and *Can-Can*, the effect being similar to being centred on the cover of *Time* or *Newsweek* in the United States (Figure 11.3).

The second form of change and development involves a connection to the art world. In June 1997, The Tokyo Metropolitan Museum of Photography presented an exhibition entitled 'Photography and Media: Forms and Functions of Portraiture'. Covering 150 years of photography, this exhibition ranged from daguerreotypes to Print Club images. More recently, Yasumasa Morimura developed an exhibition for Tokyo's Museum of Contemporary Art entitled 'Self-portrait as Art History' (25 April to 7 June 1998), in which he included 60 photographs, sculptures, videos and Print Club machines (DiPietro 1998). Morimura included special backgrounds as frames that he designed himself. Some perspective is provided by Yoko Hayashi in the accompanying catalogue:

> Print Club Machine, Morimura Version . . . is an experimental form of art but there is no distinction between the machine Morimura has prepared and the Print-club machines set up in shopping and entertainment districts of Japanese cities that young people use to make photo stickers. However I

170

Figure 11.3 Different image formats: full length frame, jigsaw, 'wanted' poster and calendar, 1998–9. (Authors' photographs.)

believe it should be properly seen as a work of art which clearly reflects ideas of importance to the artist. It is a device that functions to multiply and scatter Morimura's 'I' into the world.

(Hayashi 1998: 68)

A third set of changes focuses on the location of photo-sticker machines. They are now being placed in new and somewhat unexpected locations. In late December 1997, Print Club machines were set up for use at Kezoin temple in Takarazuka, Hyogo Prefecture, as well as at the Toji temple in Kyoto. One report stated that 'even elderly parishioners have become fans of the new device, with a considerable number of them going so far as to make their own stickers, posing with their grandchildren' (Tamaki 1998). Here we find a return to the original marketing intentions cited earlier. There is a feeling that temples and shrines may be a new market and that 'the stickers serve as good luck amulets' (Tamaki 1998).

In a more familiar frame of reference, we have noticed the common appearance of Print Club machines in a variety of tourist sites, from Tokyo Tower to popular resort locations. Frames have been customised, tailored and styled for specific tourist locations all over Japan. One good example comes from the school group seen at Miyajima, home of the well known O-Torii (Grand Gate) standing in the Inland Sea in front of the Itsukushima Shrine (Figure 11.4). Taking Print Club locations even further, and as might be expected, we are witnessing the export of Print Club into global contexts. These machines have penetrated international markets with mixed results. As of summer 1998, Atlus had about 4,000 machines in other Asian nations and had sent 2,000 to European sites. Print Club was introduced to the United States by Atlus in June 1997 (Williams 1997).[7] By 2000, variations of the original Atlus machines were well distributed through the United States.

Uses of photo-stickers

From our fieldwork to date, we find two extremes of sticker use, one private, the other public. In private contexts, which are by far the more common, we see the interpersonal sharing and exchanging of photo stickers with friends – more on this topic below. We also find people making personal collections of these images: people using their photo-stickers in appointment books, on letters and postcards, or collecting them in small albums sold specifically to hold a few hundred such pictures[8] (Figure 11.4). We also have reports of salarymen affixing photo-stickers to their business cards (*meishi*), ostensibly to help colleagues to remember the face that goes with the name. But we have no systematic findings on this activity. In addition, we have several reports of girls putting their sticker-image on their boyfriends' cell phones (Figure 11.4).

In slightly broader interpersonal contexts, we found other uses closely associated with identification functions. For instance, we have reports of high school students handing in written papers and other homework assignments with their own *Purikura* attached. In one language school in Tokyo, teachers have been asking their students for photo-stickers to attach to class enrolment lists to help to identify and remember names. In another example, we found Print Club images affixed to pages of a guest book found in the lobby of a *ryokan* (inn or guest house). And photo-stickers have even been appearing on reserved liquor bottles that Japanese bars keep for their regular

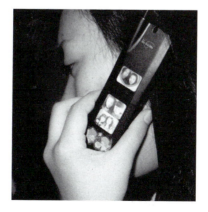

Figure 11.4 (a) A sign at a popular tourist destination offering *Purikura* of the famous Itsuku-shima Shinto Shrine, and a multiple image produced on that machine. (b) An album specially designed to carry some 200 stickers; stickers permanently displayed on a mobile phone. (Authors' photographs.)

customers. In summary, we found a growing proliferation of uses in private and semi-private contexts.

At the other extreme, featuring more public contexts, we hear of much broader distribution. In one report we read, 'They put them on their notebooks, their bags, you name it' (Joseph 1998), and in another account, 'kids could tag them onto anything that couldn't move fast' (Buckton 1998: 18). In a related practice, we also noticed that people have begun to attach their *Purikura* images to postcards.[9] The use of Print Club stickers as graffiti comes to mind.

In the most explicit examples of public exhibition, we noticed that some magazines have been accepting Print Club images in their 'personals – mate wanted' columns. Such pictures are usually accompanied by a brief biographical sketch. Finally, some new machines allow patrons to send their Print Club images from a photo booth directly to a magazine.[10]

Put a new product in front of 125 million people and one is certain to find both pro-social and anti-social uses of such a product.[11] Reports have appeared of girls using Print Club machines to 'advertise' themselves, not just to one another, but to potential boyfriends or even older men willing to pay them for sex (Anonymous 1996c). One method has been to write their pager numbers on their personal stickers and then put them on public bulletin boards, 'inviting calls from males for friendship or even financially-assisted relationships (*enjo kosai*)' (Ono 1998). In another example, Naito reports that gangsters allegedly 'use pager or phone numbers written on stickers to contact girls and lure them into shady activities by paying them small allowances' (Naito 1996; Anonymous 1996a). These shady activities include prostitution and drug use. After a series of newspaper articles documenting such activities, these bulletin boards were removed by the police.

One conclusion to this point is that Print Club images have eclipsed original projections of use and value, in both private and public venues, for many pro-social and a few anti-social reasons. In short, consumers have found many reasons to use this product. In turn, Print Club marketing has been extremely responsive to emerging market needs, most of which have been generated by an adolescent clientele. We find a steady proliferation of *Purikura* into unanticipated locations for an equally unanticipated diversity of human needs, uses and satisfactions.

Why has the Print Club become so popular?

The most common question we hear is: why has Print Club become so popular in Japan?[12] What features, for instance, of past and contemporary Japanese life might be seen to welcome, and indeed endorse, such activity, and what in the past has provided a comfortable fit? What precedents and connections, if any, lead the way? What national or international forces might be at work? We surmise that the observed popularity of Print Club should not be a mystery at all. The popularity of Print Club follows several established and fundamental Japanese traditions – familiar characteristics of contemporary Japanese culture. How and where can we begin to interpret these observations and findings? And how can we do this, avoiding stereotypes and the pitfalls of an orientalist discourse?[13]

Perhaps the most difficult yet most significant point to understand better is how Print Club finds a culturally logical place within a deeply seated and rich Japanese visual culture.[14] Importantly, Japanese attention to the visual goes far beyond the most common references in the West to aesthetic issues: 'high' visual culture interests including classic film productions (Ozu, Kurosawa), wood block prints (*ukiyo-e*), and the stereotypical not-so-high popular production of tourist photographs. For instance, we would include the regular celebration of penmanship: calligraphy contests are held on a national and annual basis. We must also acknowledge: the highest annual sales of highly visual comic books (*manga*) purchased and enjoyed by all age sectors of Japanese society; a higher hour per person and per day consumption of television than in the United States; the prominent existence of art galleries in popular department stores. In other contexts we find attention to house interior and garden designs, as well as flower arrangements (*ikebana*) and food preparation, among others, many of which are now celebrated in coffee table books flooding international markets. The visuality and visibility of personal photography, correlated with a fascination, fondness and ongoing popularity of Print Club, are logical extensions of these general interests.

This most obvious connection to the rich fabric of Japanese visual culture raises and leaves many questions for further discussion. Much has been made of Japanese marketing and consumer habits (Fields 1983; Tobin 1992; Skov and Moeran 1995; Moeran 1996; Clammer 1997). The writings of Daniel Miller (1987) have been most helpful for a better understanding of the place of Print Club in the production–marketing–consumer process. Much of his work has been about the application of ideas about objectification and material culture to modern mass consumption, with special reference to social relations. He gives much attention to the role of the consumer and the ways in which people are able to appropriate things for themselves; that is, to match their own needs and visions of preferred use. He has clarified the role(s) of consumers in relation to marketing strategies, relationships of cultural change and cultural dynamics, and sees consumer behaviours as a means of asserting personal, social and cultural identity. Within Japan much is said of the influence and power of adolescent females based on their consumer habits. Japanese industry and marketing in particular have been exceedingly sensitive to the needs of the youth segments of the population (White 1993: 138).

The introduction and success of Print Club provides us with a good example of such marketing–consumer relationships. As mentioned above, Print Club was adopted by teenagers in ways that were not initially anticipated. Sasaki Miho and the Atlus people saw a potential of this machine for family members: parents, usually the mother, having pictures made with their children, as an extension of family album photography. This has indeed happened, but only relatively recently and most certainly after the real boom occurred among adolescent girls. As we have seen, the success story of Print Club is based on adolescents adopting these machines for their own uses, and, in a very real sense, reinventing Print Club for themselves and, in turn, driving the market in their direction. As such we reintroduce Miller's perspective and see a good example of what Watts found in Japan, i.e. how 'the consumer is now at the commanding heights of the modern economy' (Watts 1998: 199).

This change, from the family content to a friends and peer group content, is not trivial. We can interpret this difference as replacing a vertical or hierarchical organisation with a horizontal orientation, representing a tension in the younger generation to reject the norm so prevalent in so much of Japanese life, namely one built on vertical organisation. Clearly, our findings favour the inclusion of girlfriends, of peer group members, of people of similar ages and of the same gender. Whether similar preferences and patterns of behavior will be found in other countries as Print Club spreads remains to be seen.

Miller helps readers to understand the inherent invisibility of what appears to us merely as highly visible product choices and material culture (Miller 1987: 215). Patterns of consumption are connected to personal and social identity but often in more indirect ways than Print Club offers. In Skov and Moeran's work on women, media and consumption, we read that 'being a consumer is a form of self-reflection offered to Japanese women by those media targeted directly at them. Such an identity ties women closely to consumer trends and simultaneously enables the market to address them in a very personal way' (Skov and Moeran 1995: 5). There is little doubt that choices of products and consumer habits in general can be interpreted as statements of identity – of claiming a relationship or connection with a particular group, or claiming to 'belong' to a specific group or taste subculture. Studying photographs generated by Print Club tends to enhance a sense of literal visibility, in that social relations become visible in new ways: relationships are more direct given the visible/visual nature of the practice and product.

Miller's suggested connections to issues of identity are also evident. Much more than a 'look at me' meta-message, we find a preference for 'look at us' or, perhaps, getting the best of two worlds, 'look at me as part of this group'. Importantly, this is a voluntary group as compared to annual school pictures, where the individual student is still part of a class-group but on less voluntary grounds and conditions. There is more on this below.

Cute consumption and *shojo* participation

Several observers of contemporary Japanese society have cited connections between consumption habits and youth culture. *Shojo* roughly equates with youth culture, more adolescent females than males, and has even been recognised as 'a definitive feature of Japanese late-model, consumer culture capitalism' (Treat 1996: 280). Youth culture is further characterised as John Treat adds: 'The word most often associated with this *shojo* culture is *kawaii* or "cute". This aesthetic value is directly linked to the consumer role that *shojo* exist to play' (Treat 1996: 281). When writing about 'cuties', Sharon Kinsella notes, 'Adolescent women (*shojo*) provide the exclusive model for cute culture . . . and have been transformed into an abstract concept and a sign for consumption in the Japanese mass-media and modern intellectual discourse' (Kinsella 1995: 244). In a statement that well describes the ongoing popularity of Print Club, Kinsella adds: 'Young women entered cute culture through consumption of cute goods with cute appearances and emotional qualities . . . Cute culture had to be entered and left in a matter of minutes or moments, which lent it to construction by ephemeral products and places of consumption of goods and leisure services' (Kinsella 1995: 245). The Print Club usage we have been describing conforms to this pattern quite well.

The role of Print Club in *shojo* has been basically one of consumption, but of a different order: different from more familiar forms, namely buying trendy items of clothing – the latest Mikimoto necklace or Moschino handbag – or types of music, or eating at the latest fast food outlet, and the like. Japanese youth consumes Print Club through a model of participant–production–consumption. There is a sense of young Japanese people consuming themselves, to which we must add, seldom alone. If anything is being consumed, it is an image and statement of relationship, group membership and belonging. Granted, there is some competition regarding who have their pictures taken in the latest 'frames'. But consumer competition, as we have noted, is based on the number of times one uses the machines; or, more importantly, the number of people one is photographed with as illustrated in one's collection of stickers.

The notion and popularity of the cute is not restricted to children in Japan; the adoration of cuteness saturates a wide range of groups. According to a study by Sanrio (the Korean company that created and popularised Hello Kitty),[15] 'their items sold to Japanese girls between the age of five and the time of marriage would be bought in America only by girls from four to seven years old' (White 1993: 126). One Japanese woman in our sample stated:

> I think that people who like character goods like 'Hello Kitty' are more likely to like Print Club. They all like something which is not real. Print Club pictures which are surrounded by many cute frames are not the real you. These are imaginary things. 'Hello Kitty' never speaks or moves. This character gives people an opportunity to imagine the character the way they want to imagine. This concept is related to the fondness for cute things.
>
> (Momoko Otani 1998)

Perhaps the 'cult of the cute' is best summarised by a statement made by an American colleague who has lived and worked in Japan for over 18 years:

> If I were to speculate – really right off the top of my head – on the popularity of Print Club, I would associate it with the whole 'cherry blossom' concept of youth in Japan and the worship of Cute. High school girls, especially, seem to have the sense that they are living the one, brief, happy moment of their lives. They present themselves as adorable, cuddly little things, desperate to preserve this one instant when they are genuinely cute. What better way than to accumulate a cute little notebook full of cute little images of themselves and their girl friends, mugging into the camera and looking cute.
>
> (George Deaux, personal communication September 1998)

Print Club images are small versions of what we might prefer to be larger, simply to see better. The miniature nature of these images is immediately apparent; one can store or, more importantly, carry a large number with great ease. Symbolically, a large cohort of group members can be held together in a small space.

Other 'cute culture' features from pre-Print Club days contribute to this pattern. For instance, we must include an ongoing popular use of paper-stickers. The use of colourful fingernail-sized stickers has been very popular among Japanese females for some time as markers, reminders and decorations. As one woman suggested,

> We Japanese have a tendency to prefer small and delicate things to big and conspicuous ones . . . Twenty- and 30-year-old women used to collect eagerly

small and pretty stickers in our girlhood days. And when the girls have grown up and had a child, they are attracted by the new type of sticker – the Print Club. I suppose that they are enjoying their girlhood days again though [since] they have a reason to make photo-stickers of their children.

(Takako Yasuma, personal communication 1998)

Some interviewees even connected 'small' with a preference for being modest and unassuming and for maintaining privacy. Regardless, 'collecting the small and the cute' is a winning combination. We can see how Atlus and Sega foster these values by continually developing new frames: people feel they must collect the latest cute version of a popular character. Much repeat business – regularly making new photo-stickers – relies on this affinity, and allows and helps the photo-sticker collection to grow.

Gender bias: response and results

Another factor connected to visual culture and consumer findings directly involved questions of participation: who was using Print Club most of the time? Through solicited response from several samples of both Japanese and Americans, in both Japan and the United States, we sought to know more about patterns of preferred participation, and frequency of use.[16] We wanted to know more about the people who used Print Club and the frequency of such use. Was it fair to state that Print Club popularity was well distributed across the Japanese population? Or were specific demographically defined groups more likely to participate than others?

Published reports claim spectacular findings. In one survey conducted in the Shibuya area of central Tokyo, 98 per cent of Japanese high school girls replied that they had used Print Club, and some interviewees had collections of over 2,000 photo stickers. One Internet author stated: 'Purikura stickers are especially popular with high school girls, who have turned them into a mode of communication' (http://tomen.co.jo/we/we29/mosaic/mosaic.html).

All signs pointed towards a female bias. In our sample of Shizuoka students, for instance, 13 females (87 per cent) reported using Print Club machines more than 100 times, with seven of these 13 (54 per cent) reporting more than 300 times, and, at one extreme, one girl claimed she had used such a photo-booth more than 2,000 times. In comparison, all males in this small sample reported much less use – most, fewer than 50 times.[17]

What about high school males? As expected, results indicate that teenage males participate much less in Print Club than females. According to one published account, 'Boys see it as something that only girls do. Masatashi, a 17-year-old student stated: "I only take them when the girl I am with wants to have one." Kinji, also a student, agrees. "I only have three or four," he says. "Boys do not collect them like girls. One is good enough for me"' (Buckton 1998: 18).

We also observed that most photo-sticker images contained same-sex people, usually girls with girls, meaning girlfriends with girlfriends (the main exception occurs when boyfriend and girlfriend use Print Club together). This generally means 'classmates', which in turn speaks to the stated popularity and significance of photo-stickers at school: 'Students can not imagine school life without Print Club' (Voigt 1998: 15).

Thus, rather than finding a home in family photography, as initially predicted, Print Club generally produces pictures that reinforce peer-centred friendship communities rather than kin communities. In turn, this suggests that collections of Print Club images lend themselves to sociometric studies and analysis. Our conclusion is that Print Club is very important as a gendered practice – with high school girls predominating. This, in turn, aligns with highly gendered patterns of consumption found in Japan (Clammer 1997).

Who else has been attracted to Print Club? It is equally important to recognise collections of people who generally ignore Print Club, people who do not use these photo booths. For instance, we might ask: do salarymen (business/company employees), OLs (office ladies, similar to multitasking secretaries) or bar hostesses use Print Club with any frequency?[18] Do pre-teens, housewives or young mothers use these machines?

Information remains sketchy on these questions. From several reports and observations, we learned that while OLs will use Print Club for themselves, salarymen are much less inclined. Marcos and Asahina interviewed several OLs in Okinawa, specifically on Park Avenue in Okinawa City, a popular location for the use of many Print Club machines. They spoke with Takano, 21, and Sachiyo, 21, who came to Okinawa City from Naha to shop for the day: Takano is quoted as saying 'Today's a holiday . . . We've used these machines more than 30 times. I have about 60 stickers from my friends' (Marcos and Asahina 1997).

We also noticed that salarymen and OLs might use it together. As one female interviewee observed, 'It is hard to imagine that a group of male salarymen use Print Club without being with OLs.' This follows the observed pattern of male teens taking pictures with girlfriends but not by themselves.

Our sense is that Print Club is popular with pre-teens but much less so than with junior and high school students. This appears strange because so many of the frames seem to be designed with very young people in mind, including the appearance of many juvenile cartoon characters, and especially Hello Kitty – we return to this point below. However, we do not have any documented frequency figures on this pre-teen–teen comparison.

From reports and observations, older housewives do not appear to be heavy users of Print Club. Younger ones, however, especially young mothers with very young children, are much more likely to use Print Club. One Japanese woman in her early thirties reported:

> *Purikura* is also *very* popular among Japanese young mothers being in [their] twenties and thirties who have little children . . . although all of them didn't like using it . . . Some of them use *Purikura* unwillingly because their children ask them to or because they are asked to do so by the mother of their children's friend who happened to be with them. They say they find *purikura* machines so often in the place where children are expected to come – for example, on the floor where they are selling toys or clothes for children in the department store or a big supermarket. The other type is mothers who are willing to use *purikura* very frequently and [like to] collect stickers.

> (Takako Yasuma, personal communication 1998)

We found other evidence that the Print Club craze is not limited to young people, and that another sector of adults who initially shunned the hobby may be giving new attention to these machines. For instance, we found an observation about a preference for grandchild–grandparent participation:

> For example, grandmothers are posing for sticker portraits with their grand-children while mothers are taking portraits with their children to swap with other mothers. This suggests that the *purikura* phenomenon is more than just a short-term fad and that it may be turning into an established part of Japanese culture.
>
> (http://tomen.co.jo/we/we29/mosaic/mosaic.html)

Again, we find mention of the delight and pleasure participants feel in taking pictures together. We have some evidence of an adherence to the original marketing ideas of Ms Miho and Atlus – but in much smaller quantities than initially anticipated.[19]

Recognised social functions

First, we found that females were generally more articulate about functional relationships than their male counterparts. The teenage Japanese students surveyed for this study recognised that several social and cognitive functions were built into their Print Club practice. In addition to claiming that they were 'something for fun', and 'something to kill time', they acknowledged that these pictures provided a way for them to commemorate a special event or interpersonal relationship and, in turn, provided a way to 'make a memory'. Others have mentioned and valued the memory-making function: 'The *purikura* phenomenon begins to make sense when one reads the analysis by sociologist Shinji Miyadai, who observes: "When you get a picture, you see in it you and your friends smiling at the machine only 50 seconds ago. Each passing moment quickly turns into a memory. Girls use the machine not because now is supreme but to make it supreme"' (Anonymous 1997b).

We also heard how *Purikura* images provided Japanese teenagers with a topic for conversation and 'a way to make friends'. While most photo-stickers are shown and exchanged in school (Kurita 1999), several interviewees reported how easy it was to share their Print Club pictures with new people. This has become an accepted way of meeting and getting to know potential friends, and of ensuring that you remember new friends. For example, one female high school student from Shizuoka told us in 1997:

> I think the reason for people exchanging *Purikura* is that you want people to remember you. Especially when you meet new people, and you don't want to forget them, about the time you spent with them and this new encounter. And it actually works! When I meet new people, we exchange our purikura to remember each other's face. And I never forget the face as long as I have their *purikura* pictures. I think this is the reason for people exchanging *purikura*.

Here, we find important connections between what are frequently seen as adolescent insecurity, calculation of social worth and number of photo-stickers. Kurita (1999) reported that more stickers meant more personal confidence, as suggested in the first quotation in this chapter: 'The more [photo] stickers I have, the more comfortable I feel about my relations with others . . . This notebook [photo-sticker album] is proof I have lots of friends' (teenage female interviewed in a Tokyo arcade, June 1996; Naito 1996). Kurita (2000) even heard one female teenager say: 'Keeping "Print Club" pictures heals loneliness'.

Clearly, issues of trade and currency come into play. As noted, high school girls are very fond of collecting as many images as possible: 'the more Print Club photo-stickers they can collect, the more currency their popularity carries' and students 'try to widen their circle of friends for photo-stickers' (Voigt 1998: 14). Ono (1998) speaks of Print Club as 'a social tool' for school girls: 'they are motivated to assemble these photo stickers with as many of their friends as they can. They want to show how many friends they have by posing with them on these stickers. And they show these stickers to their friends and share gossip.' In these instances, stickers, as information, serve as a commodity for exchange between members of friendship groups (White 1993). One conclusion here is that *Purikura* practice tends to solidify a social network of friend-ships with proof that people were together or hung out together. In turn we find connections between consumerism, youth culture and cute culture, all in the interests of producing viable and visible pieces of social organisation.

Sharing photographs

Being together in physical space has its counterparts in symbolic space. In a related form of explication, we would include the connection of Print Club to the popular practice of making and sharing snapshots. Another immediate reference point is the presumed affection Japanese people have for making their own snapshot photographs. We certainly do not want to invoke or dwell on stereotypes, but, in fact, international marketing figures and statistics do indicate that the Japanese take many photographs relative to other societies and cultures.[20]

Exchanging and sharing snapshot photographs are also widespread habits in Japan, in this case among all age groups and not just female teenagers. Snapshot photographs are very frequently duplicated and exchanged among people who attend the same party or travel together.[21] Print Club plays an important role in this context. For example, a male high school student from Shizuoka said in 1998:

> I like Print Club because it is easier than pictures [taken] by [a traditional] camera. If you take pictures with a camera it takes time to see the pictures since you have to get pictures developed. Moreover, you have to make extra copies for people who are in the pictures. It costs more. Compared to this way, Print Club is much easier . . . I think this ease is a very attractive point of Print Club.

The need to make and share photograph copies applies to members of family groups, travel groups, various sports groups and clubs, and even groups of salarymen visiting, perhaps, a satellite company office. In Japan, this practice appears less an option and more of an obligation. This connection was well stated by a recent graduate of Temple University and one of our interviewees in Philadelphia:

I think the reason for people exchanging Print Club stickers is not because everybody wants to do that. I think [this happens] because this is some sort of ceremony people are supposed to do among high school girls. They assume that you have to give your stickers if you are given them by others. This practice reminds me of the *meishi* [business card] system. People exchange *meishi* as a system in Japan. It doesn't matter if you would like to know the person better or not. You just give it to them and you get their *meishi* automatically. On the macro level. *Purikura* practice also reminds me of *oseibo*, too. People exchange gifts among one another. This is an established system in Japan. I think *Purikura* practice is very similar to those two [aspects of] Japanese traditional culture.

(Makiko Kawahima 1998)

In turn, we are led to relevant speculations of reifying interpersonal relationships and group memberships. Notions of social currency and social capital again become directly applicable to Print Club practice.

Another context of exchange is seen in the use of photography by go-betweens, people who arrange marriage partners in both formal and informal ways. One observer noted that Print Club stickers have been used 'to set up introductions to the opposite sex. "Print Club *miai*" occurs when a friend gives her photo stickers to another friend who shows them to a prospective boyfriend. They decide to meet or not by looking at their photo stickers' (Ono 1998). We discovered a slightly more indirect practice in one of our interviews in 1998:

I have a cousin who has a boyfriend. The reason they started dating is that one of my cousin's friends showed her *purikura* to a boy – he fell in love with my cousin from the picture and asked to be introduced to my cousin. That's the way they met. My cousin told me that it happens every day in Japan now.

Conclusion

A statement by art critic Hiromi Nakamura lets us return to the 'framing' reference in the title of this chapter. He states: 'The *Purikura* stickers are becoming a medium for linking people to one another. The stickers are a window that expresses one's own existence. The *Purikura* window (frame) is not just an adornment' (Nakamura 1998: 21). We have been making primary reference to choices of background frames in Print Club machines. But, secondly, we feel that Print Club images and collections of these images are, in fact, serving teenage patrons as framing devices. Print Club promotes the visualisation of a social framing of membership in a community or network of friends – many of whom might be seen or met in passing on a daily basis, but who can be 'virtually' united in photo-stickers held in album form. Kurita (1999) quotes one member of his sample as saying: 'Print Club is a microcosm of friendship. Because this is a form I actually can see with my eyes, it makes me feel secure.'[22]

Borrowing from a more flexible sense of framing, one closer to that proposed by Goffman, James Valentine (1997: 7) notes: 'The social construction of identity in Japan involves the sharing of self with others who are deemed to belong *uchi* (inside). Belonging is conceived in terms of flexible frames.' We propose that practising *Purikura* represents a modern way of framing, one of several that take place on a regular basis in everyday life. Maintaining a sense of belonging, in a horizontal social sense, but with diminished social verticality and permanence, Print Club offers opportunities to visualise or make pictorially manifest the dimensions of frames, whether used in context of friendship groups, school groups, business groups, company OL groups or other groups. Our point is a simple one: the fascination with and appreciation of the visual/pictorial in Japanese society and culture is not new. The pictorial symbolic worlds of Japan are historically rich and multilayered. The sustained attention to and appreciation of Print Club is a modern manifestation of the significance of visual culture in general, and has both implicit and explicit connections to social communication.

Several points are clear: Print Club has remained a popular and evolving practice in Japan and seems much more than its classification as fad would suggest. As one junior high school student commented, 'It's more than just a fad. It's a different type of photography. We do it to remember certain events, like when we meet people or make new friends. And then we reminisce about it later. It makes good memories' (Tomohiro Kawamura, Keio University 1997). From our discussion of Print Club as multilayered and well connected, we feel comfortable agreeing that 'the *purikura* phenomenon is more than just a short-term fad and that it may be turning into an established part of Japanese culture' (http://tomen.co.jo/we/we29/mosaic/mosaic.html). *Purikura* is a meaningful form of material culture that is intimately connected to visual culture and pictorial communication. The embeddedness of Print Club in contemporary Japanese society and visual culture is significant and signals a lasting impact, one deserving of continued academic attention.

Afterword

During the past five years, the popularity of Purikura has changed in interesting ways. The number of operating Print Club machines has decreased from a total of 50,000 located in video game centres, shopping centres and photo shops at the height of the boom in 1997–8. As expected, original patterns of use have also changed and one no longer sees people waiting in long lines for the latest machine. Some machines now display a sign saying 'Men are not allowed to enter alone', hoping to gain more profit by focusing on women as well as men and women together. However, Print Club remains very popular among its key constituency, namely high school girls. Some features have undergone improvements and created new interest. Hitachi engineers developed new and improved lighting methods (some with four settings) to soften the light, reduce shadows and hide facial imperfections sometimes caused by acne. The introduction of new software means the machines are now little different from digital cameras.

In an article titled 'Print club instant-photo booths seeing new boom', *The Japan Times* (13 August 2002) reported: 'The latest boom has made the instant picture sticker business a 50 billion yen industry and the government's Postal Services Agency is preparing to get on the bandwagon with plans to sell stamps carrying people's photographs . . . Its idea is to use digital cameras to take photographs of users at post offices and integrate the photographs into stamps using personal computers.'

Importantly, we find a new convergence of technologies, not uncommon to other parts of the world. With the rapid growth of Internet access in Japan, the most recent Print Club machines are connected to websites. Patrons can post their own favourite *Purikura* images to specific websites that allow viewers to vote for one's favourite picture. Results are announced on these sites as top ten *Purikura* lists each week. Many high school girls are eager to have their pictures on the top ten lists. Viewers can also chat with someone on these websites by showing each other's *Purikura* pictures. New technology also facilitates another popular activity whereby patrons can use these Internet connections to send their *Purikura* pictures to a third agent in this convergence, namely their friends' mobile phones.

Evidence mounts for believing that if Print Club were just a fad, it would have disappeared a long time ago – especially in Japan, a country where technology and consumer trends can change so rapidly. However, with modified formats and convergent technologies, *Purikura* practice has remained vibrant for almost a decade. We continue to find evidence for how Print Club has become an enduring part of Japanese visual culture.

Notes

Unless otherwise noted, all the photographs were created by one of this chapter's co-authors. The authors wish to thank Donald Richie, Richard Boyle, Robert Mason and David Plath, as well as two anonymous reviewers, for earlier readings of this chapter.

1 One notable exception in Japanese scholarship is Kurita (1999).
2 For a brief illustrated history of the photo booth by Thomas Rockowski, specifically a 'photo-machine' manufactured by General Electric, dated to 1912, see http://ourworld.compuserve.com/homepages/autophoto/history.htm
3 We have an example of *shinhatsubashi* (launching of a new or updated product) with parallel features to those Jonathan Watts (1998) describes for the introduction of the J League (professional football) in Japan. But we must realise that Japan most certainly did have photo booths before 1995, much as we would find in the United States or United Kingdom, namely machines sometimes located in train stations, stores or places that advertise self-made instant passport photographs. While these machines were used for serious identification purposes, they were also 'played with' by young people. Certain, however, is the fact that these machines have never approximated the extraordinary attention given to Print Club.
4 For an additional historical sketch, see http://atlus.co.jp/am/printclub/history.html
5 There is some evidence that choice of background frame may even take precedence over choice of photo partner (Kurita 1999). However, the choice of 'anyone' is highly unlikely.
6 Several exceptions have been noticed. For instance, one frame shows two boys 'surrounded by steaming, Technicolor piles of *unco* ("poop"), or two girls sweetly smiling above bold letters spelling "F__k You" complete with a colorful border of manga hands extending the middle finger in each corner of the photo' (Voigt 1998: 14). In more recent times, new action-oriented backgrounds have been added to attract male participants.
7 Predictably, the most successful initial penetration has been in Hawaii and West Coast states, but we also hear of machines in the north-east corridor (La Ferla 1998). For a report of usage in the SoHo district of New York City, see Joseph (1998).
8 Personal thanks go to Alison Nordström for this reference.
9 This practice proved problematic during a New Year mailing when postal machines began jamming because these photo-stickers either made the card too thick or began to fall off the cards.

10 The best example we found was a section of a magazine called *Street Snap*. Magazine editors would select a sample from all contributions and add comments for a monthly publication.

11 For a description of a similar phenomenon associated with Polaroid instant cameras, see Edgley and Kiser (1982).

12 This is similar to Brian McVeigh's (2000: 237) question: 'Why is Hello Kitty so popular?'

13 It may, in fact, be impossible to escape totally an orientalist criticism, generally due to alternative readings. However, this perspective is decidedly not the intent of the authors.

14 Growing interest in formalising the general concept of visual culture can be seen in volumes by Mirzoeff (1998, 1999) and Walker and Chaplin (1998). We note that visual sociology and visual anthropology play minimal roles in these programmatic accounts.

15 For an overview, see McVeigh (2000).

16 For instance, we handed out survey questionnaires to 20 high school students (15 female and five males) living in Shizuoka, Japan. We also conducted in-person interviews with a small sample of Japanese college students studying in the United States (mostly at Temple University in Philadelphia with American college students studying in the United States, mostly at Ohio State University, and with some American graduate students who worked in Japan.

17 Comparative figures for collecting photo-stickers vary in an expected way. Twelve of the 13 females in the sample (92 per cent) reported having more than 100 stickers; and eight of these 12 (67 per cent) claimed to have more than 2,000 stickers. In comparison, all males in this sample reported having fewer than 100, most with many fewer than 100. Kurita (1999) found an average of 425 photo-stickers among 15–17-year-old females.

18 For instance, Ono (1998) reports Ginza bar hostesses putting their photo-stickers on their business cards to help customers to remember them.

19 Further analysis could well reveal an age-graded diversity of meaningful functions, from 'girlhood' to female adolescence to womanhood, as suggested by McVeigh (2000).

20 Clearly this stereotype, grounded in the intimate connection between being Japanese and amateur photography, persists. When trying to explain the subject of this research and the popularity of Print Club to an American adult friend, she immediately said: 'Oh that's just what they need – more photographs!'

21 The availability of Print Club at popular domestic tourist sites – as previously described – is seen as another clever marketing strategy in this context.

22 This is not the same as what Chie Nakane (1970: 1–22) suggests as her now classic notions of 'frame' and 'attribute' – ways of understanding the social organisation of Japanese society and culture. When discussing personal identity, Nakane stresses the preference for stating membership in a particular organisation or institution – e.g. company or school – rather than stating a particular role or occupation. Nakane (1970: 7) states: 'the formation of social groups on the basis of fixed frames remains characteristic of Japanese social structure'.

12

PHOTOGRAPHIC MATERIALITY IN THE AGE OF DIGITAL REPRODUCTION

Joanna Sassoon

Digital images are produced without the intermediaries of film, paper or chemicals and as such 'never acquire the burden of being originals because they do not pass through a material phase' (Bruce 1994: 17). The invention of digital technology represents the first revolutionary change for photographic methods since Talbot's invention of the calotype, which introduced the negative/positive process and transformed the photograph from being a unique item to one that was reproducible. By the direct conversion of light into a digital format to create a stable image, 'photographs' that only exist in the digital form can be seen in one context as a truer version of photography (writing with light) than those that require the creation of a physical intermediary to view the image in a material form. While the notion that an original photograph has a unique value precisely 'because of its status as a physical object' needs re-evaluation in the digital context (Bruce 1994: 17), this chapter looks at the effects of digitising on photographs which, in their original form, are material.

Under the dual guises of increased access and improved preservation outcomes, many custodial institutions are undertaking bulk digitisation of their photograph collections. At one level it can be argued that digitising provides for increased equity of access independent of geography, once the technology is available. However, the object being digitised – the photograph – is a finely tuned material equation between being a cultural and being a technological object. At the heart of analysing the effect of the digitisation process on this balance lies a discussion of the origins and emanation of photographic meaning, the importance of materiality to the study of photographs and the relationships between the original photographic object and its digital referent.

The way in which photographic meaning is being reframed by custodial institutions through the use of new digital technologies is a continuation of the way institutions frame the meanings of all materials they house. Specifically, the manner in which photographic materials are managed is coming under pressure to change alongside the introduction of digital surrogates for access purposes. In this new digital context, with its concomitant focus on image content, institutions are redefining the key features of the photographic object. Patricia Hayes argues that this shift, which also occurs in the material environment, amounts to 'a massive dehistoricisation and decontextualisation which, if it had occurred with documents, would create a massive scandal' (Hartmann *et al.* 1998: 6). Thus, she suggests not only the way in which institutions privilege the integrity of textual over visual materials, but ultimately their influence over the way in which visual materials can be used for research. Therefore, this investigation necessarily leads to an inquiry into whether digitisation provides seamless, enhanced access to collections, and whether what appears to be a technical transformation from the material to the digital should in fact be seen as a cultural process.

Digital reproduction technology

In his prescient analysis of the effects of mechanical reproduction on art works, Walter Benjamin saw that the existence of multiple reproductions of art works increased access to their image content. This increased access changed the status and role of art works from that of ritual and elitism to being 'based on another practice – politics' (Benjamin 1985b: 224). In this context, politics is understood in relation to the development of an increasingly democratic process, and to the concomitant increase in access to the content of the art works once they are able to be reproduced. However, Benjamin fails to identify that it was the ownership of the printing press that determined the politics of the use of and access to the images, rather than the mere production and acquisition of multiple reproductions. With the increasing visual literacy of those who produce and consume the images, the effects of an image-based culture are such that it can be argued, converse to Benjamin, that mechanical reproduction has allowed politics to develop a parasitical dependence on the image. While Benjamin applauds the increasing accessibility of art work that results from the availability of reproductions, he fails to understand the power relationships required to enable the transformation of status of an image from the artistic to the political arena – a power that has equal potential to be democratising and passive, or repressive and active.

Like Benjamin, John Tagg saw the status of photography as a technology that 'varies with the power relations which invest it. Its nature as a practice depends on the institutions and agents which define it and set it to work' (Tagg 1988: 63). However, Tagg studied mechanisms by which institutional power exploits the verisimilitude of the photograph to engender social change in the context of repressive and juridical institutions. Thus he saw what Benjamin failed to recognise; that is, the ability of those who control the technology to control the image content and reproduction. It will be argued here that, contrary to Benjamin's thesis, mechanical reproduction has allowed cultural institutional politics to develop a parasitical dependence on the image.

While written in the 1930s in response to the increasing availability of mechanically reproduced images, Benjamin's thesis can be understood independently of a specific technology. Like its mechanical antecedents, digital reproduction technology can be seen on one level as democratic, fulfilling demands for increased access to collections while preserving the status of the original object. However, it can also be seen as an insidiously repressive technology enabling institutional control over what is made accessible, with criteria as to what is appropriate to be made public through digitising rarely being discussed. The debate regarding digital images has incorporated such issues as intellectual and legal control over the uses and the fidelity of the digital images (Kusnerz 1998). However, there has been less discussion about what is lost in the process of digitising original photographs and the impact of this loss on research based on photographs.

Digitising

A purely technical approach sees photography as 'the intersection of two distinct procedures; one of a chemical order: the action of light on certain substances; the other of a physical order: the formation of an image through an optical device' (Barthes 1993: 10). However, this definition belies an understanding that photography is inextricably linked with and goes far beyond either the technology or the role of the photographer. As will be discussed, it is no longer an accepted canon that a photograph is merely a print on paper, nor is it a simple and uncomplicated translation between reality and its mechanical representation. Likewise, the digitising process can no longer be seen as merely changing the physical state of a photograph from the material to the pixel. If a photograph can be seen as a more complex object than simply an image, digitising can be seen as more than simply a transformation of state, or a transliteration of tones. The process of digitising involves a more complex cultural process of translation – or a change between forms of representation.

If the process of digitising pre-existing photographs is seen as a translation, then questions as to the subsequent change in nature of and relationships between the original and its translation must be examined. In writing that 'any translation which intends to perform a transmitting function cannot transmit anything but information – hence something inessential', Benjamin (1985a: 69–70) argues that all that is essential in a literary work is contained within its information. While this case is debatable even for literary works, it does not apply to the quintessential nature of a photograph, where its meaning is derived from relationships that are external to the photographic object.

At one level, that of image content, the process of translating a photograph from a material to a digital form appears to be neutral, transparent and unmediated, albeit with some loss of image quality. That is, the image is simply transformed from one physical state to another. However, as Benjamin writes, 'the extent to which a translation manages to be in keeping with the nature of this mode is determined objectively by the translatability of the original' (Benjamin 1985a: 81). In determining the translatability of a photograph, it is necessary to investigate how 'a specific significance inherent in the original' (Benjamin 1985a: 71) survives the digitising process. These features are identified as the materiality of the photographic object as well as its sources of meanings and contexts.

When writing that 'no translation would be possible if in its ultimate essence it strove for likeness of the original', Benjamin (1985a: 73) accepts that fundamental change occurs during the translation process. Equally, successful translation serves to express the 'central reciprocal relationship' (Benjamin 1985a: 72) between two products, and if an assessment of the relationship between the material photograph and its digital referent is based on image content alone, then the digital translation can be seen as a substitute for the material item. However, when comparing their materiality and sources of meaning, the dissonant relationship between the ethereal and liminal digital representation of its tangible and material source becomes more marked. As will be argued, the nature of the photographic object and institutional practices that surround it means that translation from the material to the digital becomes a cultural, rather than simply a technological, process.

Photographs and their digital referent

The search for a single set of properties of a photograph belies the diversity of the medium and the vigour of the debate that this multifaceted nature brings, as it is precisely the polysemic nature of the photographic medium which continues to engender a dynamic body of theory, practice and criticism. For example, in discussing the effects of the verisimilitude of the photographic image, Abigail Solomon-Godeau (1991: 180) argues that 'phenomenologically, the photograph registers as pure image, and it is by virtue of this effect that we commonly ascribe to the photograph the mythic value of transparency'. While this perception of transparent photographic truth is implicit in the way many use photographs as a documentary record or as illustration, photographic theorists have rarely assumed that 'optical precision . . . is . . . a guarantee of documentary neutrality' (Schwartz 1995: 44). For Tagg, 'what makes a photograph real is the fact that the photograph is more than merely print and paper . . . what is real is not just the material item, but also the discursive system of which the image bears its part' (Tagg 1988: 4). He challenges the notion of the neutrality of the camera by arguing that it is the combination of the evidential force of an image with the 'power of the state apparatus which is controlling both the content of the images and then their power to stand as evidence or register a truth' (Tagg 1988: 62–3).

Three important features of the photograph are central to many debates about the complexity of photographs: the materiality of the photographic object, the concept of the original photograph and the origin of photographic meaning. It is therefore appropriate to consider a photograph as a multilayered laminated object in which meaning is derived from a symbiotic relationship between materiality, content and context. From this foundation it is possible to investigate how these aspects of the photograph are altered during the digitisation process.

There has been much hyperbole about the potential of digitising to enliven trajectories of photographs beyond current institutional boundaries. For example Peter Robinson (1996: 47) argues that 'the possibilities of image digitisation have captured the imagination of humanities scholars, to the extent that no electronic publication project seems complete unless it plans to include images'. In saying this, it is important to understand that the processes at work in the translation from the material to the digital image serve to change the nature and the very experience of seeing photographs in contradictory ways.

Materiality

With its delicate relationship between light and shade, its negative and paper forms, and its back and front, the very physicality of a photograph provides important information for understanding its technical origins. Embedded within the original photographic object are clues visible to the trained eye that reveal the subtle relationships between negatives, printing papers and processes used to produce the image physically. Visually, the proportions of photographic objects are an indicator of the camera, negative size and date of production, and the textures and tonal ranges are clues to the photographic processes used to produce the print. These, in their turn, point to social usages.

In addition to the physical dimensions of the object, details such as captions, retouching details, cropping instructions or markings on the backs of the photographs may reveal additional information that needs to be read in association with the image content. The physical condition of the object, the dirt and damage, is evidence of its other lives. Therefore, as Batchen (1997: 2) argues, the photograph is an image that can have 'volume, opacity, tactility and a physical presence in the world' – in essence an aura of materiality or of 'the thing itself' that emanates from the complexity of the original photographic object. While present in original photographic objects and vintage prints, such auratic qualities, which derive from the original materiality and the balance between technical and physical qualities, are hard to replicate and often lost completely in copies using modern photographic materials.[1]

As Benjamin (1985a: 79) argues, 'a real translation is transparent; it does not cover the original, does not block its light, but allows the pure language, as though reinforced by its own medium, to shine upon the original all the more fully'. Translating photographic images into digital form is, by necessity of the technology, a standardising process during which a variety of physical distinctions between different types and forms of photographs are eliminated. Fundamentally, what were once three-dimensional physical objects become one-dimensional and intangible digital surrogates, with the tactility and materiality of the original object being reduced to both an ephemeral and an ethereal state. Likewise, those important and diverse material and visual cues embedded in original photographs, such as original technologies and social uses, as I suggested above, are transformed by the nature of the viewing technology into a unity of a predetermined size, quality and tonal range of the digital image. Thus photographic sizes that lend meaning to the original object may be cropped to the proportions of standard computer screen formats.

As a result of such a process, both the fidelity and authenticity of digital images are open to question. During digitisation all features of the photograph including the top layer of the laminate of the photographic object, its image content, are open to alteration by the custodial institution. This can be undertaken digitally unbeknownst to the viewer and without leaving visible trace. The omnipresent possibility of photographic content and condition being electronically enhanced for aesthetic purposes leaves open to question whether the physical condition of photographs can be used as evidence of former lives in the digital context and, indeed, whether the digital image can itself be trusted as authentic or reliable evidence.[2] Thus the careful balance of inherent material characteristics and cultural origins is shifted radically in the creation of a digital ghost.

By its nature as a visualising medium, digitisation encourages a shift from thinking about the complexity of the material object to viewing the visual surface of an image. At once the technology reduces the subtlety of the material features of the individual photographic object and highlights the homogeneous nature of the digital image. Likewise, it reduces the complexity of the photographic object to a single dimension, with the backs of the photographs, where additional information lends further meaning to the image content, rarely being digitised.[3] This encourages a focus purely on subject content, and the production of a digital image database whose 'philosophical basis lies in an aggressive empiricism, bent on achieving a universal inventory of appearances' (Sekula 1983: 197). This concentration on the visual nature of the digital image at the expense of other material features of the photograph is further emphasised in the viewing of images through an intermediate and universalising technology.

While the digital medium emphasises the aesthetic qualities and image content of a photograph, this again obscures the subtleties of visual clues that originate from the materiality of the photograph and have become an automatic part of the lexicon of reading an original photographic object.[4] Consequently, in digitising programmes the aesthetics of the photograph tend to be privileged in the selection of images for placement in a digital collection. This leads to an assumption that it is necessarily the image content that is of prime importance. In itself this raises important questions about what happens to photographs that are not aesthetically pleasing but are intellectually important, such as family photographs and snapshots, or research where the aesthetics or image content are not the primary evidence. Thus it can be argued that digitisation is limiting understandings of photographs to their being an aesthetic medium rather than a document of evidence.

The 'original' photograph

The concept of 'the original' functions differently for photography and for other forms of documents or art works. In technical and photographic terms, the negative is the original, as it is the medium that records what is in front of the lens at the moment of exposure, but 'the very principle of photography is that the resulting image is not unique, but on the contrary infinitely reproducible' (Berger 1980: 291). While the negative may in fact be 'the truest record' of what was in front of the lens, perceiving this negative as the sole original in the photographic process 'emphasizes uniqueness over purpose' (Schwartz 1995: 46). It can be said that while the negative may be seen as the original in photographic terms, the document that conveys the message is the print made from the negative.

The ease with which multiple prints can be photographically produced from a single 'original' negative resulted in Benjamin conflating the notions of singularity with authenticity when he wrote that 'from a photographic negative, for example, one can make any number of prints; to ask for an "authentic" makes no sense' (Benjamin 1985b: 224). Instead, 'the fact that many prints made from a single negative or that a single print may be used repeatedly under different circumstances points to the possible existence of multiple original photographs' (Schwartz 1995: 46). However, multiple photographic originals with similar or identical image content cannot be assumed to be duplicates, as each may contain subtle material differences affecting the image, owing to variations in printing styles and papers, be enlarged or cropped, be in different physical conditions and survive in a range of contexts of equal importance. That these photographs may have been made at various times for a range of purposes therefore 'demonstrates that the meaning of a photographic document lies not in the content or the form but in the context' (Schwartz 1995: 46). Thus, the shift from seeing photographs as illustration to their being understood as documents involves shifting the emphasis from image content to the material contexts of creation, use and preservation (Schwartz 1995: 42).

Through its life, the photograph, as both image and object, can potentially move across several spaces, including the sites of production, use, reproduction and preservation, and along with each change in ownership and context, new meanings are acquired (Appadurai 1986; Pinney 1997; Poole 1997), all of which provide evidence of past uses and meanings.

Being translated into a digital image is a new stage in the life of the photographic object and a profoundly transforming one. The custodial institution removes photographic objects from the context from which their multiple meanings derived and were documented, and re-places them into a new 'digital collection'. This creates an image bank of auratic digital objects without reference to associated contexts or clues as to their previous physical embodiment. Thus, in the process of digitising, custodial institutions are explicitly changing the meanings of photographic objects. One example of this is relationships between photographs determined by prior owners; for example, serial arrangements of photographs on an album page (see Nordström, Chapter 6 in this volume) are lost in the new digital order as individual photographs are digitised, rather than the whole page. Photographs that were once drawing meanings from their contexts of creation, production and function have been relegated to content-based digital orphans, homogenised into what Sekula describes as 'a clearing house of meaning' (Sekula 1983: 194). This new artificial metonymy of the institutionally created digital collection results in collections of singular image quasi-objects obtaining an 'aura of transcendence and independence' (Stewart 1984: 159; Schor 1992: 200). At the same time, few institutions digitise the same image more than once, despite different contexts in which the photographs are found, providing a range of meanings. Thus, digitising transforms what were once variant multiple originals of photographic documents in a material form into digital duplicates of images. As digitising suspends old meanings and creates new ones in the new collections, it must be asked how the fidelity of meanings and thus authenticity are retained in the process of translation to a digital context.

The experience of viewing

Digitising profoundly alters the interactive experience of viewing photographs. In the digital environment, with its focus on the image content, the digitising process in itself serves to enhance the aesthetics of the photographs. With their requirement to be viewable on standard screens, the way we interact with a digital image is entirely different to that with an original photographic object. Using a lupe to magnify detail in an original photograph, for instance, physically draws the viewer into the core materiality of the object to interact with the larger detail under view, while almost touching the object's surface. Enlarging a digital image involves using a keyboard or mouse while maintaining physical distance from the screen image. Thus, an intermediate technology used to view a digital surrogate is unable to replicate the interactive nature and process of viewing experienced with a material object.

With such fundamental change in the experience of viewing, it becomes important to explore what is lost in the process of translation from the material to the digital. It has been argued so far that digitisation alters quintessential features of the photograph, including its vital materiality, sources of meanings and contexts. It is now important to investigate how digitisation realigns the nature of the archive and the concept of the collection for the digital environment. Through this investigation, what emerge are the implications of how the realignment of institutional practice in the digital context will have a profound effect on the kinds of research that can ultimately be undertaken. While the digitisation of photographs is being driven by the real need to increase access to the image content of collections (Klijn and de Lusenet 2000: 25), the question becomes: access to what?

Institutions

Photographs are found in a range of institutions, including art galleries, museums, libraries and archives, and the way in which photograph collections are documented in either the manual or electronic environment provides a meta-interpretation as to how custodial institutions understand and interpret the origins and ongoing importance of photographic meaning. Stewart (1984: 154) argues that 'to ask which principles of organisation are used in articulating the collection is to begin to discern what the collection is about'. This question should apply equally to the principles underlying earlier steps in this process, such as acquisition and management.

While there are fundamental philosophical differences in these processes between types of institutions, the tenet of modern archival practice is to preserve the original order and provenance of the materials. In order to maintain the authenticity and evidential value of the information, archivists defer to the contemporaneous system that produced the record. Thus in an archival context it is possible to 'see patterns emerge that inevitably would have been lost in any selection of the best images' (Nye 1985: x). Consequently, the curatorial practices that shape art galleries and museums intentionally move artefacts into new sets of relationships and thus management (Saumarez Smith 1989: 6). Likewise, libraries generally create collections of individual auratic objects, imposing layers of order that cut across a range of original patterns of creation and earlier associations between assemblages of materials. Thus, while the *archive* defers to the order imposed on it at the time of creation, a *collection* has a logic of content and organisation created by the collector (see Edwards and Hart, Chapter 4 in this volume).

In discussing the process of creating or curating a collection, Stewart (1984: 152) argues that 'once the object is completely severed from its origin, it is possible to generate a new series, to start again within a context that is framed by the selectivity of the collector'. Without documentation of the production or functional context, collections of essentially individual objects are a mere 'territory of images' (Sekula 1983: 194). Their unity and coherence comes from their single ownership, which is derived from the collector who 'constructs a narrative of luck which replaces the narrative of production' (Stewart 1984: 165), or in fact a narrative of function. Placement in a collection with new and synthetic associations and dislocated from their original contexts of meaning and use restores not the original intention of the producer, but 'an imaginary context of origin' relating to the projection of the new possessor (Stewart 1984: 150). The structure and organisation of photographic collections where image content is seen as of primary importance is such that they are homogenised with others into a collection in that 'clearing house of meaning' (Sekula 1998: 194).

The origin and importance of photographic meaning, and how the photographic object is perceived in relation to other forms of material, are revealed through the styles and content of the documentation relating to the material. In itself this can have a profound effect on the understanding of the photographs and the nature of the research questions that can be asked of the material. Therefore, while documentation can facilitate access to certain facets of the photographic object, absence of descriptions of key features, such as material process, mounts and physical condition, can restrict the value of the photograph as a historical and visual resource.

Ideally, 'understanding the characteristics of visual materials is crucial to archival practices such as appraisal, arrangement and description' (Kaplan and Mifflin 1996: 108). However, in reality there are many examples where institutional philosophies override the needs of the forms of material being managed. With their focus on the content of the individual object, photograph *collections* are reduced to, and managed as, data banks of *images*, understood to be uncomplicated, transparent and passive representations of truth (Barthes 1993). With this understanding of the self-authenticating nature of the photograph, the subject content is privileged over those contexts, as we have considered, rendering them lost. This loss is reiterated through the use of flat file data structures by most libraries and museums.[5] Information detailing relationships with other photographs and forms of materials is critical to understanding the ongoing and shifting meanings that surround photographs. Once this information becomes invisible to the researcher, the intellectual and social value, and the polysemic nature of the photographic object, is reduced. Thus, institutions that manage photographs as image-banks shift the way photographs are understood, and likewise limit the origins of photographic meaning from being contextually and materially derived to being content driven.

Conversely, Sekula has argued of *archives* that, by their structure, they 'maintain a hidden connection between knowledge and power. Any discourse that appeals without scepticism to archival standards of truth might well be viewed with suspicion' (Sekula 1983: 198). Thus in archives it is important to preserve contextual information such as provenance, history of ownership and relationships with other forms of materials, so that photographs are seen as an integral part of a communication chain as documents in their own right.

The relationship between collection management practices and photographic theory not only is close, but has a major influence on the kinds of research that can be subsequently undertaken on photographs. In order to broaden the perception and use of photographs from being seen as images to being understood as documents, and for research to be undertaken that can be sceptical about the veracity of a photograph, it is important to change the way photograph collections are documented. Schwartz (1995: 45) argues that this will occur when managers of images

> recognize that photographs, like maps, are linked to the exercise of government and business, and ask how they function as 'a silent arbiter of power', how they 'express an embedded social vision' and how they operate through the 'sly rhetoric of neutrality'.

In essence the challenge to those documenting collections is to move from understanding a photograph as a transparent representation of the truth towards an approach where the history of the truth of the image and its material forms can be traced. To this end, documentation needs to facilitate the rebuilding of prior relationships between the structures that have served to create, authenticate and preserve an image. Documenting collections to preserve the multiple functions of the photograph will then enable studies of the changes in meaning and context of images around the material stability of the photographic object.

The influence of digital technologies on institutional practice is simply a continuation of institutional management styles framing meanings of materials they house in the material environment. With their visualising tendency, digital technologies are influencing the way photographic materials are managed, but changes being wrought are not towards the archival approach advocated by Schwartz. The very essence of the definition of what constitutes an *archive* and a *collection*, as a material object in itself, is under challenge as institutional practice reflects the way digitisation encourages that shift from the contextual to image content.

If at one level digitising provides enhanced access to collection content, the process of selecting 'suitable' images for digital collections constitutes a further intellectual mediation by an institution of material that has already been filtered by the ravages of time and previous collecting decisions and documenting practices. Many photographs that are not digitised effectively disappear. Exclusions are made on the basis of similarity of image content, those that are not considered aesthetically pleasing, photographs that are physically deteriorated or photographs for which access and management strategies have yet to be completed, such as photographs of indigenous peoples. Thus institutions may provide enhanced access to specific choices of their 'treasures' that they judge to be aesthetically pleasing, rather than promote the integrity of a complete archive through bulk and non-selective digitising. From this perspective, it can be said that the digital collection can be used to increase control over access to material, rather than to enhance it.

During the process of selecting photographic images for placement in a digital collection, the image is moved by its custodian into a new discursive space – into that of the market place. This space serves to exploit and commodify the aesthetic qualities of image content rather than to promote the research potential of the photographic object. While the desire to capitalise on the revenue potential of the collections reflects the current economic imperatives and may indeed involve a genuine attempt to make collections more accessible, whether non-commercial organisations or custodial institutions should be complicit in reducing the material features of a photograph in a market-led image environment is open to question.

Websites

Commodification and homogenisation of visual materials takes on a new meaning with the ability to search several institutional websites concurrently. One example of this service can be seen on the Australian website PictureAustralia. This is a meta-crawler website of Australian and, increasingly, international image databases held mostly, though not exclusively, in libraries, archives and art galleries. This service provides concurrent searching over many significant on-line pictorial collections, with its subject focus being on Australiana.[6] At one level this site represents a milestone in technology and is of considerable assistance to a research community in locating material. However, it also raises important questions as to the manner in which digitised visual sources are understood and can be used as evidence in their own right.

Along with other image-focused international websites such as GettyImages, the very name PictureAustralia provides evidence of a philosophical underpinning that

Figure 12.1 A screen from PictureAustralia.

emphasises the individual picture or image content. On PictureAustralia (Figure 12.1), search results are displayed as thumbnail images that can then be enlarged through a direct link to a participating institution's website. The screen design for displaying the results encourages the viewer to focus on image content through individual frames as part of a broader window pane where all the images are brought together simply as a result of the search. With minimal captioning, the name of the holding institution and the possibility of further information from hosts' websites leads the viewer to see each image in the first instance as an isolated object. When venturing to a host's website there is the possibility of some sense of context, but only within the limitations of the institutional style of documentation.

This kind of meta-website responds to the picture researcher's desire for access to individual images and to the contents of a diverse and disparate set of pictorial collections. In future it may be possible to find materials scattered across institutions that might otherwise have remained unknown, though this kind of linkage is reliant on high-level documentation of photographs by individual institutions. However, those researching the evidential nature of photographs as historical objects, and those requiring knowledge of relationships between materiality, context and content, will remain dissatisfied with both the meta-crawler and the host institutions' styles of documentation until national and international standards for the thorough contextual and content-based documentation of photographs are implemented.

There are alternatives to the re-emphasis on the visual reflected in the thinking behind PictureAustralia. While its name suggests a library collection, the John Curtin Prime Ministerial Library (JCPML) is a fine example of the archival approach in the digital environment replicating the ordering schemes in the material world. The rarity of this kind of website with archival integrity raises the as yet unanswered question as to why it is that archival principles tend to be lost in the translation to the digital environment, while they are so rigidly adhered to in the material world.

On the JCPML site there is a clear understanding of the need to provide access to information in the digital environment equal to that when handing the original materials.[7] A fundamental strength of this site is its good theoretical knowledge of the nature of the material formats and their needs in the digital environment. Consequently, this site retains contextual information with digitised links to preserve relationships between materials, recognising the physicality of photographs as historically specific objects, without precluding the more common search strategy for photographs, by image content alone (Figure 12.2). It provides digitised representations of both backs and fronts of photographs where there is supplementary information, and digitises multiple originals of the same image found in different contexts and different material forms. The complexity of data structures preserves the archival relationships and adheres to archival principles, and is ample demonstration that this kind of database can easily be implemented in the digital world.

Loss

While a photograph itself sifts what is in front of the camera lens into a material and transportable object, the process of digitising a pre-existing photograph collection acts as a further filter over and above the distorted picture of the past that remains after time has taken its toll. Custodial institutions may try to minimise the value judgements they make in terms of what should be digitised. That they are complicit in the commodification of their photograph collections based on the aesthetics of the image content rather than archival material context and research value represents a failure to uphold the integrity of the historical sources they are charged with preserving. Knowing that what is being lost in terms of photographic meaning during the digitisation process is being actively destroyed by the custodial institution charged with its preservation raises ethical issues that need to be addressed.

How far is it possible to reconstitute or replace either the original contexts or the materiality lost during the digitising process? In the concern with documenting image content, it is important that the meta-data associated with this material does more

Figure 12.2 The front and reverse of a photograph of Elsie Curtin née Needham, 14 July 1942. Photographer: Susan Watkins. (Records of the Curtin Family. Courtesy of the John Curtin Prime Ministerial Library JCPML00376/15.)

than simply replicate the ordering schemes of the past. The many understandings of a photograph can be documented so as to enable the study of the multifaceted nature of photography, while allowing the retention of traditional fixed sequential readings found in the linear arrangement of the card index. However, hypertext offers the opportunity to explore new associations freely because of relationships being recreated within the ethereal sphere. In such an environment pre-existing photographic meanings are retrievable and new ones built from within the ephemeral electronic network (Boyer 1996: 50).

An archival approach to documenting photograph collections requires a transformation in the understanding of the nature of a photograph. Rather than seeing the photograph as an image and as a passive object, it can be seen as a material document that has played an active role in history. While creating robust meta-data to incorporate the 'equivocal status of the photographic object' (Nochlin 1991: xiii) and to document the discursive systems of which it was originally part is an expensive process (Tagg 1988: 4), this approach to preserving photographic meaning is central to custodial institutions' responsibilities. While the most common approach to digitising archival collections has been to concentrate on photographs, the associative powers of hypertext can be further harnessed. As the JCPML site demonstrates, it is possible to retain or rebuild prior associations between different formats of material in which original photographic meanings were once embedded, but which have been subsequently lost through subsequent separations throughout the life of the objects.

As Eduardo Cadava (1992: 17) argues,

> like the photographer who must acknowledge the infidelity of photography, the Benjaminian translator must give up the effort to reproduce the original faithfully. Or rather, in order to be faithful to what is translatable in the original, the translator must depart from it, must seek realization of his task in something other than the original itself. 'No translation', Benjamin writes, 'however good it may be, can have any significance as regards the original'.

What is produced in the process of translating a photograph from the material to digital is not an 'echo of the original' (Benjamin 1985a: 76), but a mere shadow of its former being. This digital shadow obscures the carefully documented balance of power between materiality and context that is critical to the determination of photographic meaning. Equally the digitising process translates what was once a complex multilayered laminated object into something much more ephemeral. Where once materiality and meaning were bound up in a complex, synergistic and symbiotic relationship, the resultant digital object is an ephemeral ghost whose materiality is at best intangible. During the process of translation it is the confluence of institutional power of the custodian in exploiting the aesthetic qualities and the transparency of the photograph that transforms the digital image into a new and marketable commodity. This confirms Benjamin's (1985a: 76) understanding that 'not only does the aim of the translation differ from that of a literary work . . . but it is a different effort altogether'. Seeing the digitising process in this way begs one to question the role of research institutions in defining photographic meaning by emptying the photograph of all visual clues based on its materiality and leaving it to be judged solely on its image content.

Given the rising expectation that institutions will digitise their collections, it is therefore pertinent to ask: 'is the age of mechanical reproduction of images yielding to an age of digital dematerialisation of images?' (Bruce 1994: 17). If this is so, what are the forces for and consequences of this change? Will the aura of technology lead to the ruination of the aura of materiality and the aura of alchemy of the original photographic object, perhaps at the very moment when we are beginning to understand its significance? With the imperative of the market economy encouraging custodial institutions to exploit their images in the digital market place, what are the implications for research of this loss of the evidence of materiality? While the increased access to photograph collections is important to those interested in image content alone, is the loss of the material photographic object too great a price to pay?

Trust

Digitisation is not simply a transliteration of tones or a simple technological process. With not only its changes in physical state but also the concomitant changes in meaning, digitising is essentially a cultural process. While digitising gives the illusion of enhanced access to collections, the process raises serious questions relating to the aesthetically driven selection of photographs, the potential cropping of images, the fidelity of the content and the authenticity of the digital photograph as evidence. However, what is lost in the process is, as I have argued here, cause for concern for those for whom the materiality of the original photograph is the primary source of evidence. More than this, that researchers are questioning the integrity of the digital image changes a careful balance: the fundamental trust that researchers have that custodial institutions preserve the integrity of the photographs and the sources of photographic meaning in their custody.

As Lilly Koltun (2000) has stated, like every believer before him in commenting on the revolutionary character of the new medium, Benjamin anticipated that new reproduction technologies would be used for egalitarian mass communication, for undermining institutional power, not for widening their discipline. Custodial institutions are widening their power to define our view of the past, shift our understanding away from the original material object and proscribe through management styles the kinds of research questions that can be asked. Thus, while the digitising process has the potential to enliven the trajectories of individual photographs as images beyond current institutional boundaries, the process also realigns the concept of the collection and in doing so undermines the nature of the archive. Institutions are not only framing understandings of the past through the selection of images, but framing the very way we understand historical source materials through shifting the styles of documentation from contextual to content.

The opportunity to manipulate both the subtle balance within and between archival collections and the image of the past that is presented through the digital collection is retained by those who control the means of production: the 'cultural institutions'. By amalgamating the aesthetic content of photographs with the contemporary politics of the market place economy, custodial institutions are complicit in creating new discursive systems that may obliterate previous meanings while lending their authority to a registering of the truth of the image in the new digital context. Digitising can at times be justified on the grounds of preserving the original by reducing handling while facilitating access to the image content. However, any short-term investment afforded in pursuit of the current trend towards commercialisation of photograph collections should not be at the expense of long-term preservation of the provenance of the collection or the physical object from which the digital source originates.

With the new discursive space of the market place actively contributing to the dematerialising, dehistoricising and decontextualising of the photograph, will the increased access that the virtual collection provides outweigh the experience of access to the original for researchers? Will the imperative to digitise photograph collections involve so much investment in creating access to the image content of collections that the considerable hidden investment required to prevent the physical disintegration of the original artefact be placed in jeopardy? Will financial investment for preservation programmes be shifted from the preservation of the material towards the ongoing migration and preservation of its digital referent? Will the creation of digital collections result in the ongoing preservation of the original by limiting access to originals to those for whom materiality is central to research, or will future generations become so focused on screen-based images that the original photographic object is seen as irrelevant by custodial institutions? If this is the case, how will the increasing availability of digital images affect the study of materiality and the entangled histories and relationships between artefacts in which so much of the history is embedded?

At one level digitisation should be understood as but one single point in the life and existence of a photographic object, but it is equally the point at which the very nature of the photograph undergoes profound change. The process of digitising original photograph collections reduces the complex, multifaceted nature of the photographic object to a single unitary digital form. Through this it takes researchers 'further away not just from the technology of making the image, but from the photograph's format as a material, cultural object – an object which was made in a certain way for a reason' (Edwards 1997). In the process of becoming an increasingly image-based culture, the universal equality of digital images overrides material differences between objects through the creation of a morass of digital mono-media (Rayward 1998: 214).

The power to control and create the image that we see of the past and present rests with those who own the digital technologies – in this case the custodial institutions. The technological translation of photographs that causes the loss of contextually derived meaning is of concern. Once digitising is understood as a cultural process, what may ultimately be lost will be the trust of researchers that institutions are looking after the best interests of the material above other forms of commodity-based politics. Institutions have a responsibility to provide impartial access to material in their custody, and to respond to the challenge to ensure the survival of photographic materiality and meaning in the age of digital reproduction. It is up to those interested in the materiality of photographs to ensure they uphold this responsibility.

Notes

This is an expanded version of a paper first published as Sassoon (1998).

1 There are digitally produced copies such as Iris or giclé prints, which have the ability to respond to the contracts, colour and texture and give a strong sense of the original materiality.

However, these are used for fine art prints and exhibition purposes, rather than in the digital environments discussed here.

2 For a notice relating to the authenticity of material on one website see http://john.curtin.edu.au/era/conventions.html

3 See the John Curtin Prime Ministerial Library (http://john.curtin.edu.au) for an example of the back of a photograph (portrait of Mrs Curtin by Susan Watkins).

4 For example, the University of Pennsylvania and Getty do lots of digital retouching. See their respective websites.

5 An example of a library using a relational database to preserve archival meaning is PICMAN at the State Library of New South Wales (http://www.sl.nsw.gov.au/picman/welcome.htm).

6 http://www.pictureaustralia.org/about.html (accessed 12 July 2002).

7 This site was conceived by Kandy-Jane Henderson.

REFERENCES

1 Introduction

Althusser, L. (1976) *Essays and Self-criticism*. London: New Left Books.

Appadurai, A. (ed.) (1986) *The Social Life of Things*. Cambridge: Cambridge University Press.

Attfield, J. (2000) *Wild Things: The Material Culture of Everyday Life*. Oxford: Berg.

Banks, M. (2001) *Visual Methods in Social Research*. London: Sage.

Banks, M. and Morphy, H. (eds) (1997) *Rethinking Visual Anthropology*. New Haven, CT: Yale University Press.

Barthes, R. (1984) *Camera Lucida*, trans. R. Howard. London: Fontana.

Batchen, G. (1997) *Photography's Objects*. Albuquerque: University of New Mexico Art Museum.

Baudrillard, J. (1994) *Simulacra and Simulation*. Ann Arbor: Michigan University Press.

Baxandall, M. (1988) *Painting and Experience in Fifteenth Century Italy*. Oxford: Clarendon Press.

Bourdieu, P. (1977) *Outline of a Theory of Practice*. Cambridge: Cambridge University Press.

Bourdieu, P. (1990) *Photography: A Middle Brow Art*. Cambridge: Polity Press.

Brettle, J. and Rice, S. (eds) (1994) *Public Bodies: Private States: New Views of Photography*. Manchester: Manchester University Press.

Buckley, L. (2000) Self and accessory in Gambian studio photography, *Visual Anthropology Review*, 16(2): 71–91.

Burton, C. (1889) The whole duty of the photographer, *British Journal of Photography*, 11 October: 667–8.

Clark, T. H. (1973) *Image of the People: Gustave Courbet and the 1848 Revolution*. London: Thames and Hudson.

Crombie, I. (1998) The work and life of Vicountess Frances Jocelyn: private lives, *History of Photography*, 22(1): 40–51.

Darmsteter, A. (1886) *The Life of Words as the Symbol of Ideas*. London: Kegan Paul, Trench & Co.

De Certeau, M. (1984) *The Practice of Everyday Life*. Berkeley: University of California Press.

Douglas, M. and Isherwood, B. (1978) *The World of Goods: Towards an Anthropology of Consumption*. London: Allan Lane.

Durand, R. (1995) How to see (photographically). In P. Petro (ed.), *Fugitive Images*. Madison: University of Wisconsin Press.

Edwards, E. (1992) *Anthropology and Photography 1860–1920*. New Haven, CT: Yale University Press.

Edwards, E. (1999) Photographs as objects of memory. In M. Kwint, C. Breward and J. Aynesley (eds), *Material Memories*. Oxford: Berg.

Edwards, E. (2001) Material beings: objecthood and ethnographic photographs, *Visual Studies*, 12(1): 67–75.

Focillon, M. (1984) *The Life of Forms in Art*. New York: Zone Books.

Foucault, M. (1984) Nietzsche, genealogy, history. In P. Rabinow (ed.), *The Foucault Reader*. London: Penguin.

Foucault, M. (1989a) *The Archaeology of Knowledge*, trans. A. Sheridan-Smith. London: Routledge.

Foucault, M. (1989b) *The Order of Things*. London: Routledge.

Freund, G. (1980) *Photography and Society*. London: Gordon Fraser.

Gaskell, I. (2000) *Vermeer's Wager: Speculations on Art History, Theory and Museums*. London: Reaktion Books.

Gell, A. (1998) *Art and Agency*. Oxford: Clarendon Press.

Gernsheim, H. (1969) *The History of Photography*, rev. edn. London: Thames and Hudson.

Gernsheim, H. (1988) *The Rise of Photography 1850–1880*. London: Thames and Hudson.

Gilman, S. (1988) *Disease and Representation: Images of Illness from Madness to AIDS*. Ithaca, NY: Cornell University Press.

Ginzberg, C. (1993) Microhistory: two or three things I know about it, *Critical Inquiry*, 18(1): 79–92.

Gosden, C. and Marshall, Y. (1999) The cultural biography of objects, *World Archaeology*, 31(2): 169–78.

Green, D. (1984) Classified subjects, *Ten-8*, 14: 3–37.

Guibert, H. (1996) *Ghost Image*. Los Angeles: Sun and Moon Press.

Hamilton, P. and Hargreaves, R. (2001) *The Beautiful and the Damned: The Creation of Identity in Nineteenth Century Photography*. London: National Portrait Gallery.

Henisch, H. K. and Henisch, B. A. (1994) *The Photographic Experience 1839–1914*. University Park: Pennsylvania State University Press.

Hirsch, M. (1997) *Family Frames: Photography, Narration and Postmemory*. Cambridge, MA: Harvard University Press.

Holland, P. and Spence, J. (eds) (1991) *Family Snaps: The Meaning of Domestic Photography*. London: Vintage.

Holly, M. A. (1996) *Past Looking: Historical Imagination and the Rhetoric of the Image*. Ithaca, NY: Cornell University Press.

Jaworek, W. (1998) Wahrnehmungsapparaten und Marketinginstrumente: Präsentationsmittel von Fotografie im 19. Jahrhundert, *Fotogeschichte*, 68/69: 117–30.

Jeffrey, I. (1986) Photography, history and writing. In A. L. Rees and F. Borzello (eds), *The New Art History*. London: Camden Press.

Kuhn, A. (1995) *Family Secrets: Acts of Memory and Imagination*. London: Verso.

Lalvani, S. (1996) *Photography, Vision and the Production of Modern Bodies*. Albany: State University of New York Press.

Langford, M. (2001) *Suspended Conversations: The Afterlife of Memory in Photographic Albums*. Montreal and Kingston: McGill-Queens University Press.

Lemagny, J.-C. (1987) *A History of Photography*. Cambridge: Cambridge University Press.

Lukács, G. (1971) *History and Class Consciousness*. London: Merlin.

McCauley, E. A. (1985) *A. E. A. Disdéri and the Carte de Visite Portrait Photograph*. New Haven, CT: Yale University Press.

McCauley, E. A. (1994) *Industrial Madness*. New Haven, CT: Yale University Press.

McCracken, G. (1988) *Culture and Consumption*. Bloomington: Indiania University Press.

Malraux, A. (1949) *The Psychology of Art: Museum without Walls*. London: Zwemmer.

Marx, K. (1970) *A Contribution to the Critique of Political Economy*. London: Lawrence and Wishart.

Maynard, P. (1997) *The Engine of Visualisation*. Ithaca, NY: Cornell University Press.

Miller, D. (1987) *Material Culture and Mass Consumption*. Oxford: Blackwell.

Miller, D. (ed.) (1998) *Material Culture: Why Some Things Matter*. London: University College London Press.

Morley, D. (1992) *Television, Audiences and Cultural Studies*. London: Routledge.

Newhall, B. (1949) *The History of Photography*. New York: Museum of Modern Art.

Newhall, B. (ed.) (1980) *Photography: Essays and Images*. London: Secker and Warburg.

Odo, D. (1997) Japan: an imagined geography. Constructing place through a nineteenth century tourist album. Unpublished MSc dissertation, ISCA, University of Oxford.

Pelligram, A. (1998) The message in the paper. In D. Miller (ed.), *Material Culture: Why Some Things Matter*. London: University College London Press.

Pinney, C. (1997) *Camera Indica: The Social Life of Indian Photographs*. London: Reaktion.

Poole, D. (1997) *Vision, Race and Modernity*. Princeton, NJ: Princeton University Press.

Porto, N. (2001) Picturing the museum: photography and the work of mediation in the Third Portuguese Empire. In M. Bouquet (ed.), *Academic Anthropology and Museums*. Oxford: Berghan.

Rinhart, F. and Rinhart, M. (1967) *American Daguerreian Art*. New York: Clarkson Potter.

Rinhart, F. and Rinhart, M. (1969) *American Miniature Case Art*. New York: A. S. Barnes & Co.

Ryan, J. (1997) *Picturing Empire: Photography and the Visualization of the British Empire*. London: Reaktion.

Schwartz, J. M. (1995) 'We make our tools and our tools make us': lessons for photographs from the practice, politics and poetics of diplomatics, *Archivaria*, 40 (Fall): 40–74.

Scruton, R. (1983) Photography and representation. In *The Aesthetic Understanding*. London: Routledge.

Sekula, A. (1989) The body and the archive. In R. Bolton (ed.), *The Contest of Meaning: Critical Histories of Photography*. Cambridge, MA: MIT Press.

Slater, D. (1995) Domestic photography and digital culture. In M. Lister (ed.), *The Photographic Image in Digital Culture*. London: Routledge.

Smith, L. (1998) *The Politics of Focus: Women, Children and Nineteenth Century Photography*. Manchester: Manchester University Press.

Sontag, S. (1979) *On Photography*. Harmondsworth: Penguin.

Sontag, S. (2002) *Where the Stress Falls*. London: Jonathan Cape.

Straw, W. (1998) The thingness of things. Keynote address to the Interrogating Subcultures conference, University of Rochester, 27 March (http://www.rochester.edu/in_visible_culture/issue2/straw/html). Accessed 12 December 2002.

Tagg, J. (1988) *The Burden of Representation: Essays on Photographies and Histories*. London: Macmillan.

Welling, W. (1976) *Collectors' Guide to Nineteenth Century Photographs*. New York: Macmillan.

Wolff, J. (1981) *The Social Production of Art*. London: Macmillan.

Wood, J. (1989) *The Daguerrotype: A Sesquicentennial Celebration*. Iowa City: University of Iowa Press.

2 *Un beau souvenir du Canada*

Berg, P. K. (1995) *Nineteenth Century Photographic Cases and Wall Frames*. Huntington Beach, CA: Huntington Valley Press.

Bolotenko, G. (1992) *A Future Defined: Canada from 1849–1873*. Ottawa: National Archives of Canada.

Carey, B. (1986) An imperial gift, *History of Photography*, 10(2): 147–9.

Cheal, D. (1988) *The Gift Economy*. London and New York: Routledge.

Crary, J. (1992) *Techniques of the Observer: On Vision and Modernity in the Nineteenth Century*. Cambridge, MA: MIT Press.

Daniel, M. (1994) *The Photographs of Édouard Baldus*, with an essay by B. Bergdoll. New York: The Metropolitan Museum of Art; and Montreal: Canadian Centre for Architecture.

Dimond, F. and Taylor, R. (1987) *Crown and Camera: The Royal Family and Photography 1842–1910*. Harmondsworth: Penguin.

Edwards, E. (1999) Photographs as objects of memory. In M. Kwint, C. Breward and J. Aynsley (eds), *Material Memories*. Oxford: Berg.

Edwards, E. (2001) *Raw Histories: Photographs, Anthropology and Museums*. Oxford: Berg.

Greenhill, R. and Birrell, A. (1979) *Canadian Photography, 1839–1920*. Toronto: Coach House Press.

International Center of Photography (1984) *Encyclopedia of Photography*. New York: Pound Press.

Kopytoff, I. (1986) The cultural biography of objects. In A. Appadurai (ed.), *The Social Life of Things: Commodities in Cultural Perspective*. Cambridge: Cambridge University Press.

Krainik, C. and Krainik, M. (1988) *Union Cases: A Collector's Guide to the Art of America's First Plastics*. Grantsburg, WI: Centennial Photo Service.

Kwint, M. (1999) Introduction: the physical past. In M. Kwint, C. Breward and J. Aynsley (eds), *Material Memories*. Oxford: Berg.

Langer, S. K. (1957) *Philosophy in a New Key: A Study in the Symbolism of Reason, Rite, and Art*, 3rd edn. Cambridge, MA: Harvard University Press.

McCauley, E. A. (1994) *Industrial Madness: Commercial Photography in Paris, 1848–1871*. New Haven, CT: Yale University Press.

Miller, D. (1994) Artifacts and the meaning of things. In T. Ingold (ed.), *Companion Encyclopedia of Anthropology*. London and New York: Routledge.

National Archives of Canada, Ottawa. Paul-Henri de Belvèze Papers/MG 24, F 42.

Phillips, R. B. (1998) *Trading Identities: The Souvenir in Native North American Art from the Northeast, 1700–1900*. Seattle: University of Washington Press; Montreal: McGill-Queen's University Press.

Phillips, R. B. (1999) Nuns, ladies and the queen of the Huron. In R. B. Phillips and C. B. Steiner (eds), *Unpacking Culture: Art and Commodity in Colonial and Postcolonial Worlds*. Berkeley: University of California Press.

Phillips, R. B. (2001) Quilled bark from the central Great Lakes: a transcultural history. In C. F. Feest (ed.), *Studies in American Indian Art: A Tribute to Norman Feder*. Altenstadt: European Review of Native American Studies.

Rinhart, F. and Rinhart, M. (1969) *American Miniature Case Art*. New York: A. S. Barnes & Co.

Schwartz, J. M. (1995) 'We make our tools and our tools make us': lessons from photographs for the practice, politics, and poetics of diplomatics, *Archivaria*, 40 (Fall): 40–74.

Schwartz, J. M. (2000) 'Records of simple truth and precision': photographs, archives and the illusion of control, *Archivaria*, 50 (Fall): 1–40.

Stewart, S. (1984) *On Longing: Narratives of the Miniature, the Gigantic, the Souvenir, the Collection*. Baltimore: Johns Hopkins University Press.

Stewart, S. (1999) Prologue: from the museum of touch. In M. Kwint, C. Breward and J. Aynsley (eds), *Material Memories*. Oxford: Berg.

Taché, J. C. (1856) *Le Canada et l'Exposition Universelle de 1855*. Toronto: des presses à vapeur de John Lovell.

Thomas, N. (1991) *Entangled Objects: Exchange, Material Culture, and Colonialism in the Pacific*. Cambridge, MA: Harvard University Press.

Wood, J. (1989) Silence and slow tome: an introduction to the Daguerreotype. In J. Wood (ed.), *The Daguerreotype: A Sesquicentennial Celebration*. Iowa City: University of Iowa Press.

3 Ere the substance fade

Anon (1856) *Elegant Arts for Ladies*. London: Ward and Lock.

Barthes, R. (1977) *Image–Music–Text*, trans. S. Heath. New York: Hill and Wang.

Barthes, R. (1980) *Camera Lucida: Reflections on Photography*, trans. R. Howard. New York: Hill and Wang.

Barthes, R. (1985) *The Grain of the Voice: Interviews 1962–1980*, trans. L. Coverdale. Berkeley: University of California Press.

Batchen, G. (1997) *Photography's Objects*. Albuquerque: University of New Mexico Art Museum.

Batchen, G. (2001) *Each Wild Idea: Writing, Photography, History*. Cambridge, MA: The MIT Press.

Batchen, G. (2003) Fearful ghost of former bloom: what photography is. In D. Green and J. Lowry (eds), *Photography/Philosophy/Technology*. Brighton: University of Brighton.

Burns, K. (1999) Urban tourism, 1851–53: sightseeing, representation and 'The Stones of Venice'. Unpublished PhD thesis, University of Melbourne.

Burns, S. (1995) *Forgotten Marriage: The Painted Tintype and the Decorative Frame 1860–1910: A Lost Chapter in American Portraiture*. New York: The Burns Press.

Cooper, D. and Battershill, N. (1973) *Victorian Sentimental Jewellery*. New York: A. S. Barnes & Co.

Derrida, J. (1976) *Of Grammatology*, trans. G. Spivak. Chicago: University of Chicago Press.

Derrida, J. (1981) *Positions*, trans. A. Bass. Chicago: University of Chicago Press.

Dimond, F. and Taylor, R. (1987) *Crown and Camera: The Royal Family and Photography, 1842–1910*. New York: Penguin.

Durand, R. (1995) How to see (photographically). In P. Petro (ed.), *Fugitive Images: From Photography to Video*. Bloomington: Indiana University Press.

Edwards, E. (1999) Photographs as objects of memory. In M. Kwint, C. Breward and J. Aynsley (eds), *Material Memories*. Oxford: Berg.

Fink, D. (1990) Funerary, posthumous, postmortem daguerreotypes. In P. Palmquist (ed.), *The Daguerreian Annual*, 56.

Foster, H. (1990) The archive without museums, *October*, 77: 97–119.

Frank, R. J. (2000) *Love and Loss: American Portrait and Mourning Miniatures*. New Haven, CT: Yale University Press.

Frizot, M. (ed.) (1998) *A New History of Photography*. Cologne: Könneman.

Hall, S. (1990) Cultural identity and diaspora. In J. Rutherford (ed.), *Identity: Community, Culture, Difference*. New York: Lawrence & Wishart.

Henisch H. K. and Henisch, B. A. (1994) *The Photographic Experience 1839–1914: Images and Attitudes*. Philadelphia: Pennsylvania State University Press.

Isenburg, M. (1989) *American Daguerreotypes: From the Matthew R. Isenburg Collection*. New Haven, CT: Yale University Art Gallery.

Jaworek, W. (1998) Wahrnehmungsapparaten und Marketinginstrumente: Präsentationsmittel von Fotografie im 19. Jahrhundert. *Fotogeschichte*, 68/69: 117–30.

Kaplan, D. (1998) Pop photographica in everyday life, 1842–1968, *The Photo Review*, 21(4): 2–14.

Kappler, H. (1982) Fotoschmuck: Fotografie in Dekorativer Fassung, *Fotogeschichte*, 44(12): 11–22.

Keenan, C. (1998) On the relationship between personal photographs and individual memory, *History of Photography*, 22(1): 60–4.

Kliot, J. and Kliot, K. (eds) (1994) *Campbell's Self-instructor in the Art of Hair Work: Hair Braiding and Jewelry of Sentiment with a Catalog of Hair Jewelry (1875 Edition)*. Berkeley, CA: Lacis Publications.

Krauss, R. (1984) *The Originality of the Avant-Garde*. Cambridge, MA: MIT Press.

Krauss, R. and Foster, H. (1996) Introduction, *October*, 77 (Summer).

Laqueur, T. (1992) Clio looks at corporal politics. In *Corporal Politics* (exhibition catalogue). Cambridge, MA: MIT List Visual Arts Center.

Lowry, B. and Lowry, I. B. (1998) *The Silver Canvas: Daguerreotype Masterpieces from the J. Paul Getty Museum*. Los Angeles: The J. Paul Getty Museum.

Luthi, A. L. (2001) *Sentimental Jewellery: Antique Jewels of Love and Sorrow*. Princes Risborough: Shire Publications.

McDannell, C. (1995) *Material Christianity: Religion and Popular Culture in America*. New Haven, CT: Yale University Press.

Meinwald, D. (1990) *Memento Mori: Death in 19th Century Photography*. Riverside, CA: California Museum of Photography.

Morley, J. (1971) *Death, Heaven and the Victorians*. Pittsburgh: University of Pittsburgh Press.

Moxey, K. (2001) *The Practice of Persuasion: Paradox and Power in Art History*. Ithaca, NY: Cornell University Press.

Newhall, B. (1982) *The History of Photography*. New York: Museum of Modern Art.

O'Day, D. (1982) *Victorian Jewellery*. London: Charles Letts Books.

Palmquist, P. (1980) Timely likeness, *History of Photography*, 4(1): 60.

Peirce, C. S. (1985) Logic as semiotic: the theory of signs (*c.* 1897–1910). In R. Innis (ed.), *Semiotics: An Introductory Anthology*. Bloomington: Indiana University Press.

Pointon, M. (1999a) These fragments I have shored against my ruins. In K. Lippincott (ed.), *The Story of Time*. London: Merrell Holberton and National Maritime Museum.

Pointon, M. (1999b) Materializing mourning: hair, jewellery and the body. In M. Kwint, C. Breward and J. Aynsley (eds), *Material Memories*. Oxford: Berg.

Prown, J. D. (1982) Mind in matter: an introduction to material culture theory and method, *Winturthur Portfolio*, 17 (Spring).

Rogoff, I. (1998) Studying visual culture. In N. Mirzoeff (ed.), *The Visual Culture Reader*. London: Routledge.

Rosenblum, N. (1984) *A World History of Photography*. New York: Abbeville Press.

Ruby, J. (1995) *Secure the Shadow: Death and Photography in America*. Cambridge, MA: MIT Press.

Sekula, A. (1983) Photography between labour and capital. In B. Buchloh and R. Wilkie (eds), *Mining Photographs and Other Pictures 1948–1968*. Halifax: Press of the Nova Scotia College of Art and Design and the University College of Cape Breton Press.

Snyder, D. G. (1971) American family memorial imagery, the photograph, and the search for immortality. Unpublished MFA dissertation, University of New Mexico, Albuquerque.

Solomon-Godeau, A. (1998) Rubrics cubed, *Bookforum (Artforum)*, Fall, 3: 39–40.

Sontag, S. (1977) *On Photography*. New York: Penguin.

Spies, J. (1997) Collecting 'photographic jewelry': this jewelry is picture perfect!, *Warman's Today's Collector*, July: 36–40.

Sturken, M. (1997) *Tangled Memories: The Vietnam War, The AIDS Epidemic, and the Politics of Remembering*. Berkeley: University of California Press.

Terdiman, R. (1993) *Present Past: Modernity and the Memory Crisis*. Ithaca, NY: Cornell University Press.

Trasko, M. (1994) *Daring Do's: A History of Extraordinary Hair*. Paris/New York: Flammarion.

Wendell Holmes, O. (1859) The stereoscope and the stereograph, *The Atlantic Monthly*, 3 June: 728–48.

West, L. and Abbott, P. (1990) Daguerreian jewelry: popular in its day, *The Daguerreian Annual*, 136–40.

4 Mixed box

Asad, T. (ed.) (1973) *Anthropology and the Colonial Encounter*. London: Ithaca.

Barringer, T. and Flynn, T. (eds) (1998) *Colonialism and The Object: Empire, Material Culture and the Museum*. London: Routledge.

Burrow, J. W. (1968) *Evolution and Society*. Cambridge: Cambridge University Press.

Bennet, T. (1995) *The Birth of the Museum: History, Theory, Politics*. London: Routledge.

Blackwood, B. (1970) *The Classification of Artifacts at the Pitt Rivers Museum, Oxford*. Occasional Papers on Technology 11. Oxford: Pitt Rivers Museum.

Bryson, N. (1992) Art in context. In R. Cohen (ed.), *Studies in Historical Change*. Charlottesvillle, VA: University of Virginia Press.

Coombes, A. (1994) *Reinventing Africa: Museums, Material Culture and the Popular Imagination*. New Haven, CT: Yale University Press.

Derrida, J. (1996) *Archive Fever*, trans. E. Prenowitz. Chicago: Chicago University Press.

Dias, N. (1997) Images et savoir anthropologique au XIX siècle, *Gradhiva*, 22: 87–97.

Edwards, E. (1997) Ordering others. In C. Isles and R. Roberts (eds), *In Visible Light*. Oxford: Museum of Modern Art.

Edwards, E. (1998) Photography and anthropological intention in nineteenth century Britain, *Revista de Dialectologia y Tradiciones Populares*, 53: 23–48.

Edwards, E. (2001) *Raw Histories: Photographs, Anthropology and Museums*. Oxford: Berg.

Elsner, J. and Cardinal, R. (eds) (1994) *The Culture of Collecting*. London: Reaktion.

Foucault, M. (1989) *The Archaeology of Knowledge*. London: Tavistock.

Foucault, M. (1991) Neitzsche, genealogy, history. In P. Rabinow (ed.), *The Foucault Reader*. London: Penguin Books.

Grimshaw, A. (2001) *The Ethnographer's Eye*. Cambridge: Cambridge University Press.

Hinsley, C. (1981) *Savages and Scientists*. Washington, DC: Smithsonian Institution Press.

Isles, C. and Roberts, R. (eds) (1997) *In Visible Light: Photography and Classification in Art, Science and the Everyday*. Oxford: Museum of Modern Art.

Kopytoff, I. (1986) The cultural biography of things. In A. Appadurai (ed.), *The Social Life of Things*. Cambridge: Cambridge University Press.

Kuper, A. (1973) *Anthropologists and Anthropology*. London: Allan Lane.

Langham, I. (1981) *The Building of British Social Anthropology*. Dordrecht: D. Reidel.

Latour, B. (1986) Visualization and cognition: thinking with eyes and hands, *Knowledge and Society*, 6: 1–40.

Lubar, S. B. and Kingery, W. D. (eds) (1993) *History from Things: Essays on Material Culture*. Washington, DC: Smithsonian University Press.

Malraux, A. (1949) *The Psychology of Art: Museum without Walls*. London: Zwemmer.

Maynard, P. (1997) *The Engine of Visualization*. Ithaca, NY: Cornell University Press.

Museums and Galleries Commission (1986) *Curatorial Standards for the Care of Photograhic Collections in Museums*. London: HMSO/MGC.

Pinney, C. (1992) The parallel histories of anthropology and photography. In E. Edwards (ed.), *Anthropology and Photography 1860–1920*. New Haven, CT: Yale University Press.

Pitt Rivers Museum (1932–50) *Annual Reports*. Oxford: University of Oxford.

Poole, D. (1997) *Vision, Race and Modernity: A Visual Economy of the Andean Image World*. Princeton, NJ: Princeton University Press.

Richards, T. (1993) *The Imperial Archive: Knowledge and the Fantasy of Empire*. London: Verso.

Samuel, R. (1994) *Theatres of Memory*. London: Verso.

Sekula, A. (1989) The body and the archive. In R. Bolton (ed.), *The Contest of Meaning: Critical Histories of Photography*. Cambridge, Mass: MIT Press.

Shelton, A. (1990) In the lair of the monkey: notes towards a post-modern museology. In S. Pearce (ed.), *Objects of Knowledge*. London: Athlone Press.

Stocking, G. (1968) *Race, Culture and Evolution*. Chicago: Chicago University Press.

Stocking, G. (1985) Philanthropists and vanishing cultures. In *Objects and Others, History of Anthropology 3*. Madison: University of Wisconsin Press.

Temple, R. C. (1886) The function and uses of an anthropological museum, *Journal of the Anthropological Society of Bengal*, 1: 168–86.

Theye, T. (1989) Wir wollen nicht glauben sonderns schauen: zur Geschichte der Ethnographischen Fotographien im deutschsprachigen Raum im 19 Jahrhundert. In *Der Geraubte Schatten*. Munich: Staatsmuseums.

Theye, T. (1994/5) Einige Neuigkeiten zu Leben und Werk des Brüder Carl Victor und Friedrich Dammann, *Mitteilungen aus dem Museum für Völkerkunde Hamburg*, 24/25: 247–84.

Vergo, P. (ed.) (1984) *The New Museology*. London: Reaktion.

5 Making meaning

Alinder, J. (ed.) (1979) *Carleton E. Watkins: Photographs of the Columbia River and Oregon*. Carmel, CA: Friends of Photography.

Appadurai, A. (1986) *The Social Life of Things: Commodities in Cultural Perspective*. Cambridge: Cambridge University Press.

Bertrand, A. (1997) Beaumont Newhall's 'Photography 1839–1937': making history, *History of Photography*, 21(2): 137–46.

Crary, J. (1990) *Techniques of the Observer*. Cambridge, MA: MIT Press.

Darrah, W. (1977) *The World of Stereographs*. Gettysburg, PA: William C. Darrah.

Duncan, C. (1995) *Civilizing Rituals*. London: Routledge.

Edwards, E. (1999) Photographs as objects of memory. In M. Kwint, C. Breward and J. Aynsley (eds), *Material Memories*. Oxford: Berg.

Gasser, M. (1992) Histories of photography 1839–1939, *History of Photography*, 16(1): 50–60.

Harris, N. (1999) The divided house of the American art museum, *Daedalus*, 128(3): 33–56.

Hooper-Greenhill, E. (1992) *Museums and the Shaping of Knowledge*. London: Routledge.

Hooper-Greenhill, E. (2000) *Museums and the Interpretation of Visual Culture*. London: Routledge.

Kantor, S. G. (1993) Harvard and 'The Fogg Method'. In C. H. Smyth and P. Lukehart (eds), *The Early Years of Art History in the United States*. Princeton, NJ: Princeton University Press.

Kantor, S. G. (2002) *Alfred H. Barr, Jr. and the Intellectual Origins of the Museum of Modern Art*. Cambridge, MA: MIT Press.

Keller, U. (1984) The myth of art photography: a sociological analysis, *History of Photography*, 8(4): 249–75.

Keller, U. (1985) The myth of art photography: an iconographic analysis, *History of Photography*, 9(1): 1–38.

Kopytoff, I. (1986) The cultural biography of things. In A. Appadurai (ed.), *The Social Life of Things*. Cambridge: Cambridge University Press.

Krauss, R. (1989) Photography's discursive spaces. Reprinted in Richard Bolton (ed.), *The Contest of Meaning*. Cambridge, MA: MIT Press.

Langford, M. (2001) *Suspended Conversations: The Afterlife of Memory in Photographic Albums*. Montreal: McGill University Press.

McCauley, E. A. (1997) Writing photography's histories before Newhall, *History of Photography*, 21(2): 87–101.

Naef, W. and Wood, J. (1975) *Era of Exploration: The Rise of Landscape Photography in the American West, 1860–1885*. Boston: New York Graphic Society.

Newhall, B. (1937) *Photography 1839–1937*. New York: Museum of Modern Art.

Newhall, B. (1938) *Photography: A Short Critical History*. New York: Museum of Modern Art.

Nickel, D. R. (1999) *Carleton Watkins: The Art of Perception*. San Francisco: Museum of Modern Art.

Phillips, C. (1989) The judgment seat of photography. Reprinted in R. Bolton (ed.), *The Contest of Meaning: Critical Histories of Photography*. Cambridge, MA: MIT Press.

Preziosi, D. (1996) Brain of the Earth's body: museums and the framing of modernity. In P. Duro (ed.), *The Rhetoric of the Frame*. New York: Cambridge University Press.

Sekula, A. (1983) Photography between labor and capital. In B. Buchloh and R. Wilkie (eds), *Mining Photographs and Other Pictures 1948–1968*. Halifax: Press of the Nova Scotia College of Art and Design and the University College of Cape Breton Press.

Sekula, A. (1986) The body and the archive, *October*, 39: 3–64.

Sherman, D. and Rogoff, I. (1994) *Museum Culture: Histories Discourses Spectacles*. Minneapolis: University of Minnesota Press.

Solomon-Godeau, A. (1991) Calotypomania: the gourmet guide to nineteenth-century photography. Reprinted in *Photography at the Dock*. Minneapolis: University of Minnesota Press.

Spence, J. and Holland, P. (eds) (1991) *Family Snaps: On the Meaning of Domestic Photography*. London: Virago.

Straw, W. (1998) The thingness of things. Keynote address to the Interrogating Subcultures Conference, University of Rochester, 27 March (http://www.rochester.edu/in_visible_culture/issue2/straw.htm).

Swann Galleries (1979) *Rare Books Auction*, Sale 1141, 10 May, items 226 and 227.

Swann Galleries (1989) *Photographs and Photographic Literature*, Sale 1497, 24 April, lot number 492.

Tassel, J. (2002) Reverence for the object, *Harvard Magazine*, 105(1): 48–56.

Wallach, A. (1998) *Exhibiting Contradiction*. Amherst: University of Massachusetts Press.

Weil, S. (2002) Courtly ghosts aristocratic artifacts. Reprinted in S. Weil, *Making Museums Matter*. Washington, DC: Smithsonian Institution Press.

Willumson, G. (1998) The Getty Research Institute: materials for a new photo-history, *History of Photography*, 22(1): 31–9.

6 Making a journey

Adam, H. C. and Fabian, J. (1983) *Masters of Early Travel Photography*. New York: The Vendome Press.

Adams, H. (1982) *The Letters of Henry Adams, Volume III: 1886–1892*. Cambridge, MA: Harvard University Press.

Aldrich, T. B. (1883) *From Ponkapog to Pesth*. Cambridge, MA: Riverside Press.

Bogdan, R. (1988) *Freaks: Presenting Human Oddities for Amusement and Profit*. Chicago: University of Chicago Press.

Brown, A. (1895) *From Vermont to Damascus*. Boston: George Ellis.

Clifford, J. (1997) *Routes: Travel and Translation in the Late Twentieth Century*. Cambridge, MA: Harvard University Press.

Daily Eagle (Brooklyn) (1898) William Vaughn Tupper – obituaries, 17 June: 16; 18 June: 18.

Edwards, E. (1999) Photographs as objects of memory. In M. Kwint, C. Breward and J. Aynesley (eds), *Material Memories*. Oxford: Berg.

Frizot, M. (1998) *A New History of Photography*. Cologne: Könemann Verlagsgesellschaft.

Grewal, I. (1996) *Home and Harem: Nations, Gender, Empire, and the Cultures of Travel*. Durham, NC: Duke University Press.

Hopkins, J. S. (1887) *A Winter's Journey up the Nile, 1886–87*. Birmingham: Gazette Co. Ltd.

Jacobson, M. F. (2000) *Barbarian Virtues: The United States Encounters Foreign Peoples at Home and Abroad, 1876–1917*. New York: Hill & Wang.

Kaplan, C. (1996) *Questions of Travel: Post-modern Discourses of Displacement*. Durham, NC: Duke University Press.

Kasson, J. S. (2000) *Buffalo Bill's Wild West: Celebrity, Memory and Popular History*. New York: Hill and Wang.

Langford, M. (2001) *Suspended Conversations: The Afterlife of Memory in Photographic Albums*. Toronto and Kingston: McGill-Queens University Press.

McClintock, A. (1995) *Imperial Leather: Race, Gender and Sexuality in the Colonial Contest*. London: Routledge.

Nordström, A. (2001) Voyages (per)formed: photography and tourism in the gilded age. Unpublished doctoral dissertation, The Union Institute, Cincinnati, OH.

Perez, N. M. (1988) *Focus East: Early Photography in the Near East, 1839–1885*. New York: Harry N. Abrams.

Poole, D. (1997) *Vision, Race and Modernity*. Princeton, NJ: Princeton University Press.

Pratt, M.-L. (1992) *Imperial Eyes: Travel Writing and Transculturation*. London: Routledge.

Schwartz, J. M. (1995) 'We make our tools and our tools make us': lessons from photographs from the practice, politics and poetics of diplomatics, *Archivaria*, 40 (Fall): 40–74.

Stoddard, J. L. (1897) *Lectures, Complete in Ten Volumes*. Boston: Balch Brothers.

Taft, R. (1964) *Photography and the American Scene: A Social History, 1839–1889*. New York: Dover Books.

Willumson, G. (1998) The Getty Research Institute: materials for a new photo-history, *History of Photography*, 22(1): 31–9.

Zannier, I. (1997) *Le Grand Tour in the Photographs of Travelers of the 19th Century*. Venice and Paris: Canal and Stamperia Editrice.

7 Photographic playing cards and the colonial metaphor

Bezemer, T. J. (1931) *Indonesische Kunstnijverheid. Platenatla*. The Hague: Nederlands Indië Oud en Nieuw/Koloniaal Instituut.

Bloembergen, M. (2002) *Koloniale vertoningen. Nederland en Indië op de wereldtentoonstellingen (1880–1931)*. Amsterdam: Wereldbibliotheek.

Botman, M., Jouwe, N. and Wekker, G. (2001) *Caleidoscopische visies. De zwarte, migrantenen vluchtelingen-vrouwenbeweging in Nederland*. Amsterdam: KIT Publishers.

Clancy-Smith, J. and Gouda, F. (eds) (1998) *Domesticating the Empire: Race, Gender and Family Life in French and Dutch Colonialism*. Charlottesville: University Press of Virginia.

Cohn, B. S. (1996) *Colonialism and Its Forms of Knowledge: The British in India*. Princeton, NJ: Princeton University Press.

Cooper, F. and Stoler, A. L. (1997) *Tensions of Empire. Colonial Cultures in a Bourgeois World*. Berkeley: University of California Press.

Edwards, E. (ed.) (1992) *Anthropology and Photography 1860–1920*. New Haven, CT: Yale University Press.

Edwards, E. (2001) *Raw Histories. Photographs, Anthropology and Museums*. Oxford: Berg.

Edwards, E. (2002) Material beings: objecthood and ethnographic photographs, *Visual Studies*, 17(1): 69–75.

Fabian, J. (1991) *Time and the Work of Anthropology. Critical Essays 1971–1991*. Amsterdam: Harwood Academic Publishers.

Grever, M. and Waaldijk, B. (1998) *Feministische Openbaarheid. De Nationale Tentoonsteling van Vrouwenarbeid in 1898*. Amsterdam: IISG/IIAV.

Jongejans, J. (1922) *Uit Dajakland. Kijkjes in het leven van den koppensneller en zijne omgeving*. Amsterdam: Meulenhof.

Jongejans-van Ophuijsen, C. J. (1947) *Vrouwen in Indië*. Amsterdam: Koloniaal Instituut.

Kunst, J. (1946) *De Volken van den Indonesischen Archipel*. Leiden: Brill.

Kunst, J. (1994) *Indonesian Music and Dance. Traditional Music and Its Interaction with the West*. Amsterdam: Royal Tropical Institute/University of Amsterdam.

Legêne, S. (2000) Identité nationale et 'cultures autres': le musée colonial comme monde à part aux Pays-Bas. In D. Taffin (ed.), *Du musée colonial au musée des cultures du monde. Actes du colloque organisé par le musée national des Arts d'Afrique et d'Océanie et le Centre Georges-Pompidou, 3–6 juin 1998*. Paris: Musée national des Arts d'Afrique et d'Océanie, Maisonneuve et Larose.

Legêne, S. (2002) Twee kanten van het spel. Kwartet van de koloniale verbeelding, *Historica*, 25(3): 20–3.

Legêne, S. and Waaldijk, B. (2001) Reverse images – patterns of absence. Batik and the representation of colonialism in the Netherlands. In I. van Hout (ed.), *Drawn in Wax. 200 Years of Batik Art from Indonesia in the Tropenmuseum Collection*. Amsterdam: KIT Publishers.

Locher-Scholten, E. (2000) *Women and the Colonial State. Essays on Gender and Modernity in the Netherlands Indies 1900–1942*. Amsterdam: Amsterdam University Press.

Newton, D. and Peltier, P. (1998) *The Tropenmuseum Ethnographic Collections: A Report*. Unpublished report, Amsterdam.

Pattynama, P. (1998) Secrets and danger. Interracial sexuality in Louis Couperus's *The Hidden Force* and Dutch Colonial Culture around 1900. In J. Clancy-Smith and F. Gouda (eds), *Domesticating the Empire. Race, Gender and Family Life in French and Dutch Colonialism*. Charlottesville: University Press of Virginia.

Pemberton, J. (1994) *On the Subject of Java*. Ithaca, NY: Cornell University Press.

Poole, D. (1997) *Vision, Race, and Modernity. A Visual Economy of the Andean Image World*. Princeton. NJ: Princeton Univerity Press.

Said, E. W. (1993) *Culture and Imperialism*. New York: A. Knopf.

Stewart, S. (1993) *On Longing. Narratives of the Miniature, the Gigantic, the Souvenir, the Collection*, 6th edn. Durham, NC: Duke University Press.

Stoler, A. L. (1995) *Race and the Education of Desire. Foucault's History of Sexuality and the Colonial Order of Things*. Durham, NC: Duke University Press.

Taselaar, A. (1998) *De Nederlandse Koloniale Lobby. Ondernemers en de Indische Politiek 1914–1940*. Leiden: Research School CNWS.

Thomas, N. (1991) *Entangled Objects: Exchange, Material Culture, and Colonialism in the Pacific*. Cambridge, MA: Harvard University Press.

Tichelman, G. L. (1948) *Indonesische bevolkingstypen*. Rotterdam: Nijgh & van Ditmar.

Tilley, R. (1973) *A History of Playing Cards*. London: Studio Vista.

van Duuren, D. A. P. (1990) *125 Jaar verzamelen. Tropenmuseum Amsterdam*. Amsterdam: KIT-Uitgeverij.

van Eerde, J. C. (1924) *Koloniale Volkenkunde I: Omgang met Inlanders*, 4th edn. Amsterdam: Koninklijk Koloniaal Instituut.

Wiggers, H. and Glerum, H. (2001) *Speelkaarten*. Amsterdam: MusArte.

Woudsma, J. (1990) *The Royal Tropical Institute: An Amsterdam Landmark*. Amsterdam: KIT-Press.

8 'Under the gaze of the ancestors'

Annual Reports of the Dundo Museum (1936–58) Archive of the Ex-Diamang, Diamonds Company of Angola. Coimbra: University of Coimbra Museum of Anthropology (unpublished).

Duncan, C. (1995) *Civilizing Rituals: Inside Public Art Museums*. London: Routledge.

Edwards, E. (1997) Beyond the boundary: a consideration of the expressive in photography and anthropology. In M. Banks and H. Morphy (eds), *Rethinking Visual Anthropology*. New Haven, CT: Yale University Press.

Faris, J. C. (1996) *Navajo and Photography: A Critical History of the Representation of an American People*. Albuquerque: University of New Mexico Press.

Gell, A. (1998) *Art and Agency: An Anthropological Theory*. Oxford: Clarendon Press.

Gordon, R. J. (1997) *Picturing Bushmen: The Denver African Expedition of 1925*. Athens: Ohio University Press.

Green, D. (1984) On Foucault: disciplinary power and photography. In J. Evans (ed.), *The Camerawork Essays: Context and Meaning in Photography*. London: Rivers Oram Press.

Kopytoff, I. (1986) The cultural biography of things: commoditization as process. In A. Appadurai (ed.), *The Social Life of Things: Commodities in Cultural Perspective*. Cambridge: Cambridge University Press.

Latour, B. (1989) Joliot: a história e a física misturadas. In M. Serres (ed.), *História das Ciências, volume III, De Pasteur ao Computador*. Lisbon: Terramar.

Latour, B. (1991) *We Have Never Been Modern*. Hemel Hempstead: Harvester Wheatsheaf.

Machado, A. B. (1995) Notícia sumária sobre a acção cultural da Companhia de Diamantes de Angola. In MAUC, *Diamang, Estudo do Património Cultural da Ex-Companhia de Diamantes de Angola*. Coimbra: University of Coimbra Museum of Anthropology.

Margarido, A. (1975) Le colonialisme Portugais et l'anthropologie. In J. Copans (ed.), *Anthropologie et Impérialisme*. Paris: Maspero.

Pinney, C. (1997) *Camera Indica: The Social Life of Indian Photographs*. London: Reaktion Books.

Reynolds, B. (1987) Material systems: an approach to the study of Kwandu material culture. In B. Reynolds and M. Stout (eds), *Material Anthropology: Contemporary Approaches to Material Culture*. Lanham, MD: University Press of America.

Sekula, A. J. (1986) The body and the archive. In R. Bolton (ed.), *The Contest of Meaning: Critical Histories of Photography*. Cambridge, MA: MIT Press.

Slater, D. (1980) The object of photography. In J. Evans (ed.), *The Camerawork Essays: Context and Meaning in Photography*. London: Rivers Oram Press.

Tagg, J. (1988) *The Burden of Representation: Essays on Photographies and Histories*. London: Macmillan.

Thomas, N. (1994) *Colonialism's Culture: Anthropology, Travel and Government*. Cambridge: Polity Press.

Walker, J. A. (1980) Context as a determinant of photographic meaning. In J. Evans (ed.), *The Camerawork Essays: Context and Meaning in Photography*. London: Rivers Oram Press.

9 The photograph reincarnate

Anderson, B. (1983) *Imagined Communities: Reflections on the Origin and Spread of Nationalism*. London: Verso.

Appadurai, A. (ed.) (1986) *The Social Life of Things: Commodities in Cultural Perspective*. Cambridge: Cambridge University Press.

Appiah, K. A. (1994) Identity, authenticity, survival. In C. Tayler (ed.), *Multiculturalism: Examining the Politics of Recognition*. Princeton, NJ: Princeton University Press.

Barthes, R. (1984) *Camera Lucida*, trans. R. Heath. London: Fontana.

Bell, C. (1946) *Portrait of the Dalai Lama*. London: John Murray.

Belting, H. (1994) *Likeness and Presence: A History of the Image before the Era of Art*. Chicago: Chicago University Press.

Benjamin, W. (1955) The work of art in the age of mechanical reproduction. In H. Arendt (ed.), *Illuminations*. London: Fontana.

Bourdieu, P. (1990) *Photography: A Middle-brow Art*. Cambridge: Polity Press.

Cardinal, R. (1992) Nadar and the photographic portrait in nineteenth century France. In G. Clarke (ed.), *The Portrait in Photography*. London: Reaktion Books.

Chöyang (1991) *The Voice of Tibetan Religion and Culture*. Dharamsala, India.

Connerton, P. (1989) *How Societies Remember*. Cambridge: Cambridge University Press.

Das, V. (1995) On soap opera: what kind of anthropological object is it? In D. Miller (ed.), *Worlds Apart: Modernity through the Prism of the Local*. London: Routledge.

De Vos, D. M. (1981) The refugee problem and Tibetan refugees, *Tibet Journal*, 4(3): 22–42.

Gell, A. (1998) *Art and Agency: An Anthropological Theory*. Oxford: Oxford University Press.

Harris, C. (1999) *In the Image of Tibet: Tibetan Painting after 1959*. London: Reaktion Books.

Harris, C. (2001) The politics and personhood of Tibetan Buddhist icons. In C. Pinney and N. Thomas (eds), *Beyond Aesthetics*. Oxford: Berg.

Hoskins, J. (1998) *Biographical Objects: How Things Tell the Stories of People's Lives*. London: Routledge.

Huber, T. (1999) Putting the *Gnas* back into *Gnas-skor*: rethinking Tibetan pilgrimage practice. In T. Huber (ed.) *Sacred Spaces and Powerful Places in Tibetan Culture*. Dharmsala: Library of Tibetan Works and Archives, pp. 77–104.

Mackenzie, M. A. (1991) *Androgynous Objects: String Bags and Gender in Central New Guinea*. Philadelphia: Harwood Academic Press.

Miller, D. (1987) *Material Culture and Mass Consumption*. Oxford: Blackwell.

Norbu, J. (1993) *The Works of Gongkar Gyatso*. Exhibition catalogue. Dharamsala: Amnye Machen Institute.

Parkin, D. (1999) Mementoes as transitional objects in human displacement, *Journal of Material Culture*, 4(3): 303–20.

Pinney, C. (1997) *Camera Indica: The Social Life of Indian Photographs*. London: Reaktion Books.

Poole, D. (1997) *Vision, Race and Modernity*. Princeton, NJ: Princeton University Press.

Smith, H. D. (1995) Impact of 'god posters' on Hindus and their devotional traditions. In L. A. Babb and S. Wadley (eds), *Media and the Transformation of Religion in South Asia*. Philadelphia: University of Pennsylvania.

Stoller, P. (1989) *The Taste of Ethnographic Things: The Senses in Anthropology*. Philadelphia: University of Pennsylvania Press.

Strathern, M. (1988) *The Gender of the Gift: Problems with Women and Problems with Society in Melanesia*. Berkeley: University of California Press.

10 'Photo-cross'

Banks, M. and Morphy, H. (eds) (1997) *Rethinking Visual Anthropology*. New Haven, CT: Yale University Press.

Edwards, E. (2001) *Raw Histories: Photographs, Anthropology and Museums*. Oxford: Berg.

Edwards, E. (2002) Material beings: objecthood and ethnographic photographs, *Visual Studies*, 17(1): 68–75.

Evdokimov, P. (1990) *The Art of the Icon: A Theology of Beauty*. Redondo Beach, CA: Oakwood.

Freedberg, D. (1989) *The Power of Images: Studies in the History and Theory of Response*. New York: Columbia University Press.

Ginzburg, C. (1983) Clues: Morelli, Freud and Sherlock Holmes. In U. Eco and T. Sebeok (eds), *The Sign of the Three: Dupion, Holmes, Pierce*. Bloomington: Indiana University Press.

Gosden, C. and Marshall, Y. (1999) The cultural biography of objects *World Archaeology*, 31(2): 169–78.

Hanganu, G. (forthcoming) The social lives of the Romanian Orthodox icons. Unpublished DPhil thesis, University of Oxford.

Nicolescu, C. (1971) *Icones Roumaines*. Bucharest: Meridiane.

Ouspensky, L. (1992) *Theology of the Icon*. Crestwood: St Vladimir's Seminary.

Pinney, C. (1997) *Camera Indica: The Social Life of Indian Photographs*. London: Reaktion.

St John of Damascus (1980) *On the Divine Images*. Crestwood: St Vladimir's Seminary.

St Theodore the Studite (1981) *On the Holy Icons*. Crestwood: St Vladimir's Seminary.

Stefanescu, I. D. (1973) *Iconografia artei bizantine si a picturii feudale Romanesti*. Bucharest: Meridiane.

Ware, T. (1997) *The Orthodox Church*. London: Penguin.

11 Print Club photography in Japan

Anonymous (1993) I love cuteness, *Yomiuri*, 10 September.

Anonymous (1996a) 'Ko-gals': are they real? The inside story of their indecent lives, *Weekly Post*, 29 January to 4 February (http://www.weeklypost.com/960129/960129b.htm).

REFERENCES

Anonymous (1996b) Printo Kurabu Meka Gosha Tsuzu (Five companies join Print Club), *Asahi Shinbun*, 15 September.

Anonymous (1996c) Teen-age girls are stuck on new photostickers, *Mainichi Daily News*, 5 November.

Anonymous (1996d) Success lures competitors to sticky photo business, *Asahi Evening News*, 17 September.

Anonymous (1997a) Purikura goes political, *Japan Times*, 25 December.

Anonymous (1997b) Print Club, *What's Cool in Japan*, April–June (http://www.jinjapan.org/kidsweb/cool/97-04-06/purikura.html).

Anonymous (1998a) Note, *Yomiuri Shinbum*, 9 January.

Anonymous (1998b) Ruy-chan purikura ni gomanetsu [Ryu (Hashimoto) is happy with his Print Club (frame)], *Focus*, 21 January.

Anonymous (1998c) Camera fever!, *What's Cool in Japan*, April–June (http://www.jinjapan.org/kidsweb/cool/98-04-06/camera.html).

Anonymous (1998d) Corporate sponsors everywhere at Olympic Village, *Asahi Evening News*, 24 January.

Buckton, N. (1998) A passion for Print Club, *Tokyo Classified*, 7 March.

Chalfen, R. (1996) The case of *doubutsu no haka no shashin*: the use of snapshots in Japanese pet cemeteries. Paper presented at the Annual Meeting of the International Visual Sociology Association, the University of Bologna, Bologna, 8–12 July.

Cohen, A. (1997) Americans say 'cheese' as Print Club grows in popularity, *The Daily Yomiuri*, 10 November.

Clammer, J. (1997) *Contemporary Urban Japan: A Sociology of Consumption*. Oxford: Blackwell.

DiPietro, M. (1998) An artist fools around, *Asahi Evening News*, 1 May.

Edgley, C. and Kiser, K. (1982) Polaroid sex: deviant possibilities in a technical age, *Journal of American Culture*, 5(1): 59–64.

Fields, G. (1983) *From Bonsai to Levis*. New York: Macmillan.

Hayashi, Y. (1998) Morimura Yasumasa: self portrait as art history. In Y. Hayashi, A. Obigane and K. Yamamoto (eds), *Morimura Yasumasa: Self Portrait as Art History, Volume 1*, trans. S. N. Anderson. Tokyo: Museum of Contemporary Art.

Joseph, R. (1998) Striking a colorful pose in the digital era of photo booths, *The New York Times*, 10 September.

Kawamura, T. (1997) Communicating through 'Print Clubs' and pagers (http://www.childresearch.net/key/kmedia/yrp/video.htm).

Kinsella, S. (1995) Cuties in Japan. In L. Skov and B. Morean (eds), *Women, Media and Consumption in Japan*. Honolulu: University of Hawaii Press.

Kurita, N. (1999) The iconic communication through 'Print-club', *Journal of Mass Communication Studies*, 55: 131–52.

La Ferla, R. (1998) It's not necessary to be Japanese at Yaohan Plaza, *The New York Times*, 5 July.

McVeigh, B. J. (2000) How Hello Kitty commodifies the cute, cool and camp, *Journal of Material Culture*, 5(2): 225–45.

Marcos, D. and Asahina, R. (1997) Print Club to appear in U.S. (http://www.japanupdate.com).

Miller, D. (1987) *Material Culture and Mass Consumption*. Oxford: Blackwell.

Mirzoeff, N. (ed.) (1998) *The Visual Culture Reader*. London: Routledge.

Mirzoeff, N. (1999) *An Introduction to Visual Culture*. London: Routledge.

Moeran, B. (1996) *A Japanese Advertising Agency: An Anthropology of Media and Markets*. Richmond: Curzon Press.

Naito, Y. (1996) Latest fad has teenagers stuck on stickers, *The Japan Times*, 27 June.

Nakamura, H. (1998) One world – photography in contemporary Japanese art: predictions and revelations. In *Medialogue – Photography in Contemporary Japanese Art 98*. Tokyo: Tokyo Foundation for History and Culture.

Nakane, C. (1970) *Japanese Society*. Berkeley: University of California Press.

Oga, T. (1998) Print Club, *Nikkei*, 9 January.

Ono, P. (1998) Photospot – Print Club, *PhotoGuide Japan* (http://photojpn.org/spot/purikura.html).

Rockowski, T. (n.d). Picture the fun forever (http://ourworld.compuserve.com/homepages/autophoto/history.html).

Shein, J.-E. (1991) Hello Kitty as stylemaker: advertising and popular culture in Japan, *Japan Society Newsletter*, February.

Skov, L. and Morean, B. (1995) Introduction. Hiding in the light: from Oshin to Yoshimoto Banana. In L. Skov and B. Morean (eds), *Women, Media and Consumption in Japan*. Honolulu: University of Hawaii Press.

Tamaki, K. (1998) Buddhist temples becoming havens of high tech, *Mainichi Daily News*, 13 May.

Tobin, J. J. (ed.) (1992) *Re-made in Japan: Everyday Life and Consumer Taste in a Changing Society*. New Haven, CT: Yale University Press.

Treat, J. W. (1996) Yoshimoto Banana writes home: the shojo in Japanese popular culture. In J. W. Treat (ed.), *Contemporary Japan and Popular Culture*. Honolulu: University of Hawaii Press.

Valentine, J. (1997) The framing of identity through Japanese media representations of marginality, *Japan Foundation Newsletter*, 25(1): 7–10.

Voigt, K. (1998) Joining the (Print) Club, *Mangajin*, 70: 12–15.

Walker, J. and Chaplin, S. (1998) *Visual Culture: An Introduction*. Manchester: Manchester University Press.

Watts, J. (1998) Soccer *shinhastubai*: what are Japanese consumers making of J League? In D. P. Martinez (ed.), *The Worlds of Japanese Popular Culture*. Cambridge: Cambridge University Press.

White, M. (1993) *The Material Child: Coming of Age in Japan and America*. New York: The Free Press.

Williams, M. (1997) Japan's Print Club to follow Tamagotchi to United States, *Newsbytes News Network*, 9 June (http://www.newsbytes.com).

12 Photographic materiality in the age of digital reproduction

Appadurai, A. (ed.) (1986) *The Social Life of Things: Commodities in Cultural Perspective*. Cambridge: Cambridge University Press.

Barthes, R. (1993) *Camera Lucida: Reflections on Photography*. London: Vintage Books.

Batchen, G. (1997) *Photography's Objects*. Catalogue of exhibition at University of New Mexico Art Museum, Albuquerque, 26 August to 31 October. Albuquerque: University of New Mexico.

Benjamin, W. (1985a) The task of the translator: an introduction to the translation of Baudelaire's *Tableaux Parisiens*. In H. Arendt (ed.), *Illuminations*. New York: Shocken Books.

Benjamin, W. (1985b) The work of art in the age of mechanical reproduction. In H. Arendt (ed.), *Illuminations*. New York: Shocken Books.

Berger, J. (1980) Understanding a photograph. In A. Trachtenberg (ed.), *Classic Essays on Photography*. New Haven, CT: Leete's Island Books.

Boyer, C. (1996) *Cybercities: Visual Perception in the Age of Electronic Communication*. Princeton, NJ: Princeton Architectural Press.

Bruce, R. (1994) Will the digital image change curatorial practice?, *Image*, 37(1/2): 17–25.

Cadava, E. (1992) Words of light: thesis on the photography of history, *Diacritics*, 22(3/4): 84–114.

Edwards, E. (1997) The History of Photography list (photohst@asuvm.inre.asu.edu), 22 May.

Edwards, E. (2001) *Raw Histories: Photographs, Anthropology and Museums*. Oxford: Berg.

Hartmann, W., Silvester, J. and Hayes, P. (eds) (1998) *The Colonising Camera: Photographs in the Making of Namibian History*. Cape Town: University of Cape Town Press.

Kaplan, E. and Mifflin, J. (1996) 'Mind and sight': Visual literacy and the archivist, *Archival Issues*, 21(2): 107–27.

Klijn, E, and de Lusenet, Y. (2000) *In the Picture: Preservation and Digitisation of European Photographic Collections*. Amsterdam: European Commission on Preservation and Access.

Koltun, L. (2000) The promise and threat of digital options in an archival age, *Archivaria*, 47: 114–35.

Kusnerz, P. A. (1998) Digital photography in print: a select bibliography, *History of Photography*, 22(1): 27–30.

Nochlin, L. (1991) Introduction. In A. Solomon-Godeau (ed.), *Photography in the Dock: Essays on Photographic History, Institutions and Practices*. Minneapolis: University of Minnesota Press.

Nye, D. (1985) *Image Worlds: Corporate Identities at General Electric 1890–1930*. Cambridge, MA: MIT Press.

Pinney, C. (1997) *Camera Indica: The Social Life of Indian Photographs*. London: Reaktion Books.

Poole, D. (1997) *Vision, Race and Modernity: A Visual Economy of the Andean Image World*. Princeton, NJ: Princeton University Press.

Rayward, W. B. (1998) Electronic information and functional integration of libraries, museums and archives. In E. Higgs (ed.), *History and Electronic Artefacts*. Oxford: Clarendon Press.

Robinson, P. (1996) Image capture and analysis. In C. Mullings *et al.* (eds), *New Technologies for the Humanities*. London: Bowker Saur.

Sassoon, J. (1998) Photographic meaning in the age of digital reproduction, *LASIE: Library automation systems information exchange*, 29(4): 5–15.

Saumarez Smith, C. (1989) Museums, artifacts and meanings. In P. Vergo (ed.), *The New Museology*. London: Reaktion Books.

Schor, N. (1992) Cartes postales: representing Paris 1900, *Critical Inquiry*, 18(2): 188–244.

Schwartz, J. M. (1995) 'We make our tools and our tools make us': lessons for photographs from the practice, politics and poetics of diplomatics, *Archivaria*, 40 (Fall): 40–74.

Sekula, A. (1983) Photography between labour and capital. In B. Buchloh and R. Wilkie (eds), *Mining Photographs and Other Pictures 1948–1968*. Halifax: Press of the Nova Scotia College of Art and Design and the University College of Cape Breton Press.

Solomon-Godeau, A. (1991) *Photography at the Dock: Essays on Photographic History, Institutions and Practices*. Minneapolis: University of Minnesota Press.

Stewart, S. (1984) *On Longing: Narratives of the Miniature, the Gigantic, the Souvenir, the Collection*. Baltimore: Johns Hopkins University Press.

Tagg, J. (1988) *The Burden of Representation: Essays on Photographies and Histories*. London: Macmillan.

Thomas, N. (1991) *Entangled Objects: Exchange, Material Culture and Colonialism in the Pacific*. Cambridge, MA: Harvard University Press.

Trachtenberg, A. (1990) *Reading American Photographs: Images as History, Mathew Brady to Walker Evans*. New York: Noonday Press.

INDEX